9/26/22   1.00

THE
WEALTH
EQUATION

THE
WEALTH
EQUATION

PETER J. TANOUS

FOREWORD BY **MICHAEL PRICE**

CHAIRMAN, FRANKLIN MUTUAL SERIES FUNDS

NEW YORK INSTITUTE OF FINANCE

NEW YORK • TORONTO • SYDNEY • TOKYO • SINGAPORE

Library of Congress Cataloging-in-Publication Data

Tanous, Peter.
    The wealth equation / Peter J. Tanous
      p. cm.
    Includes index.
    ISBN 0-7352-0068-8 ISBN 0-13-021074-9
    1. Investments—Handbooks, manuals, etc. 2. Portfolio management—Handbooks,
manuals, etc.. I. Title.
HG4527.T36 1999
332.6—dc21   98-31370
                                                      CIP

Executive Editor: *Ellen Schneid Coleman*
Production Editor: *Sharon L. Gonzalez*
Formatting/Interior Design: *Robyn Beckerman*

© 1999 by Peter J. Tanous
MoneyQ questionnaires and profiles, pages 24–42 ©1998 by Shoya Zichy
Foreword ©1999 by Michael Price

Printed in the United States of America

10 9 8 7 6 5 4 3 2 1   *10 9 8 7 6 5 4 3 2 1*

ISBN 0-7352-0068-8   **ISBN 0-13-021074-9**

This publication is designed to provide accurate and authoritative information in regard to the subject matter covered. It is sold with the understanding that the publisher is not engaged in rendering legal, accounting, or other professional service. If legal advice or other expert assistance is required, the services of a competent professional person should be sought.

      *. . . From the Declaration of Principles jointly adopted by a Committee of the
American Bar Association and a Committee of Publishers and Associations.*

ATTENTION: CORPORATIONS AND SCHOOLS

Prentice Hall books are available at quantity discounts with bulk purchase for educational, business, or sales promotional use. For information, please write to: Prentice Hall Special Sales, 240 Frisch Court, Paramus, New Jersey 07652. Please supply: title of book, ISBN, quantity, how the book will be used, date needed.

 NEW YORK INSTITUTE OF FINANCE
An Imprint of Prentice Hall Press
Paramus, NJ 07652
A Simon & Schuster Company

On the World Wide Web at http://www.phdirect.com

Prentice Hall International (UK) Limited, *London*
Prentice Hall of Australia Pty. Limited, *Sydney*
Prentice Hall Canada, Inc., *Toronto*
Prentice Hall Hispanoamericana, S.A., *Mexico*
Prentice Hall of India Private Limited, *New Delhi*
Prentice Hall of Japan, Inc., *Tokyo*
Simon & Schuster Asia Pte. Ltd., *Singapore*
Editora Prentice Hall do Brasil, Ltda., *Rio de Janeiro*

She knows the meaning of selflessness;

Her personal well-being was never a high priority;

Only two things could bring her down, fatigue and a problem in the family;

She loves great books, Sondheim, and the Yankees;

She works hard at a job that does not fill her heart, but at which she wants very much to succeed;

She entertains flawlessly, but the process never comes easily;

She willingly subordinates her personal desires to the happiness of her family and those around her;

She has dreams of her own, but not the time to fulfill them;

She thought that her sacrifices went unnoticed and unappreciated. It was one of the few times she was ever wrong.

CONTENTS

Foreword by Michael Price   ix
Acknowledgments   xiii
Special Contributors   xvii

PART ONE
THE FACTORS
1

Formulating the Equation 3

Defining Your Investment Personality 17

The Common Denominators: What Makes Great Managers Great . . . 43

PART TWO
THE MULTIPLIERS
53

Master Key 1 Set Realistic Goals 55

Master Key 2 Eradicate Fear—Understand Risk 73

Master Key 3 Never Time the Market 93

Master Key 4 Speculate Intelligently; Never Gamble 103

Master Key 5 Stay Alert; Avoid "Dumb" Mistakes 131

Master Key 6 Have Faith 145

Master Key 7 Allocate Wisely 155

PART THREE
THE SOLUTION
169

Completing the Equation: Customizing Your Plan 171

Before We Part 236

APPENDIX 1
MONEY-MANAGER SURVEY   241

APPENDIX 2
PARTICIPANTS IN INVESTMENT MANAGER SURVEY   273

Index   287
About the Author   299

FOREWORD

Peter Tanous has been around the investment business for a long period of time. In his book, *The Wealth Equation*, he lays out a way for individual investors to look at themselves before they start making investment decisions.

Investment decisions are actually very personal decisions that have to be tailored to your investment needs. Whether you are investing for retirement income, long-term capital gains to pay for a child's education, a vacation home, or to endow your own foundation, investment decisions are extremely personal. You have to feel comfortable with the decisions that you make not just at the moment you make them, but over time. To be a successful investor, you have to be in sync with the stocks or funds you own. Just as you feel uncomfortable wearing a suit that does not fit, it makes no sense to feel uncomfortable with your investments. You go to the tailor and spend a thousand dollars on a suit because you want it to fit right. A stock or mutual fund portfolio may cost thousands, if not hundreds of thousands of dollars. Wouldn't it be a shame if it did not fit right?

Creating a well-fitting portfolio has many facets. One that is critical is matching an investor's risk tolerance with the investments that he or she makes. Investors sometimes confuse volatility with risk when in fact they are two different things. Tanous knows the difference is important. In *The Wealth Equation*, he gets investors to the point of figuring out whether or not and to what degree they are able to withstand risk, and also helps them determine the degree of volatility they can tolerate. This is an important first step.

He then points out some of the basics in which I, too, believe. The first is to go with track records. He says you must embrace what works, no funny formulas, no secret strategies, and no black boxes. To me, investing means stocks and bonds, which really means either owning or lending money to a company. From my point of view, if you are going to own a company, that is, buy shares of stock in a company, the value approach works best. When I buy a stock, I want to buy a stock that trades at a discount to its asset value by a significant margin. That then gives me a cushion, what we call— what Ben Graham called—a "margin of safety." Other styles suit other investors. Peter talks about that, too. He also says that although few people can replicate what Peter Lynch does or what Warren Buffett does—those people are very special people—if you know your psychological investment profile, you can determine what investment style best fits your needs. Knowing that, you can then go out and find fund managers or financial advisors who have the track record and style that fits your own.

Avoiding mistakes is a big part of successful investing. The cost of a mistake is huge. Pure investment losses can be very expensive. In addition, there is lost opportunity time, transaction costs, and sometimes tax consequences. When you are decorating a house, your interior decorator probably charges a 30% commission, but if he or she helps you pick the right drapes instead of the wrong drapes, in the long run, it can save you a lot of money. Investment involves lots more dollars than selecting drapes. It is essential to invest wisely. *The Wealth Equation* should help individual investors avoid costly errors by guiding them to the investment philosophy and style that meets their needs. (After reading *The Wealth Equation*, buy a copy of Peter's first book, *Investment Gurus,* to get a more detailed feel for various styles. If you want to look at Mutual Shares style, you could also go to several books that talk about what we do: the very bible of value investing, Ben Graham's *Security Analysis* or *The Intelligent Investor*, both of which can now be found at bookstores and libraries.)

I would like to make one last observation about how you think about investing. After you have decided whether or not you are willing to take risks, after you have looked for consistent returns, after you have done all the things smart investors should do, you need to be realistic about the rate of return you can expect. Over the last several years, stock market investors have been spoiled with 20% or more rates of return. Our funds have yielded 20% or more for something like five out of the last seven years, and that is too high. It sounds funny, but in a sense I believe that investors should look for between

10% and 15% compounded annually over long periods of time. That 15% will double your money every five years, and that, if you can achieve it without running a lot of risk, is a spectacular return. The years of 25%, 30%, and even 35% that we have seen recently are extraordinary when looked at over a century, and should not be expected to go on forever. In the real tough years, such as 1990 and 1994, if you find ways to achieve 5% or 7% instead of dropping 10%, 15%, or 20%, you will do extremely well in the long run.

Peter Tanous, too, points out the importance of realistic expectations to a sound, long-term investment strategy. Understand the risk that you are running when you buy a high-tech fund or shares in Microsoft instead of a closed-end fund with a good long-term track record at a 20% discount. Come up with ways to measure your returns versus your goals, and start to think about when you should make changes. It makes no sense to time the market—people *cannot* do it. It does not make sense to be too active in buying or selling securities; investors need to be patient. Lower turnover makes a lot of sense, but turnover at the right time is sometimes needed. The time to take action is when your investments have not met *realistic* expectations. For example, 1998 has been a difficult year for value investors, but just because it has been difficult does not mean that you should switch out of value investing. If you understand the approach and it has worked well for you over time—and these two things are key—take the attitude that this approach works in the long term. I am taking less risk than the high flyers, and it makes sense to stick around.

Do not kid yourself—I know Peter would agree—reading *The Wealth Equation* and *Investment Gurus* is only a beginning. Investing well does require some work. If you are out there investing, you owe it to yourself to stay abreast of what people are saying about the market and funds. You do not have to read every issue, but pick up a copy of *Forbes*, *Fortune*, *Business Week*, or *Money* from time to time. Pay attention to the business section of your paper or read *The Wall Street Journal* from cover to cover each day. You owe it to yourself to dedicate some time, some of your leisure time, if not some of your work time, to paying attention to where interest rates are, what the performance of the market has been this year versus your fund's performance, and how your funds have ranked in their peer group (Morningstar, Lipper, and other services provide these rankings).

Compare, in the mutual fund business, the turnover of your funds with comparable funds; compare the fees. Be aware. This is a "buyer beware" kind of business, and you owe it to yourself, if you spent the money, to go pick up a couple of books to continue your education. The mistakes you avoid today are the dollars you will compound tomorrow.

MICHAEL PRICE

Acknowledgments

I confess that I am often surprised at how many people actually read the acknowledgments in books. I am one of them. Apparently, so are you. I suppose there are a number of reasons for this peculiar habit. Some of us look to see if there are any recognizable names. Others want to find out if anybody they know is included. There are no doubt other reasons.

Sometimes I wonder if the reason serious readers peruse the acknowledgments is to find out more about the author. Indeed, when you think about whom the author thanks, and why, it does give you some insight into what the writer is like. If nothing else, you now know who and what he or she considers important. Is the spouse adequately acknowledged? After all, living with an author writing a book is no picnic. How about the children who inevitably suffer some neglect during this tedious process? Do others who contribute to the process get their fair share of thanks? Are there some hidden revelations, about which we can only guess, from the gratitude expressed in these lines? Ah, the mysteries . . .

Now it's my turn.

My staff at Lynx Investment Advisory, Inc. were all very much involved in this project from the beginning. Everyone had his or her own area of preference and expertise. Lara Mongini rode herd on the hundred managers who participated in the survey, compiled survey results, proofread pages, offered suggestions on content, was always enthusiastic and helpful—traits I have come to admire and expect from her. Christopher Odyniec helped us both by contacting managers and compiling data. Peter Forbes, CFA, added valuable insights and ideas. It was Peter who suggested I interview Peter Bernstein and Victor Niederhoffer, for which I am continuously grateful.

Ann Tanous continued in her role as "office mom" and wise counsel on a variety of topics, not the least of which was putting up with the author almost 24 hours a day. My grown children were generous with advice from their respective corners of the country: Christopher Tanous from Florida, Will Tanous from Los Angeles, and Helene Tanous Bartilucci from New York City. Since all three of my children chose interesting occupations that happened to be different from mine, my reward came when Helene married Paul Bartilucci, who manages investment accounts at Bankers Trust and speaks the same language as his father-in-law.

Help came from a great many outside sources as well. Peter Walker of *Money Manager Review* helped with the selection of managers to be included in the survey, as did Thomas H. Clark of Salomon Smith Barney. I appreciate their help and their wisdom. Linda Lyons masterminded the construction of the manager survey questionnaire and the interpretation of the results. Jennifer Schmitt of TeamVest combined art and investment expertise in creating the charts that illustrate the personal portfolios we recommend in the book.

I am grateful to the individuals who agreed to be interviewed for this book. They are all legends in their own right: Gary Brinson, Foster Friess, Josef Lakonishok, Susan Byrne, Bill Grant, Victor Niederhoffer, and one of my favorite business book authors, Peter Bernstein, who also contributed some editorial comments that I found most invaluable. My dear friend, Andrew Tobias, whose writing skills I continue to envy, also helped in several ways. Other sage advice came from Nancy and Bernie Picchi, Lily Simo, supply side guru Art Laffer, and Bill Isaac, who, in my opinion, saved the nation from serious economic peril while he served as chairman of the F.D.I.C.

The foreword to the book was written by Michael Price. You probably think that I asked Michael to write the foreword because he is so much better known than I. That, of course, is absolutely correct, but it's not the only reason. Yes, I happen to like seeing his name on the dust jacket of my book, but more important, it so happens that Michael Price is one of the people in this business I admire most. You are no doubt familiar with his extraordinary record managing the Mutual Series Funds. You may also know that he is thought to be very tough. In fact, he had the dubious distinction of appearing on the cover of *Fortune* in an issue highlighting him as "The Scariest S.O.B. on Wall Street." So, why do I admire him? Because to me, Michael Price shows the greatest loyalty to those around him, including every single one of his shareholders. What makes him angry are corporate executives who are not sufficiently motivated to earn a proper return for their shareholders. Yes, he is tough, but he does it to protect and enhance our wealth, as his shareholders. My kind of guy. As you may already know, Michael Price is retiring as CEO of the Mutual Series Funds. He told me recently that he would move down the hall and manage his own money. But don't bet any of your money that we won't hear from him again.

My agent, Theron Raines, deserves special credit for patience and perseverance, rare qualities in that field. If there is a single person responsible for my writing investment books at all, it is my editor, Ellen Schneid Coleman, who is a source of inspiration and admiration. If I knew how she did all the things she does so well, I would write a book about that. If you ever write an investment book, may you be so lucky as to have her as your editor. Also in my publishing family, I acknowledge with great pleasure the grace and beauty and hard-nosed, can-do skill and dedication of that trio of PR brio, Sally Hertz, Yvette Romero, Barbara Monteiro, and the indispensable quattro, Barbara Lombardo. What a team!

Special Contributors

Two individuals made important contributions to this book in their respective areas of expertise. The combination of their talents has been a significant factor in developing *The Wealth Equation.*

Shoya Zichy

Shoya is an Investment Psychologist and the Managing Director of New York City–based Zichy & Associates, a global company specializing in the development of marketing and sales training programs for corporations and financial institutions to implement Myers-Briggs technologies. Her work has been featured in *Fortune* and on CNN-TV.

Ms. Zichy's background includes fifteen years in the fields of international private banking and financial journalism, most recently as Marketing Director for American Express International Bank and prior to that with Merrill Lynch and Citibank. In 1990 she tapped into a long-standing interest in psychology and became qualified to administer and interpret the Myers-Briggs Type Indicator.®[1] A frequent speaker, her seminars on "The Psychology of Money" and "Sharpening Your Marketing Style" have been delivered to pension funds, money managers, 401(k) participants, and high net worth individuals. She is authoring two books: *The Leadership Style of Women* and *The Psychology of Financial Planning.* For more information, she can be reached at 340 East 64th Street, Suite 4E, New York, NY 10021; (212) 755-2849.

---

[1] MBTI and Myers-Briggs Type Indicator are registered trademarks of Consulting Psychologists Press, Inc. For further information, contact the publisher at Consulting Psychologists Press, Inc., 3803 East Bayshore Road, Palo Alto, CA 94030; (800) 624-1765.

GREGORY H. LEEKLEY

Greg is a proud Blue Innovator (you'll find out what that means as you read the book) and a founding principal and Director of Investment Management of TeamVest, LLC, in Charlotte, North Carolina. TeamVest is an investment advisory firm specializing in the management of diversified mutual fund portfolios and the 401(k) marketplace. As a sub-advisor and consultant, Greg's experience has included assisting Salomon Smith Barney's Consulting Group, Interstate/Johnson Lane, as well as several regional bank trust and investment advisory organizations in the development of 401(k) participant advisory services.

Prior to entering the investment advisory industry, Greg served as Director of Research for Muhleman Marketing, Inc., a full-service sports marketing firm also based in Charlotte. At Muhleman Marketing, Greg assisted in the effort to bring the NFL's Carolina Panthers' to Charlotte. As a result of the success of the Carolina Panthers effort and Muhleman's unique stadium financing strategies, Greg assisted Muhleman in consulting to many NFL, NBA, and MLB franchises and their owners. Greg received his degree in economics from Wofford College in South Carolina. Greg Leekley can be reached at TeamVest LLC, 4201 Congress Street, Charlotte, NC 28209; (704) 643-1331.

PART ONE

THE FACTORS

Formulating the Equation

This is an investment book for war veterans. I don't mean Korea, World War II, or Vietnam. We're talking investment wars. I think you know what I mean. You qualify as a veteran if you have read some other books, invested and lost some money in the stock market, bought stocks on tips, and never made any real money. This is a book for those who haven't given up yet; those who are still eager to learn the truth about investing; not only what really works but what it is that works for them.

Defining the Problem

To start, let's see how many of these statements apply to your own investment experience.

- I've read several terrific investment books, but my own investment performance is still lousy.
- All those "foolproof" stock market systems stop working as soon as I try them.
- I have an incredible knack for getting in and out of the market at exactly the wrong time.
- If I have a good year in the stock market, it's a cinch that next year I'll lose as much as I made this year. (Maybe more.)

3

- When I buy a mutual fund from somebody's "Top Ten" list, it's a sure sign that fund will never appear on any list again.
- My investment portfolio has never beaten the overall market.

If several of these statements seem familiar, you may take comfort in knowing that you are squarely among the majority of all investors. Deep down, you want to create wealth with your investments in the market, but the goal seems increasingly elusive. When you read about the exploits of very successful investors, you wonder why you can't achieve similar results. You've tried the "formula" approach, but that didn't work. You studied the secrets of some of the great investors who have written their own books, or who appear regularly on television, and guess what? You aren't any richer. In desperation, you sank some hard-earned money into a few surefire tips from impeccable sources, the takeover stories, the surprise earnings about to come out, the new invention or drug. Yes, you heard them all, but the opportunity to catch up with *one* big score was just too irresistible to pass up. So what happened? Nothing. Your overall investment returns today are as disappointing as ever, and you are frustrated with your inability to get onto the right track. The problem is all the more frustrating, since you and I aren't getting any younger, are we?

Take heart. First, because you are not alone; and, more important, because you are about to change your investment habits forever. Beginning today, you are embarking on the course of action that will earn you the wealth you so richly deserve. In this book I will show you the *right* way to invest by approaching the subject of investing in a way you have not seen before.

I will introduce you to the "Wealth Equation," which combines the master craft of the best money managers in America with an investment plan that is specifically engineered just for you as the individual you are. We begin by learning how the great investors do it. Learning the secrets of the great professional investors is essential to building your own personal investment program. For this book, I have selected 100 of the top investment managers in the United States and asked them a series of probing questions to find out what sets them apart from the thousands of others in the field.

Next, you learn how to apply the secrets of these great investors to a program that is *specifically tailored* to you as an individual. To do this, I introduce you to the MoneyQ questionnaire.

You will be asked to answer a short series of questions and run through some simple exercises. These will help you learn a few things about yourself that will help you determine which investment program is best for you.

By combining the wisdom of these top professionals with your own investment needs and personality traits, we will create the investment program that caters *not* to a category of investors, *not* to a type of investor, *not* to a profile of investors, but to *one* investor—you. It is from the insights gained from this poll of investment geniuses coupled with my 35 years experience in the investment business and the MoneyQ personality profile that I developed *The Wealth Equation*, which I believe is the most sensible road map to a successful investment future for every investor.

As a decorated veteran of the investment war, I know you have read several other investment books. Obviously, if one of the other books you read fulfilled its promise and your expectations, you and I wouldn't be sitting here today. To understand why *The Wealth Equation* will work for you where others failed, let's spend a few minutes talking about why the other approaches *didn't* work for you.

Did you really expect to get rich on stock tips or other forms of dubious advice promulgated in magazine articles, newspapers, and even books on investing? Many bestselling investment books are written by people who have successful investment track records. No surprise there! The idea, of course, is to share with you and me their secrets of success, what tricks they used to beat the market or otherwise compile a sterling investment record. Then, armed with this new knowledge, we are supposed to go out and do likewise. Other writers of successful books aren't even investment professionals. This group may be particularly appealing. After all, if these nonprofessionals can beat the market, so can you (or so the reasoning goes). But, you might ask, why is it that these few investors do so well, and even after I study their book, their methods, and their secrets, I don't do any better? Put another way, how many millionaires out there became millionaires by reading one of these books?

To provide the answer to these important questions, let me remind you briefly of a simple lesson in statistics. In a distribution of, say, mutual-fund performance over a period of time, most of the funds will be clustered around the average return, which might be the performance of the Dow Jones Average or the Standard & Poor 500 Index. There will also be some funds with performance records

at the extremes. These so-called "outliers" will include funds that did
very badly, and those that did very well. Now, did those who did
very well do so because they were smart or just lucky? That is one
of the most important questions in the investment business. It is the
investment-industry version of the Jesuitical debate about the number of angels who can dance on the head of a pin. Common sense
can help us here. I am quite prepared to believe that Peter Lynch,
Michael Price, and Warren Buffett are genuinely skillful. I was not
prepared to believe that those charming and lovely Beardstown
Ladies were anything but lucky, even before we learned that they
had inadvertently cooked the books and that their real performance
record was far from stellar.

I took you on this excursion for a basic lesson in statistics to
make a very important point and to answer a question that we
posed earlier. Why can't you improve your investment performance
by reading about someone else's successful investment strategy? The
simple answer is that you can't do as well as Peter Lynch because
you aren't Peter Lynch. Here's another example: Do you think that
reading a book about writing great song lyrics by, say, John Lennon,
would teach you to write a song like "Help" or "Imagine"? (I'll con-
cede that you might come up with "The Macarena.") Probably not.
So, what is the difference between John Lennon's mythical book and
Peter Lynch's in terms of your learning to do what they do as well
as they do it? Absolutely nothing. I think you get my point.

Since buying a book with some new investment scheme, or
based on someone else's great track record, will do very little to
improve your own performance, what should you do? And why
should you buy this book? For you to do well, you must rely on two
basic principles: The first is to embrace what is known to work. No
funny formulas, no secret strategies, no black boxes that spit out the
right stocks to buy and sell, no speculative strategies that could
result in your losing a sizable portion of your savings. The second is
to find the investment program that is right for you. Not Peter
Lynch's, not Warren Buffett's, not the strategy of the author of the
last investment book you read. What we need to find is *your* investment strategy—the one that will work for you. This is what *The
Wealth Equation* is about. This is the book that finally gets you
going on a realistic road to wealth.

I want to be clear about this. Time and experience prove that
there are some things that work on Wall Street and a lot that don't.

The great investors know which ones work, and they practice them religiously, but the idea is not to try to be like any *one* of these great professionals. I figured out long ago that there is no one investment program that is right for all, or even for a large group, of investors. Individuals have needs, fears, time objectives, personalities, and countless other attributes that make each of us the individuals that we are. This is not a good field for cookie-cutter approaches. For this reason, we are going to identify those Master Keys—the things that have worked for the great money managers; and then, using *The Wealth Equation*, we will combine these Keys with your own personality traits and investment perspective—fears, ambition, and skills—to create that investment program that is truly your own.

Let's begin by looking at some bad investment habits. As an informed individual, you already know that so-called "Get-Rich-Quick" schemes don't work. They prey on the unwise and unwary, and you, of course, are not one of them. If I say to you: "If it looks too good to be true. . . ," you will immediately answer: "It probably is." You are neither gullible nor uninformed.

So why have you not done better in the market?

There are several reasons. For one, the secret to doing well in the market consists of a set of basic tenets. These are the successful habits and practices of the very successful money managers. They work for them and the right combination of these practices, tailored to your specific needs and requirements, can work for you.

For reasons beyond the scope of this work, many investors who are otherwise very smart and even prescient in their own professions, turn into gullible masses of jelly when it comes to investing in stocks. They do things when it comes to investing that they would never consider in their own professions. For example, they

- Buy stocks based on tips from golfing buddies or business associates.
- Believe takeover rumors.
- Are fond of stock market "formulas," such as the Dow Ten and other "infallible" systems that beat the market every time (well, at least they have in the past).
- Buy stocks on hunches or other phenomena.

A major goal of *The Wealth Equation* is to help you acquire true investment wisdom. Investment wisdom is not learning how to read

a balance sheet or tear apart an income statement. Those are investment skills. Lots of people have them. Investment wisdom is something else.

In the beginning of our investment lives, we approach stock
market investing with a combination of enthusiasm and naïveté.
We're eager to learn all we will need to know to achieve our goal
of making a considerable amount of money in the stock market. We
read *The Wall Street Journal*, buy some books, attend seminars,
watch Wall Street Week and CNBC, and then we begin the process
of investing. Depending on our own temperament and personality,
we invest aggressively or conservatively. After a period of time, we
assess the results of our investment strategy. What we invariably find
is that in our choice of stocks, we had some winners, we had some
losers, and, by some quirk of fate, they tended to balance out over
the long run. After a while, we are neither richer nor poorer. We
have invested a considerable amount of time and effort to wind up
pretty much where we started. After trying some shortcut advice and
other gimmicks, we face the sobering reality that our own investment strategy has failed. It is time to acquire investment wisdom.

Many of us who acquire investment wisdom will acquire it after
we have suffered through the personal trials of failed investment
strategies. Life is like that. We tend to get smarter as we get older
and more experienced, guided by the real examples that life has
taught us along the way. Wisdom of the years is often nothing more
than the accumulation of unforgotten experiences. Happily, we tend
to learn from our mistakes. Fortunately, a few younger people will
acquire wisdom ahead of the scheduled time. As the father of young
adult children, if I can help them along in the process, that will make
me all the happier.

What is investment wisdom? It is the realization, both on an
intellectual and emotional level, that the ultimate successful investment strategy is based on time-tested guidelines handed down by
wizened, war-scarred investment veterans who have overcome their
own errors and have succeeded brilliantly. But there is more.
Investment wisdom also involves an understanding that there is not
a single investment program that will work for every investor. For an
investment program to truly work and be successful, it must be a
program based on the unique characteristics of the individual who
is doing the investing. Only then will the investment program stand
the test of time. It is much like a good marriage. It takes work and

effort to succeed. When a marriage fails, it is often the result of some kind of mismatch between the individuals, based on their personalities, their priorities, their goals, and their ambitions. So it is with your investment program. It must be one that is compatible with you and your personality, your goals, and all the things that make you the individual that you are. All too often, we "divorce" our investment program because it wasn't right for us. Investment wisdom demands that we choose the investment program that is just right for us as individuals. *The Wealth Equation* will help you do that.

Investment wisdom is also the accumulation of knowledge of successful investment strategies, everything that has worked over a long period of time. Investment wisdom is a set of factors that the great investors have learned and formulated. Investment wisdom is a natural product of *The Wealth Equation*.

The Master Keys

The 7 Master Keys are the first part of that Equation. You may be wondering about the use of the phrase "Master Key." I keep an eye on most of the best-selling self-help books, many of which stress "habits," "rules," and "secrets." Oh yes, they often provide "tips," not a felicitous word choice in my line of work. Obviously, books that proffer "tips" or even "secrets" must sell better than those that don't. I'd certainly be willing to pay 30 bucks for a bunch of instant stock market secrets, wouldn't you?

Our Master Keys are designed to convey something far deeper than hot tips and the like. The term Master Key can be interpreted in two ways. In one sense, it is like the locksmith's definition of a master key. A key, of course, is the instrument we use to unlock a door, a safe, and so on. A master key is a key that unlocks all the doors or all the locks in a specific environment. This is what our Master Keys do when it comes to investing your money in the stock market. These keys represent the distilled wisdom of the most successful professional investors.

Another connotation of Master Key is a key that belongs to a master. Here we mean the master of a particular discipline or science. Thus, our Master Key can also be interpreted as the gift of knowledge from the masters in our field, the top professional investors who are eager to share their secrets of success with you, the informed and serious investor.

When you think about it, the concept of Master Keys applies to most endeavors—work, the arts, sports, anything. Pick your favorite sport. What do the top performers all have in common? They go about *practicing* their skills every day, in some cases, for most of the day. In the process, they acquire the skills and knowledge necessary to perfect themselves and reject advice and practices that do not enhance and improve their performance. In tennis, the champions spend hours on the court perfecting their strokes. World-class tennis players can return a ball and hit a handkerchief-sized spot on the other side of the court. They can do this almost every time. Watch those kids playing basketball. There are always one or two who stay behind after the game is over, and they practice their shots, sometimes for hours. It's not difficult to predict which of those kids stands a chance at becoming masters.

It's the same in the arts. The greatest musicians practice for hours upon hours each day. Ask any professional. He or she will tell you the same thing. What I find fascinating is that most of us, myself included, find it difficult to tell the difference between a Chopin piano concerto played by a very good professional musician and the same piece played by one of the two or three virtuoso pianists in the world, say Van Cliburn or the late Artur Rubinstein. Could you tell the difference? Perhaps not. But *they* can. You don't work that hard without a sense of mastery.

Now, stop worrying. You haven't bought the wrong book. I'm not going to suggest that you quit your job and start practicing your investment skills. No, I am not asking you to do the kind of work the great artists, sports heroes, or even investors do. Our goal is to *take advantage* of the work the great investors do and allow their efforts to guide us in our own investment program.

As a professional investment consultant, my job is to analyze the traits and qualities of great investment minds to see who has got it right, who delivers consistently superior performance over time, and who can be depended on to provide solid investment results for my clients with a minimum of disappointment. I work with some of the greatest money managers in the country every day.

From their collective wisdom, my 35 years' experience in finance, and also the wisdom shared by the great academics who have analyzed the field of investments, I have distilled the wisdom of the great investors into 7 Master Keys to investment success that any serious investor can follow. This book is about what works in creating wealth. The Master Keys reveal what every investor needs to be successful.

IDENTIFYING THE MASTER KEYS

To identify many of the Master Keys, my staff and I, using the tools available to us in our business, screened thousands of money managers. We already knew some of them; many we did not know. We looked for managers whose long-term investment track records were not only very good, but also whose performance ranked them consistently among the top 25% of their peers. We did this over several different time periods. We invited 100 of these managers to participate in the book by answering detailed questions on their investment procedures and performance. The results of this survey have never before been revealed, and you will encounter a number of surprises throughout the book.

To amplify the ideas, once we had refined the Master Keys, I then conducted in-depth interviews with well-known investment specialists, many whose names you will recognize. These interviews add dimension to the 7 Master Keys, and offer rare and telling insight into each subject. We interviewed Gary Brinson, the well-known money manager who is the author of the asset allocation study that bears his name. We spoke with noted financial author Peter Bernstein, and with author and currency trader Victor Niederhoffer, who suffered a recent and widely reported disaster in the market. Bill Grant, former chairman of MacKay Shields, and chairman of the Galen Group offered a variety of interesting insight into the market, as did Susan Byrne, manager of the Westwood Funds. Foster Friess, the well-known manager of the Brandywine Fund, spoke about faith and investing, and raised some issues that I doubt you have heard before in this context. We also spoke with money manager and academic Josef Lakonishok, a proponent of value investing.

WHAT IS YOUR INVESTMENT PERSONALITY PROFILE?

The 7 Master Keys should be approached with zeal. We must make them a part of our lives and impress upon ourselves that this investment strategy is for keeps. I realize that it is easy for me to make a statement like that; after all, you're the one who has to do it. So I take it as my challenge to help you get from here to there (if I want to stay true to my objective, which is to make you into a world-class investor). When we are through, you will have acquired not only the knowledge to become a wise investor, but the discipline to see it through and train others.

Let's talk about our approach. Before we can implement the 7 Master Keys, we must prepare ourselves psychologically. You won't profit from this book by simply nodding as you read that maybe I'm right, or that this or that makes good sense. It has to work for you, and that probably requires a changed mindset on your part. In that way, the investment habit is like other habits—overeating, drinking, you name it. We want that magic bullet that will cure our ills and make up for all the mistakes we may have made in the past.

But, let's be realistic. You can't just read a book, even one with which you agree, and expect it to change your life. *You* have to change your life, profiting in some way from the newly acquired knowledge. Are you ready to do that? It means changing how you think and, above all, changing your investing habits and maybe a few others, too. Do I need to remind you that changing habits isn't easy? But you know you can do it.

I will grant that investing is a bit more complex and can't be so easily summarized, but the lessons are readily available to those who look. Changing your investment habits requires discipline. *The Wealth Equation* begins with our examination of the 7 Master Keys, which I derived from the practices and habits of the greatest investors in the world. We hear the voices of some of these great managers. As they recount their own stories, they share with us how they acquired their own investment wisdom and how it continues to help them excel where others fail. That alone is not enough. To make it work for us, we must be disciplined students, eager not only to learn from the greats, but also to modify our own habits and practices accordingly.

That is why there is more to the process of becoming a successful investor than simply learning the rules. The second part of the Wealth Equation is the MoneyQ questionnaire, which will help you discover not only what kind of investor you are, but also your *attitudes* toward investing. In that way, your investment program can be specifically tailored to you as an individual.

THE MONEYQ QUESTIONNAIRE

In a test developed especially for this book by noted financial behaviorist Shoya Zichy, you will learn a great deal about yourself and your own approach to investing. Zichy, who started out in finance, is a pioneer in linking personality traits to investment behavior. The MoneyQ questionnaires presented here for the first time are, in my opinion, a milestone in helping individuals understand their attitudes toward investing. Combining this knowledge with the experience of 100 great investors is, I believe, a true formula for investment success.

Do you think you know your investment profile? Don't be too sure. Our series of questions are designed to reveal just how you should invest, taking into account not only your investment objectives, but also what it is that motivates you, frightens you, or makes you want to succeed. That is part of what makes this book different: The investment program I recommend is not a generic one based solely on your age, time horizon, and all of those other traits commonly considered in (and necessary to) financial planning. The financial plan you will discover here is different because it is *your* financial plan, one designed specifically for you, given not only your age, financial situation, time horizon, and risk tolerance, but also your personality, your views of the world, your ambitions and dreams. In a nutshell, all of those things that make you *you*! That is what makes this time around different.

To get from here to your personal financial plan, I invite you to complete the MoneyQ questionnaire. Don't worry, it takes only a few minutes. The work that went into creating the MoneyQ questionnaire has been painstakingly validated in trials over the past two years both with individuals and groups at money-management conferences around the country. All of the money managers we polled for this book also took it, so you will have an opportunity to compare your personality type to that of many of the greatest money managers in America.

I hope that the idea of working a little for financial success doesn't disappoint you. *The Wealth Equation* is not a quick fix. It is not "beach reading" as we have come to know it. It is "beach reading" in the sense that the time you put into reading this book will allow you to spend the rest of your years sitting on the beach, sipping piña coladas and reading John Grisham novels instead.

WHAT IS THE WEALTH EQUATION?

You say you are ready now? Good. Let's move forward. You might wonder why I am so certain I can deliver the true path to investment success. I assure you, it is not that I am one of the greatest investors in the world myself. Indeed, there are very few great investors. What I have done, in my professional and personal investment life, is to try to identify the geniuses, the gurus, in this business, and study what it is that these superachievers have in common. What are the traits that contribute to greatness? What characteristics do the truly successful investors share, be they Warren Buffett, Peter Lynch, Michael Price, or so many others? I have studied them, and now I have surveyed 100 more of the greatest practitioners, and I believe I know the answer. That is what the Wealth Equation is about. This is what I want to share with you so that you may put into practice a personal investment program using the 7 Master Keys to forever change your own financial future.

If you read my previous book, *Investment Gurus*, you learned the process by which a variety of investment geniuses go about picking stocks for their portfolios. In this work, we advance to the next step. We distill the greatness of these and other gurus, past and present, into an identifiable set of Master Keys that the most successful investors employ. We custom-tailor their wisdom and secrets into an investment program tailor-made for you as the individual you are. If there is a magic formula for investment success, the Wealth Equation is it:

> The wisdom of the great investors, *plus* your own personal investment plan, *equals* the wealth-building program that is right for you.

That means, and this is especially important, that it is a program that is easy and comfortable for you to follow. So open your mind, put aside the investment habits of the past, and join me as we embark on a mission of discovery to learn how the greatest investors in the world approach the stock market and how we, too, can light up our financial future.

Here's my promise to you: If you adopt the Wealth Equation, complete the MoneyQ personality-profile questionnaire, identify your personal-investment characteristics, and follow the 7 Master Keys, you will shed both the bad habits and the frustrations you have experienced. More important, you will become the successful investor you always wanted to be. Remember, we are talking about what works, and then we are applying it to an investment program designed just for you.

MAXIMIZING THE RESULTS

Here are some suggestions for getting the most from this book. First, I recommend that you read the book slowly. It is always wise to let new knowledge sink in. If you read slowly and deliberately, the information you acquire will stay with you and ruminate around your brain for a spell, unencumbered by conflicting information. In this fashion are habits changed and lessons learned.

The Wealth Equation is a three-part process. In Part One, you will discover your personal MoneyQ profile. The process is both fun and revealing. Part Two of the Wealth Equation introduces the 7 Master Keys. In this section, you learn some of the guiding principles responsible for the success of 100 of the most accomplished money managers in the business today. Finally, in Part Three, you come face-to-face with your personal investment portfolio, the one designed specifically for you given both the traditional criteria of risk tolerance and time horizon, and, for the first time, incorporating your personal MoneyQ to arrive at the portfolio that is designed for you as the individual and person you really are.

As you read along, I suggest you use the information as you acquire it. Seek examples of the Master Keys in your everyday life, financial or otherwise. You'll be surprised at how many applications you find. Conversely, identify people who are making the same old mistakes, the ones the experts have learned to ignore. The practical application of the Master Keys will serve to cement their usefulness in your mind.

Finally, always remember to treat the market with respect. Here's a little fable to keep in mind. In this story, think of the lion as the stock market. A hunter traveled to the African jungle for a safari, confident in his exquisite rifle and in his abilities as a marksman. On safari, he quickly bagged a wildebeest, a rhino, and several lesser prey. At last, he encountered what he had come for—a bold, mean lion, king of the jungle. The hunter faced the lion and put the rifle to his shoulder, taking aim. Suddenly, the lion, instead of attacking the hunter or running away, bowed his head between his paws and stopped moving. Puzzled, the hunter looked up and asked: "Are you afraid, lion?" The lion looked up and responded: "No. I'm just praying before I eat."

Defining Your
Investment Personality

Why am I so confident that you will get rich by adopting the Wealth Equation? It's because it leads to an investment program that is tailored to you as an individual: a program that takes into account *your* life, *your* beliefs, *your* emotions, and all there is about you that makes you do what you do. I don't want this to sound like another pop psychology book—God knows, there are enough of them out there, but I do want you to take a self-assessment retreat with me. On this retreat you will, at last, discover the investment program that is right for you, one that will allow you to use the knowledge you will acquire about investing in the most personal way possible. This will be the investment program that takes you into account as the individual you are. This will not be a week-long or weekend retreat in some log cabin in the woods. It is a retreat you can take at any time, and it should take you no more than half an hour.

Let's start with an example: Susan and Robert, both well-paid professionals, have been at odds over money for most of their seven-year marriage. The couple frequently disagree on how much to spend and what types of investments to make. Recently they sold their house, opting to rent for the next year pending Robert's company's reorganization. As the greater risk taker, Susan wanted to put the proceeds into a balanced mutual fund. Right before the closing, she was called away on a business trip. She returned to find that her more conservative husband, fearing the loss of capital, had placed the money in a one-year certificate of deposit, thereby locking up their funds for at least 12 months. You can guess what happened. Six months of arguments and finger pointing followed.

EXPLORING YOUR MONEY MIND

To create a successful program, therefore, you must first know yourself. To do this you must *classify* yourself. We classify people all the time. It is something we do instinctively. You see someone you know, or even someone you have just met. You think: he *is efficient, athletic, competitive.* Or: she *is warm, energetic, and well organized.* We classify people just as we code categories of art or investments. It helps us group information and store it in appropriate files for future use.

I know nobody likes to be labeled, especially when those labels probe into deep recesses of our being, but the fact is money is lodged in one such recess, and the factors that influence our approach to it are complex. Knowledge, investment experience, and the amount of disposable income we possess are obviously important. The attitudes of our family, neighbors, colleagues, and the culture in which we live also play central roles, further complicating the broad mosaic of interweaving influences.

There is, however, another and, to date, little-recognized influence, broadly known as financial temperament. You will discover it in this chapter. This feature of *The Wealth Equation* is based on the research of investment psychologist Shoya Zichy. You will hear me refer to her often. It is, in my opinion, the most comprehensive, intelligent work done in this field as it applies to investment personality.

I've already touched on the MoneyQ profile. Each of us has a particular MoneyQ profile, as determined by the inner architecture of our brain. That MoneyQ, research proves, exerts a powerful influence on our attitudes toward money (of course), risk, financial planning, and many other aspects of financial behavior. So, yes, while each of us is unique, some of our attitudes are classifiable. The classifications create an organized and statistically validated system, which provides another tool to better financial management. Since many of us don't live alone, our MoneyQ must also take into account the environment in which we live, including the temperament and MoneyQ of those around us who share in these important decisions. Understanding different financial temperaments within a family can go a long way toward reducing the stress and discord that result from conflicting attitudes toward money (remember Susan and Robert).

This chapter helps you explore your individual financial temperament and how it will affect and interact with your time horizon and investment experience. This is the path to achieving your investment goal in the most realistic and practical way possible. To be just a little crass, this is how you are going to get rich.

A BRIEF HISTORY OF THE MONEYQ PERSONALITY MODEL

For more than 25 centuries, beginning with Hippocrates in 450 B.C., scientists and scholars have recognized that there are predictable patterns of human behavior, most notably in some variation of a four-part personality model. In 1921, famed Swiss psychiatrist Carl Gustav Jung went a step farther. He stated that these predictable patterns are based on preferences that are inborn or emerge early in life and become the foundation of how we approach people, tasks, and events for the rest of our life. His ideas were adopted by two brilliant American women, Isabel Myers and her mother, Katharine Briggs, who devoted the next 40 years to systematically observing people. Ultimately, they developed a psychological instrument known as the Myers-Briggs Type Indicator® (MBTI®)* which is now used in a broad range of practical applications worldwide. To date over 15 million people from corporations, governments, churches, universities, and family-counseling centers, among others, have validated their MBTI® results, thereby confirming that there are distinct categories of personalities and that these personalities are highly predictive of how we handle things, from running a company to raising our children.

In the 1950s, another enthusiast of personality typing, Dr. David Keirsey, began to explore ways of integrating personality theories with the work of Myers and Briggs. His book, *Please Understand Me*, overlaid the fourfold personality model to the Myers and Briggs profiles, thereby creating a new temperament model. Since then, his work has been expanded by his longtime student, Dr. Linda Berens, president of the Temperament Research Institute, who continues to provide a rich array of new insights.

---

*MBTI and Myers-Briggs Type Indicator are registered trademarks of Consulting Psychologists Press, Inc.

In 1995, Shoya Zichy, a former private banker turned personality-type expert, began her research linking the concepts of Myers and Briggs, Keirsey, and Berens to attitudes toward money, risk, and investment behavior. I was so impressed with her work that I asked Ms. Zichy to collaborate with me on this part of the book, and her work is offered in this form for the first time.

Shoya Zichy is a New York City-based Myers-Briggs trainer and a past president of the Myers-Briggs Association of New York. She specializes in corporate-training seminars applying the Myers-Briggs concept to management development, marketing, sales, and money and investments. Her clients include some of the largest companies in the United States. Her work has been featured in *Fortune* magazine, on CNN TV, and other media. Zichy is a frequent speaker on the psychology of money specifically as it relates to 401(k) participants and high net-worth investors. She is a past board member of the Financial Women's Association. At present, she is working on two books on psychological ramifications of leadership and financial planning.

As a frequent lecturer and Myers-Briggs facilitator to corporations, Zichy began asking seminar participants who had validated their personality type to fill out an investment questionnaire. The correlated results produced the eight MoneyQ profiles, which are presented here for the first time. These profiles provide a blueprint that explains how different people approach risk, financial planning, asset allocation, and a host of other issues that have an impact on investment behavior.

MAPPING YOUR MONEY MIND

No doubt you can see where we are heading. In *The Wealth Equation*, you learn the disciplines of the great investors. That gives you a much better understanding not only of what works, but how the great investors put this knowledge to use. But knowledge alone will do you no good unless you can put it to use in a systematic way that works for you as an individual. That is the secret to investment success.

Combining the extensive experience of the academics and psychology experts we just cited and our knowledge of investment traits and characteristics, we find out together what makes you tick in a financial sense. You will be classified into a personality type that suits you, using the techniques that have been validated on over 15 million participants. Next, we will overlay investment characteristics on top of these profiles to arrive at the investment strategy that is best suited to you as the person you are. At the end of this process you will have an investment strategy designed for your temperament and personality type. It is not someone else's investment strategy, it is *yours*, and for that reason has the best chance of working for you.

THE COLORS OF YOUR MIND

To give you a better idea of what these personality types are all about, let me take you for a stroll through a mythical village. There are four neighborhoods in this village where most of the people live. They tend to group themselves together by virtue of their common traits and characteristics. Our excursion will be a brief introduction to the personality types. You will learn much more about them as we progress. Let's go for a walk.

The four personality types we encounter as we stroll through the village are identified by color: Gold, Red, Blue, and Green. (There are two subdivisions within each category, but we'll get to that later.) You will find that you fit into one of these color categories.

The first neighborhood we encounter on our walk leads us to an area of solid, well-built houses. We notice that the children in the neighborhood are well dressed; lawns and gardens are properly groomed and well cared for. The stores in this part of town open and close on time and tradespeople arrive at the appointed hour. The volunteer fire department has a waiting list of desirable candidates, and churches and synagogues do not lack for volunteer leaders. The religious services are all well attended. Holidays are observed rigorously, and well-planned gatherings take place on the Fourth of July and Memorial Day.

We find a lot of titles in this neighborhood, doctors, lawyers, and judges. Around here, a diploma is a coveted accomplishment. Many senior bankers, military officers, and corporate executives make their homes in this part of town.

This is the **Gold** neighborhood.

As we move to another part of town, we quickly notice that the houses are sprawling, many with rooms added on. Families are larger here, and the area is alive with activity of one kind or another. Over here, a pickup basketball game is in progress. Another group rides by on bicycles, out for an excursion into the countryside. We notice that the people in this neighborhood live pretty well. We see expensive cars, cases of vintage wines and catered foods being delivered to homes, yet the neighborhood isn't the wealthiest one we will encounter. We also notice a greater number of moving vans here, suggesting that this is a fairly mobile group of people.

Around the corner, a movie-theater complex rises as well as a community theater group. In fact, we find an interesting combination of talents in this part of town. There are professional sports personalities and actor types, but we also observe a number of small business owners and self-employed individuals who tend to dislike corporate hierarchies and the attendant rules and regulations. Most of the town's wheeler-dealers live here, too.

This is the neighborhood of the **Red** profiles.

Continuing our stroll, we come upon an area of futuristic looking houses with bright vistas and large open areas. Learning seems to be very important here. We can tell by the number of bookstores and libraries. The people in this neighborhood are not the most gregarious in town; they are too busy learning—in fact, they never seem to get enough knowledge to satisfy them. Children are intellectually curious and challenge their parents and teachers. In fact, they are sometimes accused of being blunt and obnoxious.

This group places a high value on intellectual companionship. In general, they are serious and focused. Perhaps most important, the residents in this part of town are never satisfied with themselves or others. As a result, the intellectual atmosphere is filled with challenge, and that sometimes leads to confrontation. Sarcasm and intellectual jousting pepper the discussions, and these exchanges are more confrontational than good-natured (as they might be in the Red neighborhood). In general, these people have a hard time with emotional issues, which they find confusing. They are often agents of change who are willing to take risks in the pursuit of new challenges or ideas. This makes them interesting people as long as they avoid the elitism and impatience that characterize their peer group. Around here, we find the homes of CEOs, journalists, strategic planners, and some academics.

This is the **Blue** neighborhood.

As we complete our stroll, we wander through yet another community. The houses radiate warmth, with connecting porches overflowing with vegetation and thoughtful floral arrangements. The focal point of this community consists of a large community center where various cause-centered activities compete for a spot on the agenda to promote their activities. All sorts of worthwhile endeavors flourish, especially in the areas of ecological, spiritual, and physical well-being. There seems to be an unusually strong interest in cosmic issues here, including reincarnation and the afterlife. Some of the older residents have been to Eselen, the famous California institute.

Business and commerce are of secondary importance in this neighborhood. There is a bookstore focusing on spiritual and psychic topics as well as a health store specializing in vitamins and herbs, but not much else. Residents are motivated by their quality of life, which they strive to improve for themselves and others, at least in a psychological sense. They dislike confrontation. To them, power is the ability to influence others. The residents here are, understandably, gifted communicators, in both oral and written form. They dislike formal structures and are somewhat emotionally dependent on the encouragement and appreciation of others. These residents tend to be in marketing and communications, working in advertising agencies and as writers, as well as TV anchors. All the psychological fields are represented, and a high number of leaders of different causes make their homes in this neighborhood.

We have just visited the **Green** neighborhood.

WHAT COLOR IS YOUR MONEY MIND?

Perhaps you already know which neighborhood you would choose to live in. In many cases, most of us will identify with the residents of more than one neighborhood, so deciding where to settle down will be hard. Meantime, the task of determining who you are as an investor is at hand. Armed with the knowledge shared by the greatest investors, it is time for you to learn about yourself as an investor. Please get a pencil and remember, this will take only a few minutes. Don't continue with the book without completing our MoneyQ questionnaires.

There are two: MoneyQ1 will determine your personal MoneyQ profile. To complete this questionnaire, select the statement that fits you *most* of the time. You are going to find some of these harder to answer than others for the simple reason that you may think, hey, I agree with both of these statements. That's normal. We're not robots. There are times when we react one way and times when we react another. To answer questions such as these, you need to decide which of the statements applies to you *more often than the other*. Then check that statement in the unshaded box on the right or left that best describes you.

MoneyQ1

INSTRUCTIONS

- Choose the statement from the left or right column of the MoneyQ questionnaire on page 25 that best describes you at least 51% of the time.
- *If both apply* choose the one that would apply under *ideal circumstances* or *conditions of your own choosing*, as opposed to those required of you at work or home.
- Make a ✔ in the left or right column, corresponding to your choice between each pair of statements. **Answer all the questions**, otherwise your profile will be incomplete.
- Put yourself in a relaxed frame of mind and work quickly.
- Once you have answered all the questions, add up the number of checks (✔) in each column and write the totals at the bottom. Your total for all six columns should be 35.

Compare the total in column A to the total in Column B. If A has the highest number, circle A. Likewise columns 1 and 2, and columns ❑ and ∇. You will then have a "score" that looks something like this: A – 2 – ∇. Find the combination of letter/number/shape on the following chart and you will have the MoneyQ color that best describes your temperament.

GOLD	Trustee	A1 ❑	Conservator	A2 ❑
RED	Tactician	A1 ∇	Realist	A2 ∇
BLUE	Strategist	B1 ❑	Innovator	B1 ∇
GREEN	Mentor	B2 ❑	Advocate	B2 ∇

Now turn the pages and read the one that describes your particular color group.

MONEYQ1

A 1 ☐	**LEFT COLUMN**	**RIGHT COLUMN**	▽ 2 B
	Value accuracy	Value insights	
	Like to be with people of common sense	Prefer to be with imaginative people	
	Find predictable and stable is best	Find new and different is best	
	Look for practical uses	Look for innovative uses	
	Tend to be competitive	Tend to be nurturing	
	Prefer to be fair	Prefer to be compassionate	
	More often skeptical at first	More often accepting at first	
	Persuaded by objective reasoning	Persuaded by passionate conviction	
	Get things done--now	Meet deadlines at the last minute	
	Annoyed when interrupted	Accommodating when interrupted	
	Make detailed plans before you start	Handle problems as they arise	
	Make decisions quickly	Stay open to new options	
	Prefer talking about concrete situations	Prefer discussing ideas and theories	
	Like set and established procedures	Like change	
	Live in and enjoy the present	Prefer to imagine the future	
	Prize your strong sense of reality	Prize your vivid imagination	
	Value ability to logically analyze	Value ability to empathize with others	
	Try to ignore emotional aspects	Look for emotional aspects	
	Weigh pros and cons objectively	Decide by personal values	
	Always punctual and sometimes early	Tend to be leisurely	
	Want to have things settled in advance	Like to be spontaneous	
	Like to plan in advance	Like to go with the flow	
	Think facts speak for themselves	Facts only illustrate the general idea	
	Make existing methods work better	Create new and better methods	
	Handle projects one step at a time	Jump in anywhere and leap over steps	
	Concerned about underlying principles	Concerned about impact on people	
	See flaws and critique readily	Overlook flaws and support readily	
	More often head rules the heart	More often heart rules the head	
	Good at analyzing plans	Good at understanding people	
	Most often feel settled	Most often feel restless	
	Like to be scheduled	Find schedules confining	
	Like to be systematic	Stay unplanned, when possible	
	Need structure	Need freedom	
	Do best at observing facts	Do best at seeing new possibilities	
	Prefer to think concretely	Prefer to think abstractly	
	TOTALS		

GOLD TRUSTEE

FINANCIAL ORIENTATION
(reported rankings against other types)

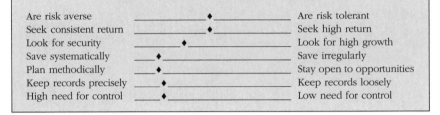

Are risk averse	Are risk tolerant
Seek consistent return	Seek high return
Look for security	Look for high growth
Save systematically	Save irregularly
Plan methodically	Stay open to opportunities
Keep records precisely	Keep records loosely
High need for control	Low need for control

Trustees are often the pillars of their communities seen by others as able to get the job done.

They prefer investments that are secure and provide a consistent return.

Meticulous in their record keeping, they rarely rely on intermediaries to ensure the accuracy of their accounts.

Realistic, grounded and responsible, Trustees are often the pillars of their communities. They are seen by others as able to get the job done. They value "the system," trust contracts, and organize their lives around procedures, providing security and stability for those in their care. They enjoy being in charge and frequently rise to positions of responsibility in their jobs and volunteer organizations. Belonging is a strong need, and service a tangible expression of their commitment to the community.

As the most defined economic realists, they excel as professionals and frequently become accountants, bankers, and administrators of all types.

They communicate in a style that is simple, direct, and frank and are usually ready with an opinion. Highly observant of details, they prefer working with real things and trusting their own experience as opposed to new theories. Inherently efficient, they are gifted at implementing policies and ensuring that things remain orderly and on track. They gravitate toward situations that allow them to plan ahead, set goals, and control the schedule.

In financial matters, Trustees are highly focused on saving and long-term planning. Often drawn to commerce or business, they tend to make or have money and preserve it. They have an above-average knowledge and interest in investments and fiscal issues.

Meticulous in their record keeping, they rarely rely on intermediaries to ensure their accuracy.

Borrowing, where possible, is avoided. Money represents both security and a measure of success in other areas of life. It is used judiciously to provide comfort, peace of mind, an elevated position, and the general well-being of the family.

Unless professionally involved in the investment industry, Trustees tend to be moderately conservative in their investment approach and usually have a relatively low tolerance for volatility. Investments that are secure and provide a consistent return make up the bulk of their portfolios. They are long-term investors, viewing their portfolio as passports to a worry-free future.

Investment ideas are well researched and thoroughly documented with established facts, including, wherever possible, a track record of performance. Stocks and government bonds are preferred over real estate and corporate bonds. Complex financial structures and untested products are of less interest.

Typically, they prefer well-established firms and advisers that are organized, consistent, and professional. Respect is the key; liking the individual is a secondary benefit at best. Trustees, however, remain independent and in control of their accounts at all times. Many turn to no-load mutual funds as a cheaper alternative to advisers.

GOLD CONSERVATOR

FINANCIAL ORIENTATION
(reported rankings against other types)

Are risk averse	◆_____	Are risk tolerant
Seek consistent return	___◆_____	Seek high return
Look for security	_____◆_____	Look for high growth
Save systematically	___◆_____	Save irregularly
Plan methodically	___◆_____	Stay open to opportunities
Keep records precisely	__◆_____	Keep records loosely
High need for control	__◆_____	Low need for control

> They strive to maintain a harmonious environment,
> always looking to stabilize the family, unit,
> or organization under their care.
>
> Conservators are organized and in full control
> of their cash flow.
>
> Like everything else in life, they feel a disciplined approach
> works best, and follow procedures consistently.

Warm, orderly, and conscientious, Conservators focus their energy on ensuring the welfare of those under their care, something they start doing early in life. Always curious about people, they are highly observant and quick to make others feel at ease. They are usually very affirming people.

Like all Golds, they have a highly developed work ethic, taking commitments and obligations with utmost seriousness. They are involved in details, want everything organized, and excel at anticipating what needs to be done. They enjoy following through and mobilizing others to accomplish concrete goals.

Conservators respect authority, history, and tradition. The conservation of resources remains a high priority throughout their lives. They do not enjoy change, abstract concepts, and untested theories. In fact, when they start imagining things, they are usually sure the worst will happen. This can lead to depression and self-doubt.

As leaders, their contribution is significant, yet they remain modest. They strive to maintain a harmonious environment, always looking to stabilize the family, unit, or organization under their care. Focused on the here and now, they are not usually interested in change or future possibilities. Their warmth, people orientation, and sense of responsibility frequently direct them to careers or volunteer activities where they are of service to others.

In financial matters, Conservators are organized and in full control of their cash flow. They are not likely to go into debt or squander hard-earned resources. In fact, they abhor misuse of resources by anyone. Saving for emergencies is a top priority.

While inherently good with facts and figures, they typically gravitate toward investments of lower risk and more consistent return. Like everything else in life, they feel a disciplined approach works best, and they follow procedures consistently.

Money is viewed as a tool for empowering and providing services for others. If the Conservator *is in charge of the family finances* or *is a key income producer,* then financial education and long-term planning become a top priority. If not, they are just as happy to leave the management of investments to others.

Conservators seek to establish a comprehensive relationship with an adviser. It is important to them that they *like as well as respect* that individual, that the adviser be orderly, systematic, and accurate, and that suggestions be backed by solid research. They enjoy investing in stocks directly, particularly blue-chip stocks, have an above-average interest in bonds, a moderate interest in real estate, and an above-average interest in investments with a guaranteed return.

RED TACTICIAN

FINANCIAL ORIENTATION
(reported rankings against other types)

Are risk averse	◆___ Are risk tolerant
Seek consistent return	◆___ Seek high return
Look for security	◆___ Look for high growth
Save systematically	◆___ Save irregularly
Plan methodically	◆___ Stay open to opportunities
Keep records precisely	◆___ Keep records loosely
High need for control ·	◆___ Low need for control

Realistic and pragmatic, they trust only what they know
and have personally observed, with little interest
in long-term projects.

They are unusually adept at sizing up problems and
moving in for the solution.

Tacticians are born to be risk takers. Where possible, they
prefer to invest in the stock market directly rather than in
mutual funds.

Unusually effective in times of crisis and change, Red Tacticians are active, independent, and seek the unexpected. When they are around, something usually does happen. They function best in small collegial teams where hierarchy is secondary to getting the job done. They often live on the edge, seeking action, and thus are frequently found among athletes, show-business types, promoters, small-business owners, field-rescue teams, and troubleshooters of all types.

Realistic and pragmatic, they trust only what they know and have personally observed with little interest in long-term projects so important to Golds and in abstract concepts dear to Blues. They excel at observing details and have a particularly acute visual memory. They enjoy a broad variety of people and activities, often operating outside the norms followed by others.

Tacticians are highly independent. They trust their own instincts and are unusually adept at sizing up problems and moving in for the solution. They prefer immediate rather than long-term problems and are gifted negotiators when called upon to make logical and difficult decisions. They are adaptable individuals who speak clearly without hidden agendas.

In financial matters, Tacticians are born to be risk takers. With enough disposable income and exposure to investments, they can become very adept at managing money. As in other areas of life, however, they will operate in their own way, outside the mainstream of established practice. Tacticians develop a broad-base storehouse of practical knowledge and, with their acute powers of observation, will often pick up investment cues others may miss. Rarely, however, do they have an interest in extensive research and written materials on their investments, preferring instead to respond to their "gut" instincts.

This ability combined with above-average flexibility enables them to respond opportunistically to new investment ideas. Most Reds have a high tolerance for risk and volatility. They also like the thrill of investing in the stock market and usually prefer investing in stocks directly rather than in mutual funds. Time constraints or lack of sufficient knowledge may require that they invest in mutual funds, but, at heart, Reds do not like relying on professionals. They have a keen interest in high-growth stocks and also may find real-estate investments with their hands-on-improvement potential attractive, most especially when they can negotiate a bargain.

Building wealth is a high priority for Tacticians, who like to live well. Record keeping, administration of assets, and detailed planning are usually of less interest to this spontaneous group, who prefer to plunge in and get the investment under way. Unless restrained by family constraints, money is viewed as another source of fun and excitement.

RED REALIST

FINANCIAL ORIENTATION
(reported rankings against other types)

Are risk averse		Are risk tolerant
Seek consistent return		Seek high return
Look for security		Look for high growth
Save systematically		Save irregularly
Plan methodically		Stay open to opportunities
Keep records precisely		Keep records loosely
High need for control		Low need for control

Resourceful, spontaneous, and adaptable, Realists are
found where there is fun, stimulation, variety, and
immediate tangible rewards.

Temperamentally, they are "high rollers" who like
to speculate.

When knowledgeable, they respond opportunistically to
new investment ideas and have a higher risk tolerance
than most.

Resourceful, spontaneous, and adaptable, Realists are found where there is
fun, stimulation, variety, and immediate tangible rewards. Members of the
"now generation," they look for and find enjoyment in everything they do,
pulling others in behind them.

They have diverse friends and interests, including a genuine and proactive
love of animals, nature, and children. Hollywood is home to many in this
group, as are emergency fields, crisis counseling, and all areas requiring
their highly developed negotiating and entrepreneurial skills.

Fun apart, they are realistic and down to earth, preferring to respond to
things as they come up rather than to plan ahead. They prize their common sense and the ability to solve immediate problems even though their
approach is frequently unconventional.

They avoid routine, seek excitement, value freedom, need activity, and prefer to *work harmoniously with others in an optimistic and humor-filled environment*. Long-term planning so dear to the Golds and abstract concepts so necessary to the Blues are of no interest to our more improvising Reds, who respond opportunistically to the challenges of the moment while often keeping *many* balls in the air at the same time.

In financial matters, Realists share the views of their other Red cousins that money is a tool, usually adding excitement and always a way to enhance the enjoyment of life. *Temperamentally*, they are "high rollers" who like to speculate—win big and lose big. Tomorrow is another day and usually another opportunity to earn another dollar. Money is something that must be enjoyed *now*.

Long-term planning, along with budgets and record keeping, are usually avoided.

Despite this seemingly haphazard approach, however, financially educated Realists who need to handle money are very capable investors. They respond opportunistically to new ideas, have a higher risk tolerance than most, and like the thrill of discovering investment opportunities. Picking stocks directly is frequently more attractive to the Red Realist than investing through mutual funds or investment advisers. Time constraints or lack of sufficient knowledge may require some mutual-fund investments, but, at heart, Red Realists prefer to pick their own investments. They do, however, have a close relationship with their trusted advisers, whom they use principally for research, execution, and record keeping.

They have a keen interest in high-growth stocks and also often find the hands-on-improvement potential of real-estate investments very attractive. Real estate is also suited to these gifted negotiators who are particularly adept at getting a bargain.

Building wealth is a priority for Reds who like to live well and plan to do so far into their future. The administrative aspect of their investments is best left to others.

BLUE STRATEGIST

FINANCIAL ORIENTATION
(reported rankings against other types)

Are risk averse	♦	Are risk tolerant
Seek consistent return	♦	Seek high return
Look for security	♦	Look for high growth
Save systematically	♦	Save irregularly
Plan methodically	♦	Stay open to opportunities
Keep records precisely	♦	Keep records loosely
High need for control	♦	Low need for control

They gravitate to the world of theories, future possibilities, and bold new designs.

They like being in charge and having the control necessary to carry out their vision.

They place a high value on asset allocation and solid long-term planning to achieve aggressive financial goals.

Independent, complex, intuitive, and focused, Strategists create visions, devise strategies, establish plans (and contingency plans), and then act decisively, often disregarding the skepticism and discouraging remarks of others. *Strategists have faith in their insights.*

They gravitate to the world of theories, future possibilities, and bold new designs. They *love to compete and challenge existing systems.* They enjoy learning new things and adding to their impressive store of skills. They drive themselves and others, often pushing to a degree that makes others uncomfortable.

Their communication style is especially clear and precise. They *like being in charge* and having the control necessary to carry out their vision. They can, however, quickly become frustrated when having to deal with details or facts that are unrelated to their insight and vision. Intellectually creative, they are often found leading organizations, or as lawyers, judges, management consultants, and executives of all types.

In financial matters, Strategists usually have an above-average interest and understanding of financial and investment issues. They excel at maneuvering finances to achieve their goals. Money is viewed as a source of power and proof of competency in other areas. Building wealth is a top priority.

Global in perspective and patient with complexity, they are usually willing to consider investment ideas that are new, international in scope, and/or structurally complicated.

They demand *unusually* high intellectual competence of their financial advisers and will challenge most of the accepted investment strategies. Since they tend to be "big-picture" people, they do, however, need the help of others to monitor the details of their investments and accounts. Only infrequently will a Strategist undertake his or her own research, preferring to quickly appraise the work of others. Mutual funds are attractive to some in this group, who value both the high degree of control and sophisticated range of choices. Others set up their own plans and pick securities accordingly.

Aggressive but not the highest risk takers, they place a high value on asset allocation and solid long-term planning to achieve aggressive financial goals. Asset-allocation plans are reviewed on a periodic basis and compared against the latest market models.

Strategists, for the most part, have a low level of anxiety about their investments, which they view as one more force to be harnessed and managed.

BLUE INNOVATOR

FINANCIAL ORIENTATION
(reported rankings against other types)

Are risk averse	⬥_____	Are risk tolerant
Seek consistent return	⬥_____	Seek high return
Look for security	⬥___	Look for high growth
Save systematically	⬥_____	Save irregularly
Plan methodically	⬥___	Stay open to opportunities
Keep records precisely	⬥__	Keep records loosely
High need for control	⬥_____	Low need for control

With their intellectual energy and compelling interest
in everything around them, they remain forever alert
to new opportunities.

As a group, they are dichotomous. While naturally drawn
to math and science, Innovators either *avoid dealing
with money* (inventors and professors) or can be
some of the *most sophisticated financiers*
(arbitrageurs and currency traders).

Their ability to access and process information
from many sources makes them prime candidates
for cutting-edge investments.

Inventive, insightful, and mentally stimulating, Innovators are constantly searching the universe for new and unusual ideas.

With their intellectual energy and compelling interest in everything around them, they remain alert to new opportunities. Independent and highly resourceful, they are not afraid of taking controversial positions. They enjoy debating issues from both sides.

Diversity is the key to their satisfaction. They are most at home in a flexible environment, which will allow them to critique, improve, and redesign whatever project has caught their interest. Whether others agree, understand, or support them is irrelevant. They look for difficult problems, always confident of their ability to improvise as needed. Following through once the project has been launched, however, is of less interest. Their unusual insights make them, at times, almost psychic about future developments. These traits enable Innovators to succeed in a variety of entrepreneurial activities. They are also found in strategic planning, currency trading, academia, and all aspects of computer technology.

In financial matters, Innovators are *potentially* among the highest risk takers. As a group, however, they are dichotomous. While naturally drawn to math and science, Innovators either *avoid dealing with money* (inventors and professors) or can be some of the *most sophisticated financiers* (arbitrageurs). They excel at understanding money flows and the impact of events on the future of investments.

Historically, they have been the most interested in stocks, which they analyze with the same zest as they analyze business opportunities. They take pleasure in either personally finding or having their advisers find undervalued situations. They will compare industries and companies with great insight and are among the most interested in currency opportunities, options, and other vehicles with potential for above-average return. Building wealth is a top priority, but beating the odds is equally interesting.

Innovators are competitive, often viewing investments as one more area in which to excel. Their ability to access and process information from many sources makes educated Innovators prime candidates for high-growth investments, unusual tax shelters, and complicated currency transactions. They have an above-average tolerance for both risk and volatility.

Day-to-day administration of the account, however, is not of interest and is best handled by a professional. Like their other Blue cousins, Innovators require unusually high levels of competence from their advisers. They will look for well-presented summaries, new investment ideas, and advanced financing concepts. Real estate is also of interest as long as the administrative details are handled by others.

GREEN MENTOR

FINANCIAL ORIENTATION
(reported rankings against other types)

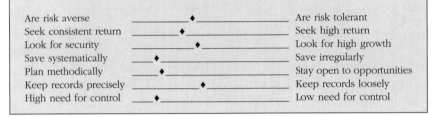

Are risk averse		Are risk tolerant
Seek consistent return		Seek high return
Look for security		Look for high growth
Save systematically		Save irregularly
Plan methodically		Stay open to opportunities
Keep records precisely		Keep records loosely
High need for control		Low need for control

Intuition, foresight, and compassion drive the Mentors,
who excel at leading others to achieve their potential.

As "big-picture" thinkers, they are insightful, able to
project the trends and pitfalls of the future.

Disciplined planners, they will set goals and measure their
progress on a regular basis.

Social investing is an area of interest.

Intuition, foresight, and compassion drive the Mentors who excel at leading others to achieve their potential. They operate best in a people-focused environment, requiring the fellowship of a harmonious group. Their enthusiasm, tenacity, and organizational skills enable them to achieve whatever they set out to do, but they function best with order and goals.

Gifted communicators, they have an unusual ability to manage without appearing to do so; not by means of direct orders, but by influencing through their own passion and positive expectations. Mentors are very loyal to individuals, causes, and institutions they admire. They expect a high degree of loyalty in return and may be opinionated.

They enjoy areas that optimize their ability to exercise their considerable "emotional intelligence" and intuitive ability to project the future's trends and pitfalls. Marketing, public relations, fund raising, social services, human resources, sales, and organizational development are some of the areas satisfying to Mentors.

In financial matters, given a choice, Mentors prefer to deal with other matters in their lives. They are not interested in money per se, but as a tool to improve the quality of life for their family and to support their own aspirations. However, they have a strong sense of responsibility for the financial security of individuals and institutions under their care. As a result, unless someone they trust takes over, they will devote all the time and energy necessary to work out their financial plan, retirement program, and other fiscal objectives. At the end of the day, many actually begin enjoying the process and the intellectual challenge of predicting investment trends, which they do well.

They are effective in managing cash flow, while being moderately conservative in their investments and are often more frugal than not in their use of money. They tend to be less comfortable with the volatility of high-risk investments and will normally favor balanced investments and a sizable liquid account. They save systematically and effectively, thereby satisfying their need for stability and order. Security is a higher priority than building wealth.

Disciplined planners, they will set goals and measure their progress on a regular basis. They also understand the long-term horizon of their investment strategy. Mentors tend to have specifically developed plans for their retirement.

Otherwise, they prefer to leave the day-to-day details of their accounts to financial professionals with whom they establish warm and trusting relationships. Unless dictated by other circumstances, Mentors prefer working with advisers rather than investing in mutual funds or in stocks directly. Many Mentors are beginning to express an interest in social investments.

GREEN ADVOCATE

FINANCIAL ORIENTATION
(reported rankings against other types)

Are risk averse	◆	Are risk tolerant
Seek consistent return	◆	Seek high return
Look for security	◆	Look for high growth
Save systematically	◆	Save irregularly
Plan methodically	◆	Stay open to opportunities
Keep records precisely	◆	Keep records loosely
High need for control	◆	Low need for control

They are free spirits by nature, who are intrigued by the
unusual and who love to be recognized for their
originality and unique contributions.

Keen and penetrating observers, they have a strong sense
of what motivates others.

Advocates go in streaks. They are either almost psychic in
their investment capabilities, or totally disinterested.

When "financially activated," they transfer their high-risk
appetite to the investment area.

Energized by new ideas, Advocates are warm and creative. They are free
spirits who are intrigued by the unusual and who love to be recognized for
their originality and unique contributions. Frequently unconventional, they
admire other nonconformists.

Keen and penetrating observers, they have a strong sense of what motivates others and a particular aptitude for seeing life as a cosmic pageant
with endless possibilities for human development. They usually remain
optimistic whatever the circumstances.

Adaptable and playful, they love a challenge, dislike routine, take life as it
comes, and tend to change projects and goals more frequently than others
do. They are gifted communicators, and many take up writing and speaking at some point in their lives.

As big-picture thinkers, they are insightful and able to project the trends and pitfalls of the future. They are interested in many areas, focusing in particular on those that have an impact on people and global concerns. Advocates, however, have an intense dislike of bureaucracy, in principle and practice, and they gleefully fight it at every chance possible. Many are writers, television anchors, journalists, public-relation specialists, trainers, leaders of causes, and counselors of all types.

In financial matters, Advocates go in streaks. They are either almost psychic in their investment capabilities, or totally disinterested. Like other Greens, they are not interested in money, except as a vehicle to empower themselves and others. When someone they trust takes charge of the financial planning, they will happily redirect their energy elsewhere and keep their investments in vehicles requiring minimum attention. If, however, they are responsible for the well-being of others—a family, philanthropy, or company—or for their own financial security, their attitude toward investments changes rapidly. They remain, however, disinterested in the nitty-gritty details of their accounts.

Advocates are moderately high risk-takers in general, with an almost bohemian approach to relationships, career goals, and life itself. When "financially activated," they transfer their appetite for risk to the investment area. Once armed with financial education and resources, they are open to "cutting-edge" investment ideas, have an above-average tolerance for volatility, are responsive to new technologies, and are patient with complex financial structures.

Sporadic savers and planners at best, Advocates leave the day-to-day administration of their accounts to others. They rely on the advice of financial professionals, with whom they need to establish warm and trusting relationships. Professionals are also required for record keeping and administration, which Advocates abhor. Typically they prefer to work with an adviser rather than investing in stocks directly. Most Advocates have an interest in social investing.

YOUR MONEYQ

Did you agree with your MoneyQ description? Good. If you did not agree with the description, chances are some of your scores in the categories are close, for example, 8 in one column and 7 in the corresponding column. Realize that while personality groups are innate and do not change throughout our lives, sometimes we frame, or react to, questions according to the expectations of our employer or our family, rather than according to our true preferences. Keep in mind that since "distorted framing" can lead to inaccurate results, only you can accurately determine your "inborn" temperament.

MY PERSONAL MONEYQ PROFILE:

COLOR: _____

TYPE: _____

THE WEALTH EQUATION——PART ONE COMPLETED

You have completed Part One of the Wealth Equation. You now know your MoneyQ profile, and you are familiar with the history of MoneyQ and Shoya Zichy's work in developing it.

It is time for Part Two.

Part Two of the Wealth Equation will reveal the 7 Master Keys to investment success. The Master Keys are a collection of the distilled wisdom of 100 top money managers we surveyed, along with my advice as an investment consultant with more than 35 years experience in the financial industry. This group of managers has one thing in common—success. They are all top investment professionals who possess a record of superior investment achievement. You will learn what they consider important to achieving that success. You will also learn how to apply this wisdom to your own investment program.

In Part Three of the Wealth Equation we invite you to take MoneyQ2, a short questionnaire that will address your risk tolerance, age, and investment-time horizon.

The Common Denominators: What Makes Great Managers Great

In our survey of top investment professionals, we discovered a number of surprising traits and common interests. Many of the characteristics the great managers share are also traits we can apply when we select a manager or when we adapt their practices to our own investment program. I have divided the data into five different areas of the managers' lives: their personality types, personal backgrounds, their professional lives, their relationship to their clients or investors, and the advice these top professionals have for you, the investor.

Portraying the Top Managers

PERSONALITY PROFILE

In the preceding chapter, we took a mythical walk down the streets of a fictitious village to visualize how each of the different personality groups might live. Studies show that the personality groups divide among the population at large as follows:

GOLD	38%
RED	38%
GREEN	17%
BLUE	7%

Based on the MoneyQ profile (the same one you just took), we discovered that the breakdown of money managers is, in certain respects, quite different from that of the population as a whole. In fact, successful managers ended up almost exclusively in two groups, Gold and Blue. Here is how their distribution broke down in our survey:

GOLD	42%
RED	9%
GREEN	5%
BLUE	44%

The first thing that surprises you when you compare these results is that while the number of Golds is approximately the same in both groups, the Blues, who represent only 7% of the population as a whole, represent 44% of the money managers in our survey. Remember, the Golds are those who are the community leaders and top professionals. They lead orderly lives and are looked up to by their peers. The Blues are more introverted and highly intellectual. They tend to study a lot and are serious and focused. These two groups comprise the vast majority of the successful managers we interviewed, and it is likely that this breakdown prevails among larger groups of money managers as well.

As we go along, I will point out to you those results that struck me as particularly interesting and revealing.*

PERSONAL PROFILE

Not surprisingly, almost all of the top managers are college graduates. Of the group, 25% received some of their education at an Ivy League school (31% of the Golds were Ivy League graduates). You may recall an earlier study by Glenn Ellison and Judith Chevalier, themselves Ivy League professors. They found that fund managers who attended the more selective schools (read: Ivy League) had better performance than managers who attended Podunk State. Our sample seems to bear this out. Ivy League schools are a tiny fraction

---

*A complete recap of survey results can be found in Appendix 1.

of the total number of colleges and universities in the United States, yet a quarter of our top managers had some Ivy League education.

Of the top managers, 69% had advanced degrees, mostly MBAs (59%), while 8% had other kinds of master's degrees and 2% had PhDs. Their major fields of study are not particularly surprising. Among undergraduates, 77% majored in business, finance, or economics. Among those who went to graduate school, 57% of the sample majored in business or finance, and many of the others specialized in related fields such as economics or accounting.

As to their personal philosophies, 77% described themselves "optimists" and 74% felt that they could have been successful in a job other than the one they held. Interestingly, two thirds of this group said that they had always been interested in stocks and investing.

As individuals, our managers exhibit a range of personal behaviors and even quirks, some of which are more interesting than others. For example, in the MoneyQ profile, you may recall a question that asked if you like change or if you prefer set-and-established procedures. In answer to these questions, 59% of the managers said they liked change, versus 38% who said they didn't. Here, the difference among personality types was notable: 84% of the Blues said they liked change, while only 16% preferred set and established procedures. This is consistent with what we know about the Blues' personality profiles. Golds were almost the opposite: 60% of them liked set-and-established procedures. Since both color groups are successful, preferring change to established procedures does not appear to influence investment success among managers one way or another. But it is important that you understand your own view of change. If you are comfortable with changing circumstances, you will be better prepared to live with a portfolio that is more volatile than someone who prefers established procedures and as much predictability as possible.

When we asked, [Do you] try to ignore or [do you] look for emotional aspects? 84% of all of the managers said they try to ignore emotional aspects. Of these, 93% of the Blues said they ignored emotional aspects and 81% of the Golds agreed. Clearly, no matter what the managers' MoneyQ, it seems that to be a great money manager (or investor), you must separate emotion from investing.

Interestingly, these top professionals also make time for reading outside the office: 68% of them spend at least ten hours a week reading outside the office, but 62% of that reading time is for business while the rest is for personal pleasure or other reading interests. Again, the message is clear. Whether you are researching stocks or mutual funds, there are no shortcuts to investment success. Like the great managers, you will find yourself doing a fair amount of reading and research to get what you are after.

PROFESSIONAL PROFILE

In most cases, these managers' first jobs were in the investment business. The largest percentage (42%) started as research analysts in the research department of a brokerage firm or as money managers, while 34% of the group started their careers as either a stockbroker or money manager. Thus, a total of 76% of these top professionals started their careers in the money-management business or in a field closely related to it. Clearly, the very successful money managers didn't go into this career by happenstance. This bears out what I heard from such gurus as Michael Price, Peter Lynch, Richard Driehaus, and Laura Sloate, all of whom became interested in investing as youngsters or adolescents. I am impressed that so many started in the investment business, stayed in it, and went on to be successful. Determination and early interest appear to be traits strongly linked to success in this field.

I expect you will not be surprised to learn that most of the top people have been doing it for a long time. There are not a lot of talented youngsters here. As in many other professions, a true craftsperson emerges after many years of practice and refinement of skills. The money-management business is no different. The mean number of years on the job for the group was 20. Only 17% of our sample had been managing money for ten years or less. Experience counts.

A mentor helped 43% of the group develop their skills early on in their professional careers. More than half said that failure along the way was an important learning experience for them, and 59% described themselves as team players.

Don't be surprised that the truly successful, as in most other fields, work long hours. Only 11% of our group said they worked a 40-hour week, and 26% admitted to working over 60 hours per week. The mean was 54 hours. (Are you still looking for shortcuts to investment success?)

What talents and attributes does it take to be a successful money manager? The most important factor to our group was an inquisitive nature. This was followed closely by investment-management experience, then intelligence, and knowledge of financial analysis. In addition, a large percentage (90%) of the managers considered self-discipline an important factor in investment success.

Other interesting points, not just for the investment-management business, but for life in general: 77% of the top managers thought that "avoiding dumb mistakes" was "very important" to success. What's a dumb mistake? Letting their emotions control their investment decisions, *not* doing their homework, *not* sticking with their investment principles, and *not* staying focused were among the dumb mistakes our managers cited. This was followed by securities selection, which 74% of the group rated highly as a contributing factor. I would hardly expect anything less than that from people whose job it is to pick stocks and make money.

Now, most investment managers do not make asset-allocation decisions since most managers are married to a particular style of investing at which they excel (for example, growth stocks or value stocks, large cap or small cap, domestic or international, and so forth. No one is good at *everything*). As a result, most managers do not need to concern themselves with the asset-allocation decision. Nevertheless, when we asked about asset allocation, fully 60% of the managers said that asset allocation was "very important" to investment success. Get the message? We're on to something!

At the other end of the scale, only 8% of great managers said that market timing was important to success as a money manager. This is an important point and one you'll hear more about: The reason so many of the top managers, starting with Peter Lynch, do not believe that market timing contributes to investment success is that you cannot do it successfully with any consistency. To dot the Is and cross the Ts: For most mortals, market timing doesn't work!

We asked the managers a number of questions about their methodology. For example, most investors know, often from painful personal experience, that deciding when to sell a stock or mutual fund is often much more difficult than deciding when to buy. How do the great managers know when to sell? Is it some special gut instinct they have, or do they use a disciplined approach to the selling process? We asked them those questions. Specifically, we asked if they would be more likely to rely on a specific sell discipline or "gut instinct" to sell a stock in their portfolio. An overwhelming 90% said that they relied on their sell discipline.

Avoiding failure was considered very important by 44% of the managers but, interestingly, 50% of the Blues in this category considered avoiding failure important while only 41% of the Golds felt the same way. This confirms what we know about Blues: that many of them are risk averse and believe in asset allocation to reduce risk and increase predictability. If you are a Blue, you may identify with this approach.

We wanted to know what the managers' principal goal was in managing money. Was it to beat a benchmark, beat the market, achieve their clients' financial goals, or simply to avoid failure? As you might expect, 96% of the managers thought it was very important to achieve their investors' goals, 91% either agreed strongly or agreed somewhat with the statement that their main goal was to beat a benchmark, and 49% said that beating the market was important to them in their investment strategy. Interestingly, on this score, 60% of the Golds considered beating the market "very important" compared to 41% of the Blues. Given my profile, that might tempt me to choose a Gold money manager, other things being equal. (Now is the time to fess up: I am a Gold profile.)

PICKING A MANAGER WHO FITS
YOUR PROFILE

Of course, others things *aren't* equal. In the first place, it is not likely that you will know what category your money manager or mutual-fund manager fits in. (Your manager may not know either, unless he or she also took the MoneyQ questionnaire.) Yet knowing your own MoneyQ type can help you pick a manager whose investment style corresponds with your views of investing. For example, if you are a Gold Trustee, you want predictability in your investments with a minimum of risk. Once you realize that, you will certainly not entrust all or part of your assets to a fund or manager with a volatile investment style. On the other hand, if you are a Red Tactician, your personality is the opposite of Golds. You are aggressive, you understand and accept risk, and you just might want to venture into a hedge fund or some other risky investment where you expect a big return, and you understand and can accept the risk you are taking to try to get it. Blues, on the other hand, understand risk very well, they just wish it would go away. While Reds and Golds see trees, Blues see the forest. They are Big Picture people. Greens are also Big Picture types, but they recognize their need for financial counseling, and will not hesitate to seek advice before making an investment decision.

Relationship with Clients/Investors

We were understandably interested in the relationship between these high-achieving money managers and the clients they serve so we asked them some questions about their relationships with clients. We also asked them what advice for achieving investment success they would offer investors who were not their clients.

One of the thorniest problems professional investment advisers face is client expectations. In one survey, Montgomery Asset Management asked 750 mutual-fund investors what they expected to earn in the stock market in each of the next ten years. The answer was an astounding 22.2%! That compares with the 15.2% return the stock market produced (using the S&P 500 with dividends reinvested) for the five-year period from 1992 to 1996, which itself was historically very high. This isn't healthy and can lead to disastrous results if you invest with these expectations. (You can imagine how the money managers feel about it!) In a nutshell, most investors expect too much from their mutual funds, their investment managers, the market, and ultimately themselves.

We asked our sample group this question: For investors who characterize their risk profile as moderate, what do *you* think is a satisfactory gross annualized return over a ten-year period assuming a 4% inflation rate? We followed up with: What do *most investors* think is a satisfactory gross annualized return over a ten-year period assuming a 4% inflation rate? Not surprisingly, the money managers' expectations were lower than what they thought their clients (or other investors) expect. The spread, however, was not as dramatic as in the Montgomery Asset Management survey.

In our study, the managers' mean (and median) response to the first question about what they think is a satisfactory return was 10%. Remember, that's *before* inflation. The same managers believed that their clients' (or other investors') expectations were closer to 12%—far less dramatic than in some of the other surveys. Of course, the clients of these investment managers have the advantage of being educated (or indoctrinated, if you prefer) by some of the top talent in the field, which might lead to more reasonable expectations. (Or maybe the managers are wrong about what their clients expect, and if we were able to ask them directly, we would have found that their expectations were indeed higher.) Nevertheless, inappropriate expectations create a potential problem. (Later, I will share some additional statistics with you that are positively scary.)

When we asked our managers if managing client expectations was integral to their management style, 51% said it was. Here again, we had an interesting breakdown by type: 57% of the Blues among managers answered "yes" to the question while 48% of the Golds did the same. Now if over half of the managers believe that managing your expectations is an integral part of their management style, what does that tell us about you? I think the message is clear—your expectations may not be realistic.

How do unrealistic expectations affect you? Well, on the simplest level, they may lead you to make poor decisions, to take greater risks than you should; to invest or pull out of the market for inappropriate reasons; to change your style or your manager for not meeting unreasonable expectations. If you understand your MoneyQ temperament, however, you will be better positioned to understand your own bias with respect to investment expectations. For instance, if you are a Gold, chances are you will have a realistic assessment of expectations by virtue of the way you approach the investment process, methodically, seeking predictability and lower risk. Blues, who may be visionaries as well as risk takers, may well jump on that story of a new cure for cancer and buy the stock instinctively. These are instincts Blues need to control. Reds will have similar problems. Here's the point: If you know your MoneyQ profile, you will know yourself as an investor. You will know what to look out for, know what you are likely to do well and what mistakes you are particularly vulnerable to.

In addition to having realistic expectations, understanding your risk tolerance is a very important part of your investment decision making; 42% of the managers considered it the most important factor in dealing with their clients. To get a picture of the depth of this problem, at least from a money manager's point of view, look at what happened when we asked the top managers if they felt that investors understood their own risk tolerance. A whopping 85% of them felt that investors *did not* understand their own risk tolerance. Amen. On the other hand, 66% of the managers felt that they understood their client's risk tolerance, presumably even if the investor didn't.

As a guide, here are the MoneyQ profiles ranked in descending order of risk tolerance, with the highest risk tolerance on top and the lowest risk tolerance on the bottom.*

BLUE Innovator	Higher Risk
RED Tactician	
RED Realist	
BLUE Strategist	
GREEN Advocate	
GOLD Trustee	
GREEN Mentor	
GOLD Conservator	Lower Risk

The importance of knowing your MoneyQ risk tolerance is obvious. If you are a Green Mentor, you should not be speculating like a Red Tactician. Remember that speculating always feels good when you're winning, no matter what your personality type. But when the inevitable losses come along, those who are less suited to speculating by virtue of their MoneyQ types will not only feel the worst, they might compound the problem by making dumb mistakes. Know yourself.

ADVICE FROM THE PROS

We could not let an opportunity to ask some of the top managers in the country for their advice and suggestions on how average investors might improve their chances for success. That advice is reflected in the keys we have developed. Here's a quick capsule of the combined wisdom of the great managers.

- Focus on long-term goals.
- Don't trade too often.

---

*This ranking is mitigated by the different MoneyQ types' approach to risk, which differs from one group to the other.

- Have patience.
- Make an investment plan and stick to it.
- Practice asset allocation and diversify.
- Understand your own risk tolerance and try to understand the potential loss involved in any investment.
- Invest regularly and systematically.
- Don't try to time the market.
- Be disciplined.
- Be consistent.
- Make rational, not emotional, decisions.
- Buy quality, well-managed companies.
- Set realistic goals. (Remember that losses are part of the investment process. Don't be greedy.)
- Monitor your results, reevaluate your holdings, and make adjustments whenever necessary.
- Get professional help if you can afford it.

Now on to the Master Keys to see how all of this good advice can be implemented.

PART TWO

THE MULTIPLIERS

MASTER KEY 1
SET REALISTIC GOALS

Extend your patience and shorten your greed.

GERRY HEFFERNAN
STRATTON MANAGEMENT

I expect that you will not be surprised to hear that the truly great investors do not leave to happenstance the results they expect from the stock market. We asked the great managers we surveyed about the goals they set for themselves. Over 90% of the managers pick some benchmark, such as the Standard & Poor's 500 index or the Russell 2000 small-company index, that they aim to beat. (In "The Common Denominators: What Makes Great Managers Great," we talk about the differences between the investment returns the managers expect and what their clients' expect. Guess who expects more?)

Before we get to that, let's talk about defining expectations. For example, say you are a high-school basketball player. You are the star of the team, and a lot of points are expected of you in every game. Would you realistically set your goal to score 50 points every game? I doubt it. It's not that this is an impossible goal. There are, after all, a few superstars who have done it, but only a handful. No matter how good you are, an expectation that high would be unrealistic.

The stock market is no different. In our game of making money, realistic expectations are the order of the day. Sure, there are a few cases out there of superstar investors who have earned 30% a year for an extended period, but I hope you don't think that just because they did that, you can too. (And *please* don't tell me that you heard about a new system that is going to show you how to make 30% a year in the stock market! We are not trying to recruit unrealistic and gullible investors here.) We'll get back to this shortly. Remember, the objective of *The Wealth Equation* is to make you rich by creating a sensible plan that is tailor-made for you.

Ask yourself this question: Why do you invest in stocks? Is it because you expect to find a real winner and make a lot of money in a short period of time? Are you looking for that special advantage that will earn a quick score, either because you got a good tip or were the beneficiary of some privileged information? Perhaps you know someone who is well connected at a particular company and this person gave you hot information on the company's prospects, information that perhaps others do not yet know. Let's forget for the moment the fact that if that were true, and you made some fast money, you might be counting it during a long vacation at the federal penitentiary. The fact is, you might get lucky from time to time, but luck is hardly an investment strategy you can count on. For those of you looking for "quick" profits, now may be the time to admit that you have tried some—shall we say—"investment shortcuts."

On the other hand, you may be a true long-term investor, a person who is investing in the stock market because you have a specific goal you need to meet. This might be college educations for your children, a second home at the shore, or, the ultimate savings objective common to us all, a comfortable (no—a luxurious!) retirement. In this case, your objective is more realistic if only because it is long term, and long-term objectives are easier to navigate through the choppy seas of short-term market fluctuations.

Whatever your goals, the first step to success is to define your investment expectations. Perhaps the hardest part of what we are about to do is to delve into the inner thoughts, aspirations, fears, and expectations of the most important person in the world: you. Be realistic. We're the only ones here, and I don't want you to try to impress me. I want only that you be honest with us both about who you are and what you may become. This will remain between us as we make our way through the choices that will guide you to the correct investment decisions, and when I say correct, I mean correct for nobody else but you. Along the way, I will do my best to ensure that you do not make the wrong choices or select inappropriate answers to the questions that will arise. With the help of *The Wealth Equation*, we will build your investment future from the ground up. It doesn't matter how old you are or what your education level is. All that matters right now is your sincere desire to invest intelligently and enjoy the fruits of your investment wisdom. Once you know who you are, you can realistically assess what is out there in the world of stock market investing, and what isn't.

In our manager survey, Kevin Riley of Roxbury Capital Management put it well: "Determine whether your real goal is entertainment or investing. Entertainment implies a game-oriented, aggressive trading strategy, while investing requires patience. Some people by temperament are traders, others investors." Amen.

The greatest investor of all time, Warren Buffett, has a very simple strategy. As he puts it: "We favor business and industries unlikely to experience major change. . . . We are searching for operations that we believe are virtually certain to possess enormous competitive strength 10 or 20 years from now." Would you be surprised, having heard that, that Warren Buffett has invested heavily in Coca-Cola and Gillette? Did Warren Buffett become one of the two richest men in America (net worth over $21 billion) by investing in the obvious? Well, maybe that is exactly what he did. So let's pay attention. There is nothing, I say again, nothing, about the way Peter Lynch and Warren Buffett invest that requires a master's degree in business to understand. But Buffett is a billionaire and you are not. Probably one big reason is that you are not as disciplined as Buffett is. Buffett knows what his goals are and he sticks to his strategy.

Most investors, you see, vacillate between ideas they like, techniques that appeal to them on the spur of the moment, investment fads, technical analysis, market timing, and all of those strategies that virtually guarantee that you will end up behind the investment eight ball. All these traits point to a lack of discipline and a lack of focus on realistic goals. Please keep this in mind as we delve into your personal-investment objectives. As our investment survey shows, the successful money managers have no doubt about theirs.

THE VALUE OF TIME

Defining your *realistic* investment expectations is the first step toward wealth. Note I stress realistic goals. In order to accurately define your expectations, we need to talk about your investment time horizons. We all look at time in different ways. Time is, after all, an irreplaceable commodity, one we can never recoup. Hence, time is something we should take very seriously and think about carefully. What do we do with our time? Are we satisfied with our personal utilization of the irreplaceable time available to us? Many of us often feel that there is not enough time to do all the things we want to do, and we lament the rapid passage of time, underscoring all the things we failed to do.

But in the investment arena, time can be our most valuable asset. Indeed, it is time that will turn us all into financial geniuses. When it comes to our investment portfolio, few things can be as helpful to us in achieving our objectives as the passage of time. Our job is to make the right decisions early on, formulate our investments according to a plan, and let time do the rest of the work. Time will help us, if we don't screw it up. Getting old does have its advantages!

Of course, we have different time requirements for different events in our lives. Educating children, saving for an opulent vacation, planning to purchase a vacation home, and our own carefree retirement are all worthwhile objectives, and each of them involves different time horizons. Typically, if we are saving for retirement, that objective is going to be longer term than most of the other events in our lives. Many of these objectives and the time horizons themselves will be a function of your personal MoneyQ personality. As we proceed, you will soon get to know yourself a lot better, at least as far as money is concerned! You will also learn that time horizon and risk are intimately related.

For the sake of this exercise, we will define time horizons as the latest time at which you will need to spend a significant portion of the money you invest. For example, if you were saving for the education of one or more children and the children were just starting grammar school, the time horizon might be 10 to 15 years. What is your time horizon? Please choose one of the following:

1 to 3 years

3 to 5 years

5 to 10 years

10 to 15 years

15 years or longer

Did you choose 1 to 3 years? Realistically, you should keep your money in a bank and settle for a guaranteed rate of return.

Remember, we are dealing with what works. To explain what I mean, let's look at some market data over different time spans.

Most serious investment professionals want you to have a minimum five years' investment time horizon. That's because history shows that the odds over time are stacked in your favor. All the great investors know this, and if you are not already there you should, and can easily, adopt this attitude once you change any old habits you may have acquired along the way.

"Think long term," says T. Scott Wittman of Vantage Investment Advisors. "Set your investment strategy for the long term based on long-term goals and expected returns." George Froley of Froley, Revy Investment Company adds: "Try to hold good companies for long time periods." Peter D. Wells (Kanne Paris & Hoban) chimes in: "Building wealth requires a long-term perspective." Comments on this subject echo from one great manager after another. On the subject of creating wealth long term, we come as close to unanimity as we will ever get among the great managers. Time is your friend.

Let's look at the facts. Using the Ibbotson/Sinquefield data on stock market performance for the 72-year period from 1926 to 1997, the Standard & Poor's 500 index produced positive returns in 52 years and negative returns in 20 of those years. That means that if you invested in the S&P 500 index, you made money in 72% of those years, which, most of us would agree, is a pretty good average. However, if your life savings are involved, you really don't want to take a one in four chance of even a small loss in any given year.

Now let's look at longer time periods within these same years, 1926–1997. Take five-year investment periods. There have been 68 of them between 1926 and 1997, assuming you start investing in any one of those years for five years. Since 1926, you would have made money in 61 of these 68 periods, or about 90% of the time. That's very good, and odds like that begin to justify taking a chance on investing in stocks. Looking at even longer periods over the same time span, only two ten-year investment periods (out of 63) would have produced a loss, and there are no losses in that historical time frame for investment periods of 15 years or longer. These data are for the market index. Now, if you can achieve performance that is better than the market, you can stack the odds in your favor even more. That is, of course, what we are setting out to do.

By the way, you may have heard market statistics that are different from the ones I have just shared with you. Here's why: Most large companies pay dividends to the stockholders, usually in the form of cash. When investment professionals calculate investment return, we normally include the value of those dividends in the calculation since, after all, they represent a return on your money just as the price appreciation of the stock does. But often, when a gloom-and-doom market analyst is trying to prove that the market is risky, he or she will use the same Standard & Poor's 500 statistics, but *without dividends reinvested*. (The index you see in the financial press is the raw index without dividends.) Stocks in the index pay dividends and, if you owned those stocks, you would have received those dividends and, presumably, reinvested them. Most professionals use data that include the reinvestment of the dividends that the stocks in the S&P 500 produce. The reinvestment of dividends makes a big difference in your returns over a long time period.

THE MIRACLE OF COMPOUNDING

Let's get back to defining expectations. You know that expecting an unrealistically high return will lead to disappointment and possibly cause you to make some really bad mistakes in an effort to "catch up" when you have a disappointing year. This happens most often when our expectations exceed our MoneyQ for risk tolerance or in other ways don't match our money mind. When our goals and our MoneyQ are in sync, even conservative strategies will lead to growth.

Let's have a look at some returns and the effect of those returns over different time spans. To see how different amounts of money will grow over time at the assumed rate of return, let's take an example that is typical of many IRA savings plans. Start with $10,000 and reinvest your dividends and profits. Add $2,000 of fresh capital each year for the specified number of years.

RETURN	5 YEARS	10 YEARS	15 YEARS	20 YEARS	25 YEARS
10%	$26,315	$55,812	$103,317	$179,825	$303,041
12%	28,329	64,156	127,295	238,568	434,668
14%	30,474	73,747	157,064	317,485	626,361
16%	32,758	84,757	193,974	423,367	905,170
18%	35,186	97,381	239,668	565,186	1,309,893

These are very impressive numbers, and they demonstrate dramatically the beauty of compounding returns. The results also demonstrate how well you can do if you don't have to pay taxes! Remember, we used an example here with relatively small amounts of invested dollars. Imagine, if you will, what these numbers would be like with a few thousand dollars more invested each year.

You don't have to pick a return now. We will be asking you some questions later about your expectations, time horizon, and other important characteristics that will drive your personal-portfolio asset allocation. It is not too early, however, to talk about our expectations in terms of what the market offers us.

Back to time horizons. If you are unsure of your time horizon, the questions at the end of the chapter will help you sort them out. Also, keep in mind that you need not have a single time horizon. Rolling time horizons are more realistic for most of us, since we generally have more than one long-term investment objective. There's the house to buy, the kids to educate, the second home at the beach, the fantastic vacation, and, ultimately, retirement. That's a lot of time horizons.

RISK VERSUS REWARD: DEFINING EXPECTATIONS

The next step in setting realistic goals is to determine the return you hope to earn by investing in stocks. Here again, your success depends upon your being realistic. The great investors do not set unrealistic expectations for themselves or their clients. "Do not get greedy. Be reasonable in your expectations," advises Alan B. Snyder of Snyder Capital Management. Have you noticed how some people who are ordinarily reasonable and judicious in their daily lives jump at an opportunity for a quick buck in the stock market? You Red profiles will know what I mean. Before you do that again, try to remember this advice from David L. Diamond, CFA of High Rock Capital, LLC: "Think rationally before you invest. If you cut coupons to save ten cents on a bottle of ketchup, why would you take your life savings to buy a stock on a whim?" Yeah.

This is a key to the success of great managers. They know all of the statistics, and all of them will try to beat the S&P 500 index or their own relevant benchmark. They all also know that a rising tide lifts all of the boats. What that means to you and me is that most stocks will

A TALK WITH PETER BERNSTEIN: REALITY CHECK

To get another perspective on the question of market expectations, I chatted with Peter Bernstein, the well-known investment book author and consultant. Peter's recent book, *Against the Gods*, was a worldwide best-seller, which chronicled the history of risk. A fascinating tale. He is also the author of *Capital Ideas*, perhaps the finest book on investment theory and practice ever written. Given my respect for Bernstein's views, I wanted to ask him for his thoughts on what investors might expect.

TANOUS: Peter, I think the most important issue investors must address is what return on their investment they can reasonably expect from the stock market. A recent study conducted by Montgomery Asset Management found that investors expected returns of 22% a year for the next ten years. As you know, stock market returns, as measured by the Ibbotson/Sinquefield studies, show returns of about 11% a year over the last 70 years. I don't know about you, but I find those expectations scary.

BERNSTEIN: I think it's even more complicated than that because the 11% return, or even a lower number, is a long-term average of markets at very different levels over time. If history and common sense tell you anything, it's that markets that have gone up a lot are going to have lower future returns than markets that have gone down a lot. The trees-don't-grow-to-the-sky syndrome is serious. If you simply do the arithmetic, a 20%-a-year return doubles your investment in about three and a half years. So that would be 16,000 [*Dow Jones Average*] in 2003, 32,000 in 2007… As you can see, you get numbers that are not realistically supportable in terms of what earnings, dividends, or interest rates are likely to be. The 20% figure is just silly. Even 9, 10, or 11% growth figures are not certain because those figures include a wide range of experiences. What the market is saying by going up is that we think everything is great, and we're just not going to worry. We're witnessing an evaporation of anxiety that anything really bad can happen.

TANOUS: What will cause that sentiment to change?

BERNSTEIN: The stock market at 8700 [*Dow Jones Average at the time of this interview*] is saying that we think we understand how the world works. I don't think something bad is going to happen until the world begins to work differently from the way people expect. For example: The economy weakens and the Fed lowers interest rates, but the economy keeps right on weakening. That's kind of what happened in Japan. Here's another example: Inflation reappears and the Fed raises interest rates. The first increase in rates doesn't tame the beast, and the Fed has to keep raising them and raising them. Parameters begin to burst and suddenly you don't understand what's happening, and so the only thing to do is to run for cover. As long as people understand what is happening, they're not going to worry, and the market won't go down, *but* returns can still be less than 20%.

TANOUS: Indeed. Putting this in a longer-term context, let's say for young people thinking about their retirement nest eggs, my concern is that if investors have inflated ideas of returns, they start playing catch-up, they take even greater risks, and they get into even more trouble. What sort of advice would you give someone who is building that nest egg? What can someone reasonably expect?

BERNSTEIN: I get up every morning and I remind myself that I really don't know. I just don't know. So I'm not a believer in 100% solutions. I do make judgments, but I consider that uncertainty is the real worry. We don't know. We try to draw on the past, but if you look at the past and ask what is the probability that any one of those particular episodes is likely to replay itself, the probability seems very small. Another depression like the '30s isn't likely; we've learned too much to let that happen. The probability of a replay of the inflation of the 1970s isn't likely. I think we've learned too much to have that happen. So if those things aren't going to replay themselves, the markets that followed those events are not likely to replay themselves either.

History doesn't really tell us very much unless we expect the episodes in history to replay. So we really don't know. The probabilities are that the U.S. economy will continue to grow and prosper, and therefore I would want to own a share of American business but I sure as hell wouldn't bet the ranch on it. So in spite of Jeremy Siegel, [author of *Stocks for the Long Run*] I would not be 100% in stocks, and I would own bonds. Not that I think bonds are the greatest thing. Over the long run, I suppose equities should do better, but in my run, which is maybe 20 or 30 years, I wouldn't necessarily depend on that. Here's something that follows from this: If you're 100% in equities and that turns out to be wrong, you're going to make all the wrong decisions and panic at the wrong moment. The primary reason for holding bonds is that you don't panic when the stock market goes down. You have a sense that you're still viable. In my experience, as an individual's resolve fluctuates, the greatest risk is yielding to panic when things happen that you don't understand.

TANOUS: Presumably that's an argument for shorter-term bonds with less volatility than long-term bonds, since you could panic out of those, too.

BERNSTEIN: You can panic out of that, too, so maybe you have a laddered portfolio or you don't go out over too many years. The reason that I'm against 100% anything is that you won't be able to manage when bad things are happening, and they will happen.

TANOUS: How much faith or comfort do you attach to the long-term returns in stocks?

BERNSTEIN: Not much. Because that's a very long number, and I'm not going to live for 90 years. Seriously, the segment of history that I'm going to live through isn't necessarily going to be a long-run average. That long-run average is made up of all kinds of stuff and I don't know what my particular piece of stuff is going to be. What people should expect is that things that they *don't* expect are going to happen. Somebody who is 35 or 40 years old, who is really beginning to amass some money, maybe has 25 or 30 years until retirement. That's not very long, and there can be a lot of peculiarities and unique characteristics to that particular period of time.

TANOUS: So what do you tell that man or woman on your doorstep who fits the picture you just painted?

BERNSTEIN: I say be 60/40, or be 65/35 percent invested in stocks and bonds. Be only as exposed to equities to the extent you can live with it when you're wrong, because the real danger is to panic out of the market. People will do it. We're human. To get back to the beginning of the discussion, when things are happening that you don't understand, I

rise if the market as a whole is rising. You might have an investment objective of 12% a year on average, but you also know that if the market is down 10% in a bad year, you are not likely to meet your objective that year. Likewise, if the market roars ahead, as it did in 1995, 1996, and 1997, you can reasonably expect to do better than your 12% goal, at least in those years. Bottom line: Expectations must be realistic or you will fail. Take that to the bank.

Sure, some hedge-fund managers try for very high returns, but they do so with investors who are prepared to endure much higher would remind you that there are going to be periods when what happens is beyond your comprehension. Unique events. This great wonderful [*stock market*] period we're going through was something nobody expected. It is a continuous surprise, and the market keeps going up because the surprises continue to be positive.

TANOUS: Do you have any strong views one way or the other on market timing?

BERNSTEIN: I go back to what I said before, we don't know. I think that the way to run your affairs is to say, I don't know. I'm a big believer in rebalancing. I think you do sell on the way up and you do buy on the way down.

TANOUS: In fact, that seems to be the thesis of a lot of value players.

BERNSTEIN: Are you greedy or aren't you greedy? You don't know what's going to happen. What's happened in Asia is a wonderful example of how one minute everybody felt bullish, that this was the greatest thing in the world, the next minute everybody is running for cover. You don't know what's going to happen. Don't be greedy. Greedy means you think you know. Don't panic either.

TANOUS: Your notion of protecting yourself is basically through asset allocation, isn't it?

BERNSTEIN: Right. I'm never so overexposed to any decision that I won't be able to handle it when I'm wrong. Unfortunately, the capital-gains tax is a horrendous barrier to rebalancing individual holdings or the whole bloody portfolio. But I do it anyway. At the end of the day, this is what I know. Nothing fancier.

risks than I believe the average investor should be subjected to. We have all heard of the investment wizardry of hedge-fund legends such as George Soros, Michael Steinhardt, and Julian Robertson, but there are many others whose results have been mediocre or even disastrous. We don't read articles about them except for the occasional example of someone who managed to lose *all* of his investors' money. Every last penny.

Obviously, in our pursuit of investment excellence, we are not going to subject ourselves to that kind of risk. This is a key point.

You have got to understand what you can realistically expect from
the market given your risk tolerance, your expectations, your time
horizon, and your own (or your investment manager's) skills. As
Lawrence R. Powell of Rohden Funds Management says, "Don't say
you are a long-term investor and sell everything during the first 10%
correction, or for that matter, after a 10% profit." That's why your
MoneyQ plays such an important role in how you invest.

Are your investment expectations realistic? We'll see later on.
One of the problems we face today is that investment returns over
the past ten years have been unusually high. In 1995, the stock market, as measured by the S&P 500, rose a remarkable 34%; 1996
added another 20%; and, in 1997, it rose another 31%! This is far
above historic stock market returns. One effect is that these returns
have led investors to unrealistic investment expectations.

As we said earlier, Montgomery Asset Management surveyed
750 mutual-fund investors in February and March 1997 and asked
the investors what they expected to earn in each of the next ten
years in the stock market. The answer: 22.2%! Compare that expectation with the 15.2% return the stock market has produced (again
using the S&P 500 with dividends reinvested) for the five-year period
from 1992 to 1996, which itself was historically very high. More realistically, compare that expectation of 22.2% annual returns with the
11.2% return the market has produced in the last 60 years.

Here is another example. The IAI mutual fund group, in con-
junction with Dalbar, Inc., a leading survey group, conducted a survey of 1,600 IAI customers, past and present. They found that 55%
of the investors expected annual returns of 15% or greater! And 95%
expected returns of at least 10%. Where is the reality here?

In other words, many investors expect much too much.

To compound the problem, unrealistic expectations can lead to
a combination of bad events. First, to even hope for returns such as
22% a year, an investor would have to take inappropriate and scary
risks and, in the process, jeopardize the capital that he or she needs
down the road. The other danger is that if the investor doesn't take
large risks, he'll be disappointed in the low return and do one of two
things: switch to riskier investments, or get out of the market alto-
gether. Both results are bad.

Are you beginning to see why so few investors get really rich
in the stock market? But hang on, because you *will* become rich.

Beating the Market Realistically

This brings us back to the most important question of all. *Is it realistic to expect to beat the market?* Let's talk about that. First, if you want to know what market returns are generally like, look at the 10% return set in the table on page 60. Given the history of returns for the market averages over time, that's what you could expect if you invest your money (tax-free) in the stock market indexes. As you can see, those returns are pretty good. What's more, they don't involve a lot of work. You don't need endless conversations with pushy brokers, you don't need to pore over those voluminous mutual-fund tables, and you don't need to do extensive research on individual companies looking for specific stocks to buy. All you need to do is buy an index fund that mirrors the S&P 500 and add your $2,000 to it every year. You have to admit, that's a pretty good investment plan all by itself. In fact, if you were pretty sure you couldn't beat the market, and there are a lot of people who will tell you just that, then your investment plan is going to be fairly short and sweet. (Some of you, especially you Gold Trustees and Conservators, Blue Strategists, and Green Mentors, may be tempted to stop reading right now! Don't.)

Not surprisingly, most managers expect to beat something. Of the managers we surveyed, 91% agreed to varying degrees that their main goal was to beat a benchmark, whether it is the S&P 500 or something else that may be more appropriate to their particular investment style. I believe that you can beat the market, too, but I hasten to add that it is not easy to do. So, no matter what your profile, if your expectations include an *intelligent* plan to maximize your wealth over time, and beating the market is part of that plan, stay with me. We have a way to go, but we will get to where you want to be.

THE HUMAN ELEMENT
AND THE EFFICIENT MARKET

We cannot really conclude the subject of investment expectations without some understanding of what is perhaps the greatest debate in the stock market community. It can be summed up in one question: Is the stock market efficient? This is important because investment expectations depend significantly on whether or not you believe you can beat the market. Obviously, if you can't beat the market, you have no choice but to buy a few index funds and be done with it.

Needless to say, few on Wall Street believe the Efficient Market Theory. If they did, they might as well put themselves out of business. After all, if stock prices are unpredictable, who needs brokers, or research analysts, or *Wall Street Week*, or hundreds of magazines and newsletters that tell us what stocks to buy? They can't possibly know!

As you can imagine, the Efficient Market Theory, which is hotly debated most of the time, has some problems. For one, there is ample evidence that the market can be beaten, although when you point this out to the Efficient Market proponents, they scoff. Why? Because the Efficient Market Theory assumes that the market is rational and, therefore, stocks trade at prices that reflect *everything* there is to know about them in the public domain. While that may be true, the market is also the result of the behavior of a number of people. How many perfectly rational people do you know? The fact is that most of us behave like, well, human beings from time to time, and I think we would all agree, most humans do not always behave rationally. The fact that humans behave like humans is an important and intrinsic part of the Wealth Equation. Without an understanding of human behavior, your possibility of achieving investment wealth will be relegated to chance or just plain luck.

Since the market is a reflection of the behavior of individuals, who are not always rational or, at least, not rational all of the time, I believe that there are more than a few ways to beat the market. In fact, my research shows that there are plenty of companies with hidden assets that investors have simply not recognized and that are not reflected in the price of the stock. That said, let us not delude ourselves. Beating the market is extremely difficult to do, but it can be done, and we're going to do it.

INVESTOR PSYCHOLOGY AND MARKET SUCCESS

As we've already discussed, one of the most popular new fields of investment analysis is behavioral-investment analysis. How do investors behave under different circumstances? Let's have a look.

Much of the work in behavioral analysis, as it relates to investing, is being pioneered by Professor Richard H. Thaler of the University of Chicago. As you may know, one of the biggest problems investors encounter is simple overconfidence. Here's an example: History tells us that the most successful investment strategy is to hold stocks over the long term, yet investors continually trade stocks. Despite the evidence, they think the stocks they are selling are going down and the new ones they are buying are going up. Yet, active trading for most of us results just in lower profits and higher costs (commissions and taxes).

Thaler and Yale economics Professor Robert J. Shiller concluded that many money managers and investors believe that they are better endowed to acquire information than are others and that they can use this advantage to make money picking stocks. As reported in *The New York Times*, economist Terrance Odean did a study on the trading patterns of 10,000 investment accounts at a brokerage firm over a six-year period. His findings were surprising. First, the average annual turnover rate of the stocks owned by these investors was a very high 78%. So much for buying and holding! Here's the clincher. Odean studied the results of the stocks these investors sold during the period. He found that on a one-year basis, the stocks the investors *sold* outperformed the ones they bought by an average three percentage points. That's not just overconfidence, it's hubris!

Here's what you should take home from this. Since investor behavior is not all that rational, investor psychology is an important, if hitherto not very noticed, factor in investment performance. It follows, then, that understanding your own money mind is the link to investment success that we have been missing for a long time. The MoneyQ questionnaires (there will be another later) mark an important step in a very important direction. What this means to you and me is that any successful investment program has to take into account not only the usual features, such as our age, risk tolerance, time horizon, and all those other good things, it also has to take into consideration what you and I are like as human beings. Only then can we realistically expect to have an intelligent investment program that works for each of us as individuals, one that we're comfortable with and can stick with, one that will help us avoid costly mistakes.

YOUR MONEYQ AND YOUR GOALS

The first step then is to set goals that our "money personalities" can live with. For example, an individual with a Red MoneyQ profile will not be happy with a very conservative investment strategy, since he or she is able and willing to accept considerable investment risk. Conversely, Golds will be uncomfortable with risky investments and will probably lose sleep over them, since they tend to be more conservative in their outlook toward money and life.

Different sets of circumstances can influence the choices we make, including our investment decisions. People can make different decisions on basically the same set of facts depending on how the facts are presented.

Peter Bernstein, in *Against the Gods* (John Wiley & Sons, 1996), relates the following experiment by Professor Daniel Kahneman of Princeton and the late Professor Amos Tversky: A group has $40 theater tickets. When they arrive at the theater, they discover that they have lost their tickets. Distressed, the majority decides not to spend another $40 and goes home without seeing the play. A second group arrives at the box office to buy tickets to the play. When there, they discover that $40 is missing from their wallet. As in the first case, they are all $40 poorer. But in the second case, the majority buys tickets and they go to the show anyway. What gives?

The academics call it "mental accounting." The point is that investors do not always react to events in the expected rational manner. There are other influences that determine the choices we make, and these conditions defy rational analysis.

Professor Thaler provides this example: Each person in a group was given $30 and told he or she could walk away with the money or take a chance on a coin toss. If the toss came up heads, you won an extra $9. If it came up tails, you lost $9. A majority, 70%, of this group took the chance knowing that they would end up with a minimum of $21. Another group was offered a slightly different proposition. They were not offered any money at the outset, but were told they could toss a coin where heads would get them $39 and tails $21. Or they could take $30 and not flip at all. In this case, only 43% chose the gamble. As you can see, both groups were offered the identical proposition, but it was framed differently. (If you feel like it, try this on a few people you know.)

Why did different people make very different decisions in the face of identical probabilities? Seemingly, it is not just the facts that determine our behavior as humans, it is also the way our minds process the information. To make the most use of this information, we have to get in touch with our inner selves as individuals and learn to understand how we are likely to react given certain choices. The MoneyQ questionnaires are designed to do that for you, to help you understand your own deep feelings about money and risk, which will, in turn, help you set your personal investment goals. (I need not remind you that these decisions are not limited to our investment programs, but that they shape our lives across the board.)

I hope as these examples unfold you are beginning to see why investors do not behave rationally and do not systematically become rich. Yes, there is a way to gain wealth by investing in stocks, and the first step is to chart our course and set our goals. Are our investment expectations sound and realistic? We must learn what to expect and what not to accept and chart our course accordingly. As we get to know our own investment personalities and determine our own investment expectations, we will be much better prepared to establish a truly realistic set of goals and formulate a program that is perfectly matched to our own human emotional traits, a set of goals that we can easily stick with to ensure ultimate success. We are on our way.

KEY POINTS

The first step to a successful investment program is to define your expectations. That means setting realistic objectives. To do that, ask yourself:

- ## WHAT IS MY TIME HORIZON?

    Realistic time horizons should be based on our knowledge of what the market has done over the last 70 years. You will not do yourself any good if you set completely unrealistic time horizons. The key is to put the odds of success in our favor. We need time to do that. As Bill Jurika (Jurika & Voyles) said, "Be patient. In investing, the fast way is the slow way."

- ## WHAT IS MY INVESTMENT-RETURN EXPECTATION?

    You know now what historic returns have been. You will try to do better than the average, of course, but you will also temper your return expectations with a strong dose of reality. Unrealistic expectations are the key to failure.

- ## HOW MUCH RISK AM I PREPARED TO TAKE?

Risk is the price you pay for higher return. The idea, of course, is to be rewarded for the risk you take, not penalized for it. This is where the experience of the great investors can help. By acquiring their discipline, you can learn to put the odds on your side. Remember that no one can predict market movements with any degree of accuracy. Sad to break this to you, but that includes you. Did you notice how often Peter Bernstein said that we simply don't know? A humble approach to the stock market will lead to wiser decisions. Know yourself. Study your personality MoneyQ profile. You will be better prepared to adapt the investment program that is ideally suited to you, with the amount of risk that is appropriate and comfortable for you as an individual.

Master Key 2
Eradicate Fear—Understand Risk

Emotions are the Achilles' heel of the market participant.

LAWRENCE R. POWELL
ROHDEN FUNDS MANAGEMENT

The greatest fear in investing is the fear of the unknown. Will the market crash? Have stocks risen too fast and too far? Should I wait to invest? Did I pick the right stocks or the right mutual funds? The list is almost endless. There is no shortage of things to fear.

To overcome fearful investing, you must understand the risks that you face. Each of us has some notion of what stock market risk means, at least to us. The great investment professionals are no different. In fact, almost all of the money managers we polled had something to say about risk. Steve Wilson of Reich & Tang put it simply and succinctly when he advised investors to "be patient, understand your true risk tolerance, and don't overdiversify." The problem is that there are so many different opinions and beliefs about risk that we tend to jumble them up in our brain.

Attitudes Toward Risk

When it comes to understanding risk, professionals often have a decided advantage since they live with market risk every day. The rest of us get it in little shocks; hearing the news that the market dropped 100 points on the radio on the way home from work, for example. As stockholders, that's not good for our digestion.

Let's begin our look at risk by walking through some of the ideas and notions that most people have about market risk. Later, I will share with you what I and many of the great money managers believe is the *real* risk in buying stocks. It is likely that you have not heard it explained this way before.

In its simplest form, most of us think of stock market risk in terms of stock prices; they go up, and they also go down. We want our stocks to go up, of course, and when they go down instead, the notion of risk is brought home to us in a hurry. In reality, the risk in buying stocks may occur on many levels. Sure, if we buy stock in a company that gets into some financial trouble, we are not likely to make any money on that investment, but even the stocks of very good companies go down, sometimes without explanation or reason. Often, this is the result of erratic market behavior. When the market is out of favor for whatever reason, stocks may decline generally and, in cases like that, all boats rise and fall with the tide. So, in addition to the obvious risk that we may buy a lousy company, there is the risk that the market may be out of whack, in which event our stocks may go down just because the market is going down. That's double risk, and the better you understand these risks, the better positioned you will be to craft an intelligent portfolio that neutralizes these risks as much as possible.

Academics who follow the stock market have long debated risk in portfolios. Some of their arguments are, well, academic, but others have advanced our knowledge of how the market works and how we should confront the various risks that the market portends. That is why investment professionals often pay attention to these findings, even though not everyone agrees with the conclusions. For our purposes, since you are probably not going to begin a new career based on the latest academic findings on stock market risk, let's settle on those areas of risk where both the consensus, and old-fashioned common sense, tell us how best to confront different kinds of stock market risk.

TYPES OF RISK

We used to think of *market risk* as the predominant risk in stocks. Academics soon pronounced that market risk was in direct proportion to volatility. Hence the more a stock, or the market, moved around and changed in price, the more risky it was. Thus, if you take more than the market risk, you have the right to expect more than the market return. A good example of this is the historic difference in performance between small-cap stocks (smaller companies, with lower capitalization, whose names may not be known to the general public) and large-cap stocks (stocks of the large companies whose names we generally recognize). As a general rule, we consider small capitalization companies those whose market value (i.e., the number of shares times the price of the stock) is about $1 billion or less. For example, General Motors capitalization is about $50 billion. Microsoft's is about $200 billion.

Over time, small-cap stocks have given returns that are about 2% per year higher than you get from investing in larger companies. The higher return is your reward for taking greater risk since, after all, small companies carry more risk than do large, established companies. This may seem a bit obvious, but Bill Sharpe won the Nobel Prize in economics for the Capital Asset Pricing Model on which this theory is based.

Some years later, two other academics Eugene Fama and Ken French developed the Three Factor Model, which said (basically) that the market risk in a portfolio of stocks is only one risk. There are other factors that affect the risk in a portfolio of stocks. These are *size risk* and *style risk*. That is because value stocks behave differently from growth stocks and small stocks (stocks of smaller companies) behave differently from large stocks. In other words, there are many more risks in portfolios than we originally thought.

As smart investors, we try to outsmart the market by diversifying some of this risk away. What this means is that if we understand value-stock risk, we minimize that risk by putting growth stocks in our portfolio so that the value-stock risk will be offset by the growth stocks, whose risk characteristics are different. To put it simply, if our value stocks are behaving badly, we hope their bad performance will be offset by our growth stocks, and vice versa. What we are after here is a portfolio that does not act like a roller coaster, soaring up and plunging down. That's not real good for our stomachs. What we want is a nice smooth progression of rising values, and since no one can guarantee that to us, we'll do the best we can to allocate our stock portfolio in a manner that makes the price swings as painless as possible. Say "thanks" to all those Nobel Prize winners.

Later, when we get down to constructing our optimal portfolios, we will take into account these different risks as we try to diversify to counter the different portfolio risks and increase our return.

GROWTH VERSUS VALUE

Let's pause for a moment and review the difference between growth and value stocks. Growth stocks are those characterized by a steady pattern of earnings growth. Market dominance is a nice feature as well. Classic growth stocks, which also have market dominance, are Coca-Cola, Gillette, Microsoft, many pharmaceutical companies (think of products such as Viagra, for example), and so on. Smart money managers buy them because they expect them to continue to grow in earnings and in stock price. This is the basic philosophy of all growth-style money managers. Roger Stamper's (Spyglass Asset Management, Inc.) views are typical of the top money managers who specialize in growth. "Growth works in the long term because the stock of a growing company will always go up. It works for me because I have a long time horizon, and I am willing to wait for a company's good fundamentals to be reflected in the price of the stock."

Value stocks are different. These are companies that are defined as low book-to-market value companies. That means that their stock price is often low compared to the intrinsic value of the company based on its book value.* Sometimes these companies exhibit no earnings growth; sometimes they have no earnings at all. So, why buy them? Managers who specialize in this type of company are attracted by their low cost and their potential. David Diamond of High Rock Capital, LLC, put it this way: "I believe investing should be no different from buying a house or a car. You wouldn't overpay for a house because it is in a good neighborhood or a car just because it is faster. Why buy a stock just because it grows faster? There is an inherent value that defines worth." Spoken like a true value manager.

To a value manager, the market does not recognize the value that some companies represent; therefore, they buy the stocks and wait for the rest of the world to catch on. Jim Henderson of MetWest Capital Management thinks of it like this, "Buying a stock is just like any other good, you want to feel as though you got good 'value' for

---

*Book value is the value of the company's assets less its liabilities (debt, for example).

your money. No one likes to feel they overpaid for something." Get the drift? Although he also owns growth stocks, Warren Buffett was long considered the king of value-stock investors, finding those hidden bargains before everybody else got wise to them.

One of the controversial debates about risk and return in stocks is the one surrounding the different performance attributes of growth and value stocks. There have been many studies that show how these different categories of stocks perform over time. What do you think? If you could pick only one style of stock—growth or value— which would it be? Imagine a portfolio of powerful growth companies with rising earnings, or a portfolio of asset-rich companies whose price is a bargain. What will you buy?

In terms of pure asset allocation, there is no right answer, but from the perspective of your own individual preferences, your MoneyQ profile will certainly offer a clue to the types of stocks you will have more success with. For example, Red MoneyQ profiles will almost certainly prefer growth stocks, and they will exhibit both an affinity for and possibly a talent in selecting growth stocks over value stocks. The same holds true, in varying degrees, for Blues. Greens, on the other hand, may well like to own growth stocks because of their risk-tolerant natures, but since they also tend to delegate investment responsibility to those they trust, they are unlikely to do the growth-stock research on their own. Golds, on the other hand, may well seek out value stocks, those low fliers that have been left behind by the market and offer attractive prices relative to their assets or other factors.

Which stocks should you own, value or growth? Based on what we know today, regardless of your MoneyQ, you should own *both* styles. (Perhaps in different proportions, and perhaps in funds rather than stocks. More about this in Part Three.) Their historic performance attributes, however, are different. Guess which has performed better over time: growth stocks or value stocks?

If you picked value, you win. The evidence is pretty impressive. For example, from 1964 to 1992, growth stocks grew by an annualized 10.45%, while value stocks grew 15.76% over the same period. That's not even close! Now I can hear you thinking: *Why don't I just own value stocks since their return is historically higher over such a long period?* Good question. Here the answers get controversial. Many academic thinkers believe that this is a story of risk. You expect higher returns for taking greater risks, and, they say, value stocks are riskier than growth stocks, so the returns are expectedly higher.

A TALK WITH DR. JOSEF LAKONISHOK: THE NATURE OF RISK

Dr. Josef Lakonishok combines careers in academia and money management. A professor at the University of Illinois, he is also a principal in the money-management firm of LSV Asset Management.

TANOUS: There is a debate in the investment community about value-stock investing and growth-stock investing. The evidence seems to indicate that value stocks perform better than growth stocks over time, so the question is, what is the price you pay for the better performance? Professors Gene Fama and Ken French have argued that value stocks are riskier, and your reward for the extra risk is better performance. But you did a study[*] in which you concluded that value stocks were *not* riskier than growth stocks. If that's so, and since value stocks do better, why shouldn't an investor just buy value stocks?

LAKONISHOK: First of all, although I'm a believer in value investing, how can you be sure that value strategies will work as well in the future as they have in the past? I find the Fama/French argument totally unappealing. I don't see what is so risky in value stocks. I don't find people in the business who view value stocks as more risky. Risk is not an acquired taste. It's not enough for Gene Fama to say that value stocks are risky. I visit many institutional investors; I talk to those people. They aren't scared about the risk of value stocks. However, they are less sure about the pattern of future returns.

TANOUS: How do you account for the fact that they tend to offer better returns?

LAKONISHOK: They offer better returns because the stocks are uglier, because people tend to extrapolate past performance too far into the future, because analysts are typically more in love with growth stocks and stocks with unbelievable stories. To me it really isn't so complicated.

TANOUS: The criticism some others have made is that your studies were confined to the postwar period.

LAKONISHOK: This is not a fair argument at all. A student of Andrei Shleifer checked during the Great Depression, the late '20s early '30s, how value stocks performed, so we have evidence going back a very long time. Value stocks did well during the Great Depression. We don't have any evidence, except for Fama and French's emotional appeal, that value stocks are more risky.

---

*"Contrarian Investment, Extrapolation, and Risk," Josef Lakonishok, Andrei Shleifer, and Robert W. Vishny, *The Journal of Finance*, Vol. XLIX, No. 5, December 1994.

TANOUS: What advice would you give to an intelligent investor investing for his or her retirement?

LAKONISHOK: I definitely would not advise anybody to put all his or her eggs in one basket. I believe in value investing, but I would not advise people to invest only in value stocks. There might be long periods of time when value stocks underperform growth stocks. In the last few years, value stocks did not shine all that brightly. Incidentally, Fama and French also got very excited about the size factor [*tracking the performance of small-company stocks versus large-company stocks*]. The size factor didn't work. Ten years for most of us is a very long time!

TANOUS: Are you saying that small-company stocks, which are supposed to do better than large-company stocks over time, haven't done better over the last ten years?

LAKONISHOK: Exactly. I would be surprised if the results weren't the same in other countries in the last ten years, too. Fama/French did their studies, and hypothesized that size is also a risk factor and investors should get extra compensation for investing in small-company stocks. Then for the next ten years, where's the extra compensation? [*Small-company stocks have generally underperformed large-company stocks over the past decade.*] If you had jumped on the Fama/French bandwagon and bought small stocks because of their higher expected returns, you would have underperformed. In addition, you would have had higher transaction costs, and higher fees since managers who manage small-cap portfolios generally charge higher fees. It would have been a bad idea.

TANOUS: From your point of view, what is the smart thing that an investor should do looking forward?

LAKONISHOK: I definitely favor value stocks, and I buy them with my own money. I would advise people to be very patient and not trade a lot. Trading is very costly. I definitely would advise people to look at the expenses of money managers, mutual funds, and so on, because if you give up 2 or 3% before you get started, how can you win? Markets are way too efficient to make up for such high expenses. I think if you are considering mutual funds, the first statistic I would look at is the turnover. I like funds with low turnover. Second, I like to see low management fees and expenses. I like the way Vanguard funds are run.

TANOUS: Do you think services like Morningstar help?

LAKONISHOK: I am not so sure. I did some work in this area and, as other researchers also concluded, found little persistence in performance. When a fund gets four or five stars, a lot of money pours into the fund, but the returns typically don't follow. So this is why, for many investors, a low-cost alternative makes sense. The DFA funds provide a relatively low-cost alternative.

TANOUS: Of course, those are 100% indexed.

LAKONISHOK: Yes, but they take a large value tilt and the costs are relatively low. For example, I don't want to sound like I'm recommending specific funds, but I also like Tweedy Browne's approach. They don't trade much, and they are very disciplined. I'm not a consultant and I didn't interview them, but I think that they have a deep value approach and that they are patient. My point is that if a typical professional, a lawyer, accountant, or doctor, is trying to outperform the market, his or her chances of doing so are very, very slim with trading intensive strategies.

TANOUS: In this book, we are adding psychological profiles to help people understand their approach to investing in addition to assessing their risk tolerance, which, in itself, is hard to do.

LAKONISHOK: I believe that the key to success in this business is discipline. There are many money managers who don't have strong convictions about what they are doing. The first two down quarters and their strategy might go out the window. I think you should do your homework, and then stick to your ideas. You should not bring in emotions every time that you revise your portfolio.

Well, maybe. The evidence here is a bit fuzzier. For example, *Fortune* magazine reported an Ibbotson study that analyzed value and growth stock performance during bear markets, specifically during all bear markets since 1978. The result was that while the market, as measured by the S&P 500, declined on average 18.1% during all these bear-market periods, value stocks declined 11.8% and growth stocks declined 21.1%. Makes you wonder, doesn't it? But don't give up on growth stocks completely. There are plenty of periods, including some recent ones, where growth stocks outperformed value stocks by

TANOUS: Do you assign any value to attempts to time the market?

LAKONISHOK: No. All of our clients want us to be fully invested at all times. We don't hold large cash positions. A big cash position for us would be 1%. We don't time the market because it is extremely difficult to do so over relatively short horizons. For example, most value money managers think that this market has been overpriced for quite a few years. Imagine what would have happened to us if we had acted upon our convictions and gone to 30% or so in cash. We would have underperformed in a big way and probably lost a lot of our clients.

TANOUS: Other words of advice for investors?

LAKONISHOK: I say again, be diversified. I think that international stocks should be in every investor's portfolio. International stocks are not so highly correlated with U.S. stocks, and thus can reduce the risk of the portfolio. Once more, watch expenses. Management fees and trading costs in general are higher for international stocks. Looking at some of the emerging market funds, I'm appalled when I see turnovers of 200%. How can investors expect to make money? Low turnover/low cost strategies are even more appealing when it comes to international stocks.

To go back to the original discussion about growth and value stocks, as a money manager and as an investor, the least of my worries is the risk in value stocks. I think that value investing is a strategy that makes a lot of sense especially when you look at valuations of companies such as Coca-Cola and Dell Computer. In cases like these, there has to be a lot of persistence in the earnings growth for many years to justify the current stock prices. Based on my research, such a level of persistence doesn't exist.

a wide margin. For example, for the three-year period ended March 31, 1997, growth stocks (as measured by the S&P/BARRA growth index and the similar Value index) beat out value stocks by an annualized 24.1 to 20.4%. Going back eight years, growth still won using these indexes, by 16.8% to 14.5%. The academics and others will go on debating this point for generations.

From our point of view, we now know that there are different kinds of risk in the market, but what good does that do us? Simply put, it tells us that if we are to get the optimal return from our portfolio of stocks, we have to try to counter the different risks. To do that, we had better understand them. From then on, it is up to us to use that knowledge to our advantage.

We know, for example, that any time we buy a stock, we have to put up with market risk. We can't control that. But when it comes to other kinds of risk, such as growth-stock risk and value-stock risk, and small-stock risk and large-stock risk, we can do something to control them. Smart investment professionals know that these risks can be neutralized, to some extent, by diversifying the risk away. You can do the same thing. What this means is that if you have nothing but, say, growth stocks in your portfolio, you will be subject not only to market risk in general, but also to growth-stock risk. That's two risks for the price of one! We can't do much about stock market risk as long as we are invested in the market, but we can neutralize growth-stock risk by balancing it off with some value stocks. Get the idea? Remember this later on (I'll remind you anyway), because these principles will be a mainstay of our portfolio allocation.

PSYCHOLOGICAL RISK: THE EMOTIONAL COMPONENT

Another type of risk, the kind that most investors are familiar with, is psychological. This is the risk of panicking out of the market at precisely the wrong time. "The best laid financial plans can be wiped out quickly in the midst of an irrational or emotional moment," (John C. Riazzi of Dean Investment Associates). "Tolerance of risk is the item that clients never seem to have a firm grip of. Their risk tolerance tends to move with their emotions." (Craig T. Johnson of Leonetti and Associates). Alas, how right they are. If only we could take the emotional component out of investing, how much better off we would be! Absent being able to do that, it's essential to factor the emotional component into your asset allocation, but first you have to get a handle on how emotional you are when it comes to money and investing. That is what we will continue to explore. Were you surprised by your profile? We're not always who we think we are when it comes to money. Your asset allocation must be tailored to your specific needs on every level, otherwise it's unlikely to work in the long run.

Here again, the professionals have an edge because they understand risk and the underlying market movements that cause it. More often than not, the top professionals possess the discipline that allows them to understand and react intelligently to this risk. Don't get me wrong. This does not give them any ability to predict the market movements any better than you or I could; it is just that they cope better. (Once when I was lecturing on this point, some wise guy from the audience got up and shouted: "Of course they cope better, it's not *their* money!")

Our job is to use the Wealth Equation to put together a portfolio of stocks, or mutual funds, that will serve us well over time and make us rich. We'll use what we learn from the top managers and combine that with your personal MoneyQ personality to create a plan. For now, however, even if your personality profile suggests that you are a risk taker, I do not recommend that you make a massive bet on value stocks alone. (There are better risks to take, and we will cover many of them.) Remember, there is no rule that says you have to own only growth stocks or only value stocks. In fact, we are all better served by diversifying our portfolios. That said, the evidence in favor of value stocks is compelling, and I can tell you in advance that when we create our optimum portfolios, some will have a value-stock tilt.

CONSEQUENCES: RISK AND REWARD

Let's move on to a new area of risk that is attracting some attention: The notion that our decisions have consequences. Sounds obvious, but it's not. Here's an example: If you go to Las Vegas and play the color red on the roulette wheel at your favorite casino, you know that your odds are roughly 50/50 of winning. So, if you're feeling in a "red" kind of mood, you might wager a few bucks on your hunch. Say you are pretty flush and you gamble $100 on red. The wheel turns and turns; you focus on the little white ball going round and round. It finally descends and starts clinking against the metal partitions between the numbers, until it finally comes to rest on the number 10, even, and black. You lose.

What are the consequences of this wager? You lost a hundred bucks. Life goes on. But what if you decided that you needed to double your life savings? You ask permission to put $250,000 on the color red, and the casino cheerfully agrees. Now we have the identical odds, but the consequences are very different. If you win you double your life savings; if you lose, you lose all of your life savings. That is not an acceptable bet even though the odds are identical to the odds in the previous example. Today, behaviorists are analyzing risk and return using this added dimension of consequence. In other words, not only do the odds affect our decision to invest, the possible consequences also affect that decision.

This is not a new idea. Once again, I turn to Peter Bernstein's excellent book, *Against the Gods*. He tells the story of Blaise Pascal in some detail. Pascal was a famous mathematician and philosopher who lived in France in the seventeenth century. He is known as the father of the theory of probability and is recognized as a world-class genius. In his later years, Pascal secluded himself in a monastery and reflected on religious subjects for the remainder of his life. During this period, Pascal raised the question of the existence of God. He put it in terms of a wager. This is an easy 50/50 bet: God exists or He doesn't. On the flip of a coin, where heads means God exists, and tails means He does not, which way would you bet? Here, the consequences have to enter into your decision. If you bet that God exists, and you lead a reasonably devout life, your reward will be great if you are right, an eternity in heaven. If you bet instead that He does not exist and you are wrong, eternal damnation is a stiff price to pay for your error. Not knowing the answer, you would be well advised to bet on God existing, not because the odds are any better, but because the consequences of being wrong are so severe.

This is an important new area of investment research, and its principles will be reflected in the questions we ask you later on. Your reactions and responses will help fine-tune our search for the portfolio that is just right for you.

A more modern application of this theory can be found in the studies of two noted academics Daniel Kahneman and Amos Tversky.[*] Their prospect theory, in simple terms, suggests that the pain or fear of a loss looms twice as large as the joy or benefit of a similar gain. Taking that a step further, Shlomo Benartzi and Richard H. Thaler[†] try to answer what many investment specialists have long considered an investment puzzle—the equity premium.

---

[*] "On the Psychology of Prediction," *Psychological Review* 80, 1973.

[†] "Myopic Loss Aversion and the Equity Premium Puzzle," Working Paper, Johnson Graduate School of Management, Cornell University, 1993.

Let's back up for a second and talk about the equity premium. What this means is that stocks (equity) return more than bonds. Well, we knew that, didn't we? Yes, but what puzzles these great academics is the amount by which equities return more than risk-free bonds. From 1926 to the present day, the equity premium over risk-free investments has been about 7%. Now that may not sound like a whole lot, but if you get that each and every year, through the miracle of compounding, you get very big numbers. You may be familiar with the famous Ibbotson/Sinquefield series that tracks investment returns back to 1926. In essence, it shows that if you had invested $1,000 in risk-free Treasury bills in 1926, your investment would be worth $14,250 at the end of 1997. But if you had invested the same $1,000 in large-company stocks, your return in 1997 would have been an eye opening $1,828,330, a major difference.

The basic theory is that stocks *have* to offer higher return than risk-free bonds because when we buy stocks we are taking a risk and we, as investors, demand compensation for that risk. If we are not compensated, we just won't invest. So far so good, but the academics shake their heads over why this premium is so huge. In their view, the stock market is risky, but is it *that* risky? After all, when you take a reasonably long-term view of stock market investments, the risk seems not so great. According to Benartzi and Thaler, if an investor has a 20-year time horizon, given the historic performance of stocks, the equity premium should be 1.5%, not 7%.

TIME/RISK REALITY CHECK

Benartzi and Thaler suggest an answer to this puzzle, which they have dubbed "myopic loss aversion." Let's look at a typical investor's time horizon. If we assume that most of us are saving for expensive college educations for our kids as well as our own retirement, a long-term investment plan could easily approach 20 years. But do we behave as if our investment time horizon were 20 years? Hardly! Instead, we check our stocks or mutual funds periodically, sometimes every day or every week. Even the most disciplined among us follow the market and react to the quarterly statements we get from the mutual funds we own, checking first to see if we made or lost money this past quarter, and how much.

Benartzi and Thaler explain that an investor with a 10- or 20-year time horizon often behaves as if his investment time horizon were just one year. To further explain this, they point out that an investor who receives a bonus in early January and plans to spend the money on a Christmas vacation later that year has both a planning horizon and an evaluation period of one year. They compare this investor with another who receives her bonus in early January and decides she wants to invest it toward her retirement in 30 years. Despite this 30-year horizon, she looks at her portfolio seriously every year and makes decisions accordingly. Her planning horizon is still 30 years, but her evaluation period is one year. Thus, even though both investors have very different investment time horizons, they behave in the same way.

To our academic friends, this means investors see risk inappropriately. It is a fact that the risk in investing for one year is a lot greater than it is in investing for 20 years. You can lose money in stocks about a third of the time if you invest for only one year. Because investors have this one-year view, they demand a higher return than is warranted by the risk they are *really* taking over the long term. That represents a real opportunity for intelligent investors like you and me.

Here's why: Regardless of our individual attitudes toward risk in general, if we discipline ourselves to invest and behave like long-term investors, we will both beat the odds and get a return that far exceeds the risk we are taking. Not only does that sound like an instinctively intelligent strategy, it is one of those rare points on which virtually all of the greatest money mangers agree. The advice of Bradley E. Turner (Gradison-McDonald Asset Management) says it all: "Practice benign neglect. Don't become a slave to your portfolio." This strategy is embedded in the custom-tailored portfolios you will find later in the book. One of them is just right for you, but, as in other aspects of your life, you will need to make certain decisions and, like the great money managers, have the discipline to see them through.

COMING TO GRIPS WITH RISK

In constructing our individual portfolios, each of us must take into account not only our risk tolerance in the abstract, but risk tolerance as a function of what is at stake. For most of us, the portfolio is our life savings, or a good part of it. This suggests that while we know we must take some risk to enjoy a superior return, such risk must be tempered by the realization that a total loss, or even a substantial loss, is unacceptable, no matter what the odds. It is the lesson of the roulette wheel. Since a total loss of your fortune is an unacceptable alternative, you cannot afford any investment where that is a serious possibility.

That brings me to the concept of *real risk* I promised to discuss earlier in this chapter. If you are convinced, as I hope you are, that investing in stocks is absolutely crucial to your future well-being, you must come to grips with all of the different risks you will encounter in the course of developing your plan to wealth. You must not only understand the risks, but you must adapt them to a program that allows you to deal with them as a person. Much of the advice we receive does not take into account how we react as individual human beings to different events in our lives.

But there are some events that bring us all together in their ability to inspire nearly universal joy or fear. In the context of the stock market, a new market high is generally met with universal joy by investors. (Of course, there are always some gloom-and-doom artists and short-sellers who won't be happy, but who cares?) Conversely, there are some stock market events that are met by almost universal fear.

Let's step back for a moment. We all know that the market declines from time to time. In any given year, you have about a one-third chance of a decline in the stock market, based on historic data. Since this fact is pretty well-known and appreciated by most investors, a small decline in the market rarely causes any but the most timid and timorous to change their investment program. That's why so many of us consider ourselves to be impervious to panicking out of the market. And in most cases, we are correct in thinking so.

In the survey I mentioned earlier, commissioned by Montgomery Asset Management and conducted by Intersearch Corporation, when the 750 randomly selected mutual-fund holders were asked what they would do if the Dow Jones average dropped 5% (that's about 450 points from a level of 9000), 58% percent said they would do nothing and another 13% said they would add to their holdings. Only 13% said they would switch their investments to something else. Asked the same question about a 10% drop in the Dow Jones Average, or 900 points from a 9000 level, 39% said they would do nothing, 15% said they would add to their holdings, and 21% said they would switch to another type of investment. No signs of panic selling there.

CATACLYSMIC RISK

Now, I want to talk to you about another kind of risk quite unlike the risk of a 5% or 10% market decline as in the previous example. It is what I have dubbed cataclysmic risk. This is the risk of an event, or a series of events, so cataclysmic as to shake the foundation of all of our beliefs and cause us to stray from all of our investment beliefs and practices. It is the kind of event that can shake us to our roots and cause highly emotional and even erratic behavior. What are these investment cataclysms? There have been four in this century.

The first is the stock market crash of 1929. The second is the period of stock market decline during the Great Depression in the '30s. The third was the 40% decline in the stock market in 1973 and 1974. The fourth was the October 19, 1987 crash, which caused a market decline of 22.6% in one day. Each of these events qualifies as cataclysmic in that it changed the stock market landscape that we had been accustomed to. In the process, many investors made understandable but unfortunate decisions in the face of extreme adversity.

The cataclysmic risk is the real risk of the market that most of us face. It is risk on two levels, absolute and psychological. On an absolute basis, a loss of 25% or more of our nest egg, whether it occurs in one day or over several years, is an event that many of us will not have time to recover from. If we are unlucky enough to be hit with a cataclysm just before we need the funds for retirement or some other purpose, we might consider that we are plain out of luck. The stock market decline in 1973–1974 is a case in point. After the stock market reached its high in December 1972 (based on the S&P 500 index), it took three and a half years, until May/June 1976, to reach that level again. Remember that this was a period of high inflation in the United States. If you adjust the numbers for inflation, an investor who had invested in December 1972 would have had to wait until some time in 1984 (over 10 years!) to recoup his or her money in real terms, meaning the equivalent purchasing power of the dollar at the time he or she invested in late 1972. This is quite dramatic, and many investors who happened to own the wrong stocks suffered longer and even more painfully. (The performance of small-cap stocks during this period was even worse.) Some poor investors simply did not have the time to recover before they needed to use their assets.

There is also the psychological aspect of the cataclysmic risk. Many investors were so traumatized following the 1973–1974 stock market debacle that they would not even consider investing in stocks again. All of their confidence in the stock market had vanished. The prospect of continued losses was too much to bear. It is not difficult to understand the psychological trauma that circumstances like that can breed. I understand it and empathize with it greatly. I had already been in the business for ten years at the time of the 1973–1974 decline. Although I was dealing primarily with institutional investors at the time, my few individual clients, along with family members and friends, were universally soured on the market. Nothing I could say was of much help. My encouraging words evaporated in the face of continuing declines. It's tough to build confidence if you are wrong day after day. You go on saying that stocks are a tremendous bargain, that the decline can't last, that this is a once-in-a-lifetime opportunity, but the market continues to decline, and you look like a Pollyanna at best, or a fool at worst.

It was a difficult period for the market. The quintupling of oil prices following the oil embargo changed the landscape of the American way of life. We saw a great transfer of wealth to the oil-producing countries, and that caused serious disruptions to our economy. Combine that with stock prices that had reached price-earnings levels never before seen, and you had the makings of a severe stock market decline.

The trauma in 1987 was just as real but mercifully swift. On October 19, 1987, the New York Stock Exchange suffered its largest percentage decline in history, tumbling 508 points (or 22.6% on the Dow Jones Average) in a single day. Billions of dollars of wealth were wiped out in just a few hours. Here again, many investors took their deflated assets and ran to the bank, never to venture into the stock market again. Can you blame them?

But these cataclysms do happen. It is our greatest nightmare. Like so many other horrendous events, they cannot be predicted. It is the equivalent of a 9.0 Richter-scale earthquake, a great flood, or a devastating tornado, an unpredictable calamity of nature. But just as it happens every 20 or 30 years in nature, so it is with the stock market. And just as few people move away from California to avoid being caught in an earthquake, few investors can afford to stay away from the stock market just because they want to avoid a great investment calamity that will probably occur once in a generation.

Why am I telling you this? Because three or four of these cataclysmic risks will hit each of us in our lifetime. We cannot avoid them. There is precious little we can do to prepare for them. But we must be ready. The problem they present to us is that when these events do occur, they are so scary that we fall prey rather easily to emotional and irrational behavior. Scores of authors and newsletter writers make big bucks scaring the wits out of us by predicting the next stock market crash. Do you remember this best-selling title: *On the Brink: How to Survive the Coming Great Depression 1993–2000* by Michael William Haga? The book was published in 1993. Hello? What happened to that Second Great Depression? Instead, the end of the millennium turned out to be one of the greatest periods of prosperity in American history, with rising stock prices, low inflation, strong economic growth, and the most remarkable achievement of all: a balanced budget.

You will not find a section in this book that will tell you how to avoid the next great stock market calamity. I wish there were, but there is no prescription against the cataclysmic risks I have described. What you will find is advice on how to prepare for it and endure it when it comes. We will prepare you emotionally and intellectually for a once- or twice-in-an-adult-lifetime event that will shake your beliefs to the roots and possibly cause you to panic out of stocks. If that day comes, remember that you knew it would come, and you are prepared to face it. The key is understanding what has happened and putting it into a historical perspective that you can profit from, not be panicked by. Unlike your friends and neighbors, you will not panic out of stocks; instead, you will do more research to decide how to configure your portfolio to maximize the benefits of any severe decline. There should be no doubt in your mind that you will be the ultimate winner. The cataclysmic risk does have an important and salutary side effect. It often presents the best buying opportunity most of us will see in our lifetimes. So it was in 1974. The time will come again. Be prepared.

KEY POINTS

In order to invest successfully, you must understand the nature of the risk you are taking. We've discussed *actual* risk, as well as the psychological components of risk. No matter what your MoneyQ is, these are the basics all of us need to know.

Here is what I want you to remember from this Master Key:

- **ACCEPT RISK**

  Understand that stock market risk is the price you pay to get a better return on your investments than you would get with a risk-free return.

- **DIVERSIFY INTELLIGENTLY**

  There are ways to reduce the risks inherent in investing in stocks. Here the findings of the great academics in the field are helpful. One way is to diversify intelligently. We have no control over what the stock market does day to day, but we can control size and style risk by owning both value stocks and growth stocks, small-cap stocks and large-cap stocks, domestic and international stocks. Exercise your control!

- **DON'T OVERREACT: ADOPT A LONG-TERM STRATEGY**

  Since stocks provide a greater return given their real risk, you can beat the system by not overreacting to stock market swings in your long-term investment portfolio.

- **TAKE EMOTION OUT OF YOUR INVESTMENT DECISION**

  All the great money managers agree: Take emotion out of the investment decision as much as possible. Yes, that's easier to say than to do; but you must keep your head. One of the best ways to avoid emotional decisions is to become an informed and educated investor. Knowing your MoneyQ can help guide you. Gold profiles will find it easier than others to put in the work needed to become educated. Some Blue Innovators may also find it easy, while Blue Strategists are likely to stick with asset-allocation plans in which they have confidence. Reds, on the other hand, will have to be careful, given their impulsive and "high-roller" mentality, as will Green Advocates. Green Mentors may count on their disciplined nature to guide them through emotional temptations in the market. In most cases, a trusted adviser may provide the ballast necessary to ensure both a clear course of action and a source of financial expertise to guide you along.

MASTER KEY 3
NEVER TIME THE MARKET

There are no market timers in the Forbes 400.

PETER LYNCH

One of the Master Keys to investment wealth is the proper allocation of your intellectual as well as your financial resources. Your intellectual resources are important because you simply do not have the time to do all of the research you might want to do in the pursuit of investment wealth. Thus, choices must be made.

A QUESTION OF TIME

An issue that preoccupies many investors is the decision to be in or out of the market. In an ideal world, we would be invested, or fully invested, only during periods of rising market prices. We all know how difficult it is to make money in a declining market, so it would seem that the smartest strategy would be to stay out of the market during periods of decline. I can't disagree with that. The problem, as you well know, is that it is extremely difficult to accurately predict stock-market movements over the short to intermediate term. That doesn't keep people from trying.

I was speaking to a group in Los Angeles recently where I was one of two speakers addressing the local chapter of the American Association for Individual Investors. More than 300 people showed up on a Saturday morning, a testimony to the dedication of this group of investors. During the course of my comments, I happened to mention that market timing doesn't pay, not realizing that the speaker who followed me was not only a market timer, but represented a market-timing service. Needless to say, he was not particularly happy with my comment, and when it was his turn to speak, he assured the audience that I was completely wrong and that market timing did indeed pay, assuming you were fortunate enough to subscribe to the right service—his.

I stayed for the lecture and was fascinated by it. The system seemed just about foolproof. By golly, this system told you almost exactly when to buy and sell and, sure enough, the market always did exactly as predicted. Who wouldn't want a service like that?

Would that it were that simple. Sadly, there is no such thing as a market-timing service that is right often enough to make you any real money. I stress the words "often enough" because these prognosticators will invariably be right some of the time. That's the stuff that gets into their marketing material. The problem with market timing, whether you do it yourself or subscribe to someone else's views, is that you will not be right enough often enough to make any money doing it unless you are just plain lucky.

Studies have shown that in order to profit from being in or out of the market, as opposed to being invested all the time, you would have to make the right timing decision 67% of the time. That's not easy to do. Think about it. If you were right on your market-timing decision 50% of the time, you would still be worse off than if you invested all the time.

This is one area where there is considerable consensus among great managers. Only 8% of the managers we surveyed said that market timing was important to investment success. Conversely, 92% of these managers do not consider that market timing is important to being a successful investor. I defy you to find any other area of investing where 92% of the managers will agree on anything.

You can see where this is leading, but let's press on. I have two thought-provoking examples about market timing to share with you. Here's the first: Historically, when the market goes up, it tends to do so in short, dramatic spurts. As a result, the penalty for being wrong is severe. That means that if you guessed wrong, and were out of the market during one of these dramatic rises, you would miss the entire advance. That will have a dramatic effect on your overall investment performance. To illustrate this in specific

terms, consider the following facts, which I picked up from investment guru Peter Lynch.

Over the past 40 years (through 1996), the market has risen on
average 11.4% a year. If you happened to be out of the stock market for 40 key months during those 40 years, your return sank to
2.7%. (Your bank probably offered a better return than that!) Over
the past 100 years, we have had 53 corrections of 10% or more and
15 corrections of 25% or more. This volatility is normal; it is the price
you pay for the higher return you get in the stock market. Trying to
guess when the stock market corrections are going to occur puts you
in the position, as I've said, of having to be right not once, but twice.
You have to be right by getting out of the market at or near the top
and, as you no doubt surmised, you also have to be right about
when to get back in. Good luck.

· The second example is somewhat different: Imagine that you
have $1,000 dollars to invest each year. For our purposes, we are
using a 32-year period from 1960 to 1992. You have to pick one day
to invest your money each year. Obviously, if you could, you would
want to invest the money on the day each year when the stock market hit its low point for that year. So let's assume just that. Through
a combination of brilliant timing and your unimaginable good fortune, you happen to invest your $1,000 on the day the S&P 500 hits
its low point each year from 1960 to 1992. With this fortuitous timing, your return over the 32-year period would be 10.6% a year.

Now let's assume your cousin, the black sheep in the family,
gets to perform the same exercise. He will invest $1,000 each year
for 32 years and he, too, gets to pick the day to invest each year. But
this dolt fulfills every promise attributed to him since he flunked out
of eighth grade. He actually manages to invest his $1,000 on the day
the market hit its high point each and every year from 1960 to 1992.
His return? It's 9.7%.

The point, of course, is that even with the benefit of perfect
timing, as in this example, the difference in return was not that star-
tling compared to the return you would have gotten with horren-
dously bad timing. And what are your chances of getting the timing
right with perfect accuracy?

One of the things you learn as you grow older is that you can't
fight every single battle that comes up in life. This may be one of
the most important lessons in life, not just in investing. When we are
young, we tend to take a stand on everything. Confront us with a

problem, we will immediately try to find a solution. As we get older, we realize that life consists of choices. Success is a function not only of making the right choices, but also of selecting the very decisions we want to make and passing on the opportunity to make others. Here's an example of what I mean.

You are at the car-rental counter to pick up the car you reserved to go to an important business meeting. The meeting in question is one you have been preparing for for weeks. If it goes well, it will be a feather in your cap, a contract with a new, important client. You have arranged for several colleagues to accompany you to this meeting in order to demonstrate the breadth and expertise of your team. The clerk at the counter has a compact car for you although you reserved a full-size sedan, so that you could comfortably transport your three colleagues to the meeting. You have the written confirmation. You ask for the car you reserved, but the clerk is indifferent to your needs. All she can give you is a compact at this point, and she wants you out of the way so she can take care of the next customer. The full-size car is important to you because you will be traveling with three others and you expect to discuss final preparations during the hour-long ride to the prospective client's plant.

You have two choices. You can raise your voice, demand to speak to a supervisor, complain about the service you are getting, and tell anyone at the counter who cares to listen how important your company's business is to this company. You demand that they produce the reserved car at once. You will settle for nothing less. Meanwhile, your blood pressure rises, you are clearly agitated, and all of a sudden, the car-rental company's problem with their inventory of cars at Cincinnati Airport is becoming more important to you and causing you more anxiety than your business meeting.

Or you might react differently. You know that the meeting is the most important matter on your agenda, so you make a conscious decision not to fight this battle with a clerk who truly does not give a damn about your problem. You take the compact, make a mental note to write a letter to the company when you have time, and resume thinking about your meeting. In other words, you decide not to fight this particular battle.

Such are the choices we make in life. We tend to make these decisions better when we focus on our priorities. So it is with investing. Decide what to spend time on and what not to waste time on. Pick the battles you want to fight. For the vast majority of us, market timing is a battle not worth fighting. Our time and energy is far better spent focusing on what stocks to buy, what mutual funds to choose, what money managers to hire, and the ever important matter of asset allocation. Since history shows that the odds of improving investment performance with market timing are minuscule, don't waste your time on it.

THE TEMPTATION OF TIMING

When I think of market timing and its insidious effect on investment performance, I am reminded of a true story told to me by legendary money manager Richard Driehaus. You may not have heard of Driehaus; his minimum account size is $2 million. He practices a form of management called Momentum investing, which involves buying stocks that are in a rapidly accelerating trend of rising prices and earnings. It is a very volatile way to manage money and is not for the faint of heart.

Driehaus has made a lot of money for himself and his clients over the years, but it was a different story when he started out. He was an analyst at A. G. Becker in Chicago before striking out on his own. One of the clerks at A. G. Becker took a liking to Richard and gave him all of her savings to invest, a total of $104,000, a considerable sum back in the early '70s. The early results were less than promising. The severe market decline in 1973 and 1974, combined with Richard's volatile investment style, caused the value of this portfolio to decline to $65,000. Amazingly, the woman did not panic. She stayed the course and decided to remain invested through one of the worst periods in stock market history and beyond. In 1996, that same account was worth over $8 million.

Wait a minute. I hear some of you (particularly you Blues) saying: Aren't you contradicting yourself? Didn't Driehaus succeed in spades by timing the market? Doesn't he still? If he can do it, so can I. Can't I? My answer is an emphatic *no*! Driehaus lives, eats, and breathes the market. It's his more-than-a-full-time occupation. He has access to the most sophisticated techniques and information. What's more—ask yourself, would you be like Driehaus's client or would you have panicked out of the market, never to return, having lost close to half of your assets?

A TALK WITH WILLIAM R. GRANT: ON TIMING

I first met Bill Grant in the early '60s. He was then the head of the Research Department at Smith Barney. In the course of his very distinguished career, Bill went on to become vice-chairman of Smith Barney and was chairman of MacKay-Shields Financial Corporation. Bill has served on the boards of 10 public companies, so he knows the real business world, not just the paper world of Wall Street. Today, he runs Galen Associates, a venture capital company that invests in the health care industry.

TANOUS: Let's talk about market timing, Bill. What role has it played in your career?

GRANT: Investing can be done only as a continuum over time. Here's an example from my own career. I have been on the board of directors of SmithKline Beecham for 24 years. During all those years, I put the equivalent of my quarterly director's compensation into the stock of SmithKline. Whether it was up or down, I knew I was going to be a long-term investor. That wound up being my single largest investment success, and it was done on a continuum without a lot of brainpower, but with a lot of long-term discipline.

TANOUS: One of the problems investors have is that there are so many people on radio and TV pontificating on what the market is going to do next. Unless the prognosticators happen to be clairvoyant, there's not a real good chance that they're going to be consistently right. Why do you think people listen to that stuff? Why do people who wouldn't think of calling the Psychic Hot Line listen to people talk about where the market is going?

GRANT: I think people don't pay attention when the market is down. But when the market is rising, they can't stand it anymore. They go to a cocktail party where everybody is exaggerating how well they've done in the market. Finally, you start to say, gee, I've got to get into this game. And as the market goes up, it keeps picking up people along the way, often for social reasons as well as financial reasons. Nobody wants to think about investing over a period of time. They want to make a decision and talk to their friends and family about how well they have done. There is an interesting social pattern here, and it is greater than most people think.

TANOUS: Interesting point.

GRANT: Another reason people think about market timing is that we're always looking for an easy way to do something. We're looking for somebody else to tell us when to take action. A lot of people are comfortable with that. For example, I love to have my wife organize my social life. I don't want to think about it. She says, here's what we're going to do, and we're going to go out on Friday night with tennis on Saturday, and I say that's terrific, what time? The parallel in investments is that we're all looking for simple ways to make a lot of money.

TANOUS: What's the downside of that?

GRANT: The downside is that you may not have the courage to move through the investment cycles through time. When the market was at 1000 or 3000 [*on the Dow Jones Average*], who would strike up a conversation at a party with: "Anybody interested in stocks?" The likely answer was: "What are you talking about?" Now, with the huge numbers of people involved and the pile-on of instant communication that takes place on the Internet, everybody is talking about the market.

TANOUS: You now see full-page ads in the paper offering machines that provide live stock quotes wherever you are. I wonder how healthy that is?

GRANT: The best speculators don't look at their stocks every day. Take the new drug, Viagra. The news about that drug became a matter of public information to the Wall Street analysts about 18 months ago. The analysts talk about all the new products in the pipeline all the time. There was available evidence back then from the tests that Viagra was the most potent—no pun intended—drug for people with erectile dysfunction. It was better than anything else on the market. If somebody had just thought about that, and asked if there was a market for it, they would have concluded that, yes, there's a hell of a market there. So you go back and do some homework. You don't have to be a genius

or talk to an analyst or do much research on the Internet to figure out
what Pfizer was on to with Viagra. You could have built up a position in
Pfizer over time. But you had to think about it. Now that's it's on the
front page of *The New York Times* as the most prescribed prescription
compound ever in the first week of introduction, everybody wants to
rush in. But early investors or speculators didn't care what the stock
did day to day; he or she just bought the stock on a continuum because
they believed in the story.

If it seems to you that I am beating a dead horse here, you are
probably right. Please keep in mind that we are dealing with a very
controversial subject. Think how strange it is that in one corner you
have the vast majority of professional investment managers, including me, telling you that market timing is a waste of time. On the other
side there's the lure that somehow you can do it right. I am particularly concerned about you Blues, with your predisposition to trading.
Reds and some Greens should also be wary of the temptations to
time the market. Golds are naturally predisposed to be long-term
investors and, I suspect, will find it easier to resist the temptation of
trying to time the market.

What should you do?

Look at the evidence. Not the charts and baloney in the direct-
mail pieces that cram your mailbox. Not the flaky commentators
who intone authoritative views that never pan out. Not the over-
confident broker who calls you with another not-so-sure thing. The
evidence. That is, the cold, hard facts of what market timing entails,
and any authoritative evidence that it succeeds more than it fails.
You will not find any such evidence.

"Market timing is a waste of time. It's what you buy and what you
pay for it that counts," says fund manager Donald Yacktman
(Yacktman Asset Management Co.). Mutual-fund managers such as
Yacktman are sometimes faced with the problem of investors who
trade the fund shares by buying and selling according to what they
think the market is going to do. This practice can be very disruptive to
the fund manager who then has to worry about volatile amounts of
money sloshing into and out of the fund. As a result, some fund managers ban the practice. Not Yacktman. "When I ran Selected American
Shares, I found a study had been done on the impact of market timers

An interesting perspective on market timing. Note the recurring theme about investing on a continuum of time, a refrain we have heard from countless managers in our survey. Indeed, when we hear of great fortunes that have been made by individuals, it is often a case of a person of seemingly modest circumstances who accumulated a large position in a growing stock over a very long period of time. You seldom hear of great fortunes having been made in the market by traders who buy and sell stocks continuously.

on the fund. Since the market timers created a net positive (i.e., as a group they were net wrong) for the fund, we let them buy and sell as they pleased," he told me.

If I have failed to convince you by now that market timing is futile, I suspect the reason may be that you are an incorrigible optimist or a skilled clairvoyant. I admire both qualities. For the rest of us, I urge adherence to the lesson of the car rental. Save your time and energy for the battles in life that really count. Market timing is not one of them.

KEY POINTS

The four points to remember from this chapter are:

- RESIST THE TEMPTATION TO GET IN AND OUT OF THE STOCK MARKET.

- AVOID ATTEMPTS TO TIME THE MARKET.

- DO NOT LISTEN TO ADVICE ON THE RIGHT TIME TO BUY OR SELL STOCKS.

- RECOGNIZE THAT THE PRECEDING THREE POINTS ALL SAY EXACTLY THE SAME THING.

MASTER KEY 4
SPECULATE INTELLIGENTLY; NEVER GAMBLE

*Some clients say that if the market were to take
a 20%–30% decline, it wouldn't faze them.
We think that is probably not accurate.*

JACK DARRELL
DARRELL & KING

Most investment advisers caution their clients against speculating in the market. On the whole, they are right. Most investors who speculate in stocks don't do it right. To be blunt, most investors don't know the difference between gambling and intelligent speculating. They might as well take their stash to Las Vegas or Atlantic City, where at least they give you free drinks while you lose your money.

In this chapter we explore speculating in the stock market. I did not address this subject in our survey of the top managers since so few pros believe in it. (Or at least when they do speculate, they call it something else.) So, this chapter is primarily my personal master key, culled from an accumulation of battle-scarred experience spanning over 30 years in the business. To add some perspective, you will also meet two top market pros with very different views on speculating. Their advice is, in my opinion, priceless.

Of course, not everybody is interested in speculating. Those who fall into the category of potential speculators are likely to be Reds or Blues. It is far more likely that you Golds and some of you Greens will heed the advice you've heard for so long and eschew all temptations to speculate with your hard-earned investment nest egg. Right now, it's the rest of you I am worried about. Again, if you are not driven to speculating with a small portion of your assets, don't do it. But if you, on occasion, are one of those who wants to take a flyer in some stock you heard about or gamble on the direction of the market, this chapter is designed to help you. Remember, this is speculating, not investing.

SPECULATION BASICS

Before we begin, let's define what we mean by speculating. In the context of our investment discussion, we are talking about speculating in the stock market as well as derivatives, commodities, or currencies, where the potential reward is very great and the potential loss is, well, absolute. Indeed, in some forms of speculation you risk not only the amount of money you put up, but also much more. In this chapter, we cover most of these possibilities. Then we examine the kind of speculation that might make sense for you, assuming you want to do it at all. The key to this master key is: If you are going to speculate in stocks, you must practice controlled speculation.

SPECULATIVE STOCKS

This group usually involves the shares of small companies with a story. These "story stocks" follow a similar pattern. Someone calls you and tells you that TechnoHypo has just come out with a new gizmo that doubles the speed of some neurotrendo, which will in turn revolutionize the computer industry. What's more, they have a patent on it and, as we are speaking, IBM is begging, I mean, down on their knees begging them to license their technology before any of the computer company's competitors do. Price is no object, of course. But our wise management at TechnoHypo is being cagey. They're not going to take the first offer that comes down the pike. The Japanese are formulating their own offer for the neurotrendo technology. So management is going to sit tight and hold out for the mega-offer they so richly deserve. The stock is selling at 2¼ per share, and once the licensing agreement is signed, we can expect the stock to go up to 10 and, after that, the sky's the limit.

I can see you smiling from here. Yes, I know you have heard a story similar to this before. This does not take clairvoyance on my part, I assure you. There are dozens of stories like that floating around the market every day. The problem is that these stories seem so real and so compelling that you Reds and Blues almost can't resist. To compound the problem, even a few losses don't dissuade you from listening to the next great story. Some colors never learn.

I'm not trying to make you feel bad. It is just that we need to inject some realism and common sense into our discussion. There is a reason why the great managers do not listen to hot tips or buy stocks without investigating a story in detail. Does that mean you should never buy stock in a tiny company with a potentially revolutionary new product? No. It just means you should not do what I just described. Later, I will give you some guidelines to speculate intelligently in this type of investment.

SELLING SHORT

Selling short is a technique where, if you are right, you can make money on a stock going down, rather than going up. I suspect you know this, but in case you don't, selling short involves selling stock you don't own. You sell the stock, and since you don't own it, you borrow the stock to deliver to the buyer. Later, presumably after the stock has gone down, you buy it in the stock market and return it to whomever you borrowed it from. Your profit is the difference between what you got when you sold the stock, and the cost (presumably lower) of the stock you bought back.

On the surface, selling short ought to be no more risky than buying a stock and hoping it goes up in price. The reality is very different. The problem is that when you buy a stock, even if you buy something as risky as TechnoHypo in the previous example, your loss is usually limited to the amount of money you invest. You put up $10,000, and if the company goes bust, you lose $10,000. You emerge poorer and, we hope, wiser. Not so with short sales. With short sales, your potential losses are unlimited. I say again: *unlimited.*

Here's why. When you sell stock short, you will borrow stock that you have to replace some day. Suppose you are wrong and the stock goes up instead of down. Well, every day you have a tough decision to make. Do you "cover" (buy back the stock you borrowed) or wait another day, hoping the stock will eventually go down? Let's assume you shorted TechnoHypo after the stock rose to $10 on some silly rumor that IBM was going to give a major contract to this fledgling company. After all, you remember people talking about this company when the stock was 2, and it was nothing but a silly story, right? So at 10, you figure this is a good short sale. The stock will collapse, and you will cover at 2, making 8 dollars a share, a very nice profit. So you sell 1,000 shares short at 10. A week later, the stock has climbed to 15. Ah, those rumors! Stupid people will believe anything. Just wait until they realize that it's nothing but another fabricated story.

The following Tuesday, IBM announces that it has awarded a huge contract to a new company called TechnoHypo, and the stock soars to 35. Now you've got a nasty little problem. You realize that unlike so many of the other stories, this one turned out to be true, and you happen to be on the wrong side of the trade. You decide you have to cover. You buy 1,000 shares of TechnoHypo at 35 to deliver the stock you borrowed back to the lender. Your cost: $35,000 (plus commissions). You lose $25,000, which is $35,000 less the $10,000 you got when you sold the stock short. Now remember, had you bought 1,000 shares of TechnoHypo at 10, instead of selling it short, your maximum loss, even if the stock value sank to zero, would be $10,000. Not so when you sell short. If the trade goes against you, you can be in big trouble. In our example, the TechnoHypo short sale cost you $25,000, but believe me, it could have been worse. Keep this in mind if you are considering making money when a stock goes down. A better way to bet on declining stock prices is to use options.

OPTIONS

Options give you the right to buy or sell a stock at a fixed price for a fixed period of time. There are intelligent ways to speculate in options and there are dumb ways, too. To review the basics, a *call* option gives you the right to buy the underlying stock at a fixed price for a fixed period. For example, let's assume IBM is selling at 100 today. An option to buy IBM at 100 for the next six months might cost, say, $12 a share. The $12 price is known as the "premium." It's the price you pay for the privilege of "freezing" IBM's price for six months. So (and I'm trying to keep this simple) if IBM rises above 112 a share (which is the option or "strike" price plus the $12 cost of the option), you make money. Say IBM rises to 130 in the next few months. Your option to buy IBM at 100 will be worth at least 30, plus some premium value, so you will make a very handsome return on your original investment of $12. Of course, if IBM goes down, instead of up, or, for that matter, doesn't move much at all, your options will expire worthless, and you will have lost, in this example, $12 a share.

Options to sell stocks at a fixed price over a fixed period of time are known as *puts*. They work in exactly the same way as call options, except that everything is reversed. If the stock goes down in price, your put option will increase in value.

There are two basic ways to use options. You can be a "writer" of options or you can buy and sell them. Writing options is a nifty exercise for individuals who own stock and want to enhance their returns. Say you own 100 shares of IBM, which you bought at 80, and the stock is now 100. You are happy with the profit you earned so far, but you're not sure whether you should sell it now or not. You might consider selling options on your IBM stock. Here's how it would work. Take the IBM calls we used in the previous example. They have a strike price of 100 and are good for six months. They currently sell for 12. This time, however, you are not going to buy IBM options, you are going to *write* them. That means that you are going to offer somebody the call options on your own stock. So a buyer of the call options will pay you $12 for each share of IBM, giving the buyer the right to buy your stock from you for the next six months at $100 a share. Now look at what that means to you. If IBM keeps going up, the buyer of the option will exercise his or her right to buy your stock from you at $100 per share. When that happens, you deliver your stock and get $100 a share. But you also got $12 a share for each option you sold, so, in effect, you sold your IBM not for $100, but for $112 a share, a tidy profit.

But what if IBM doesn't go up? Suppose it stays at 100 for the next six months. You will probably be just as happy. You get to keep your stock and the $12 premium as the option expires, unexercised. (The guy who bought the option from you isn't going to exercise his option to buy IBM from you at 100 unless IBM goes above 100 in the stock market.)

The only other possibility is that IBM goes down. Here again, you get to keep the $12 option money, which means that the stock can go down from 100 to 88 before you're out any more money than you would have gotten had you sold the stock at 100. That's because you got $12 for the option you sold, which you get to keep. So if IBM goes down to $88, you have the stock plus the $12 for a total of $100.

Sounds pretty good. I think so, which is why I am surprised that more investors don't use options as part of their investment strategy. Keep it in mind for your own portfolio. As you can see, this is not speculating. This is an intelligent way to use options to enhance portfolio return.

What about buying options? That is truly speculative. I am not suggesting that you shouldn't do it at all, but you should understand what you are doing. You can buy options on most major stocks, and you can also buy options to bet on the stock market indexes. Should you speculate in options? The problem with most options is not the underlying stock, or even the market as a whole. The problem is time. If you buy a call option on a particular stock, you are betting that the stock will go up enough to make up for the cost of the option and still leave you with a nice profit. Chances are, however, that the option you buy will be for three to six months. It is difficult to predict stock-price movement over that short a period of time. (Remember what we've said about trying to time the market?) Most investors know this from experience. There is nothing more frustrating than to buy a call on a stock you think is going up and lose all the money because you ran out of time, especially if the stock does rise later on, just as you predicted it would.

Still want to try your luck at options? We'll discuss some strategies later in this chapter.

PRIVATE PLACEMENTS

Private placement is a generic term used to encompass offerings of stocks that are not publicly held. These offerings can range from an elaborate presentation by a large investment firm for a sexy new company to an offering from your nephew to help finance his new computer-software retail store. In most private placements, the lure is that you can get into this great company before it goes public. When it does, you will be one of those lucky insiders listed in the prospectus whose net worth will suddenly shoot up dramatically as soon as the new stock starts trading on NASDAQ. Such is the dreamy attractiveness of private placements. The record is something else. As you might expect, the successes in these ventures are vastly outnumbered by the failures. Investing in a fledgling company just as it is getting started is inherently risky. Most fail. That is what you must keep in mind before investing in private placements or private companies.

If you do get tempted, at least try to buy private placements from reputable investment firms. That is not easy either since, when these deals are done, they usually look for minimum investments of $100,000 or more, which is beyond the means of most investors, particularly for risky investments like that. If a private deal is offered to you by a friend or relative, make sure that a shareholders' agreement is part of the deal. We will cover the need for a shareholders' agreement later in this chapter.

IPOs

I'll make a little bet that you know what IPO stands for. In the latter part of the twentieth century, we have lived though what may go down as the greatest bull market in history, and IPO is a singular component of the historic investment landscape.

IPO stands for initial public offering. It is the culmination of an entrepreneur's—and an early investor's—dream. You build or invest in a company (through the private placements we just discussed) and the successful company reaches a point where investment bankers from New York or San Francisco woo the management with the prospect of untold riches by selling shares of the company to the public.

When a company whose story excites the imagination of the investment community goes public, there is a kind of feeding frenzy on Wall Street. Brokers get calls from everybody they ever knew, pleading to be in on the deal. These issues are often referred to as "hot issues," and brokers never get enough stock to satisfy the demand. As a result, brokers allocate the stock to their best clients. Chances are you are not among them. That means that since you are unable to get shares at the offering prices, you will have to buy the shares right after the offering, when they begin trading publicly. The problem here is that when the demand for the new company's stock is hot, the shares open at a huge premium.

Take a classic example of a hot deal in the '90s: Netscape. The Internet darling went public on August 10, 1995, at an offering price of $14 (adjusted for a subsequent 2-for-1 stock split). I doubt your broker called you to offer you shares at the offering price. More likely, you called your broker and begged for some stock. Why? Because the opening transaction in Netscape was 35½, which means that if you were lucky enough to get stock at the offering price of 14, you could have more than doubled your money in one day. The stock ultimately peaked in late January 1996, at about $80. It was downhill from there. In April 1998, you could have bought all the Netscape you wanted at prices under $20 a share.

The lesson to be learned with IPOs is that you are better off being a contrarian investor when it comes to hot-stock offerings. Don't travel with the herd. If you really want to own the stock, wait until the furor dies down. In almost all cases, there will be a better opportunity to buy the stock at a lower price when the frenzy subsides. Yes, there are a few cases where the stock just keeps going up and up, but these are extremely rare. Don't risk a big loss just because you think you have identified the one exception to the rule. More often than not, what goes up really does come back down. In the vast majority of cases, you will get another opportunity to buy the stock. In fact, when that opportunity arises, you ought to reexamine the investment decision based on the most recent data and circumstances and—guess what? —you might decide you don't want to own it after all. (Remember Boston Chicken?)

COMMODITIES

Unless you are a farmer who is hedging next season's crop, the commodities market is another arena for speculation on price movements. The reason it is so speculative is that the leverage is enormous. You can control truckloads of wheat, for example, with only a few dollars. There have been apocryphal stories of investors in the commodity markets getting freight-car loads of some commodity delivered to their front door. But that never really happened.

Commodities were more popular as an investment medium a few decades ago when inflation was more prevalent and commodity prices reacted more violently to price changes. You can still get some action in various commodities by tracking rainfall and weather-satellite images across the Midwest, but do you really want to? Today, the action has moved to the options market where gamblers and speculators can get just as much action and at least have some knowledge of the underlying securities they are betting on. (How much do you really know about the market for pork bellies?)

My advice is to stay away from commodities as a speculation unless you know the underlying commodity very well.

HEDGE FUNDS

Most investors have some knowledge of hedge funds, even if they have never invested in one. After all, some of the hedge-fund managers have become legends in their own right. The granddaddy of hedge-fund managers is George Soros, who truly deserves his legendary reputation. Soros is a billionaire who does not shy away from making billion-dollar bets when he has a conviction. He is well-known for having made a 10-billion-dollar bet against the British pound in 1992 and netted a profit of $2 billion when the British currency was devalued. Then again, he bet wrong on the Japanese market in 1994 and lost $600 million. More recently, Soros has reportedly been at it again, betting heavily that the British pound will fall against the deutsche mark. He gives new meaning to that old phrase "easy come, easy go." But the fact is that Soros has done very well for himself and his investors. His principal investment medium has been his Quantum Fund, which is an offshore fund available only to non-U.S. investors with deep pockets. Other legends in the field include Michael Steinhardt (now retired), Julian Robertson, and a few others who have made fortunes for themselves and their investors.

Hedge funds are usually limited partnerships wherein the manager is the general partner and you, as an investor, are one of the limited partners. Until recently, these funds were limited to a small number of "qualified" investors, which usually meant high minimums ($1 million in many cases) and high net worths to get into the club. That has changed somewhat, and you may find that various investment advisers and brokerage firms are now offering you the opportunity to invest in hedge funds. For that reason, you need to educate yourself on the pros and cons of these investments if you have not done so already.

I, and most other advisers, qualify hedge funds as risky because they engage in investment practices that comport higher risks than just buying and selling stocks. At a minimum, hedge funds can go short. In fact, the original name for hedge funds was derived from the fact that they could "hedge" their long positions by going short stocks they didn't like. Over time, hedge funds have expanded beyond this narrow scope and have engaged in some pretty wild activities in their quest to achieve superior performance. Many of these activities can get you, the investor, into real trouble.

For example, some hedge-fund managers use highly leveraged investments and option strategies to make a great deal of money in a very short period of time. It is a way of betting the ranch on what they believe is about to happen. This is what George Soros does when he gambles on the direction of a currency. Earning a billion dollars on a single trade is what you and I would surely call a major gamble. Is that what you want your money manager to do? I don't think so.

Consider the recent example of a well-known hedge-fund manager, Victor Niederhoffer. A Renaissance man, Niederhoffer wrote a best-selling book, *The Education of a Speculator*. The success of his book no doubt encouraged investors to put money into the hedge fund of this very talented individual. But then, disaster struck. On October 27, 1997, Niederhoffer made a very large bet. He sold what are called "naked puts," betting that the market was going to go up. (You know that puts give you the right to sell a stock at a fixed price. If you decide to sell puts on something you don't own, say, a stock market index, you are betting that the market is going up and the puts, which have value to the buyer only if the market goes down, will expire worthless. If you are right, you get to pocket the proceeds of the sale, even though you never owned the puts you sold. If you are wrong, it can cost a bundle!)

Niederhoffer made a real bad bet. The market had its worst decline (in points on the Dow Jones Average) in history that day, declining 554 points. Niederhoffer's hedge fund "blew up," as they say in the business. As the market declined that day, Niederhoffer was subjected to cascading margin calls that he could not meet. With no additional collateral coming in, the broker liquidated Niederhoffer's positions, essentially wiping him out—a loss of $130 million. This happened to be all of his investors' money. The sad part is that if he could have hung on, the rally the next day would have eased his painful loss. A statement to the shareholders said,

"Right now, the indications are that the entire equity position . . . has been wiped out."

Remember, this is what happened to a very talented guy. His returns to his investors had averaged 28% for a decade. (We will talk to Victor Niederhoffer later in this chapter as part of our discussion of hedge funds.)

If you are considering investing in hedge funds, make sure you know and understand what the strategy of the investment manager is. Here's a clue: If the manager's past record includes some really outstanding years, such as being up 60% or 80%, assume that a bad year with the manager can include the same size loss. As I am fond of telling my own clients, the only thing I can say about the investment business with great certainty is that the manager you choose to manage your money is going to have his or her worst year right after you put your money with him or her. Therefore, let's pay attention to the potential downside risk of each manager.

SMART STRATEGIES FOR SPECULATORS

Since most of us don't have Niederhoffer's ability to suffer big losses, the first rule for intelligent speculation is: *Carefully define the amount of money you will use for speculative investment strategies.* Predetermine what percentage of your total assets will be devoted to speculative investment strategies. For most investors, this will usually not exceed 10% or 20% of the total. Your personal MoneyQ profile will guide you to the correct level of assets for speculative investments (if you are to speculate at all). Blues and Reds are likely to allocate a higher percentage of their assets to speculative investments, with the Blues leading the charge. Greens will have relatively small appetite for speculation, and Golds may not have any at all.

The percentage allocated to this activity will also be a function of the actual dollars involved. For example, if your investment portfolio consists of all the money you will need for retirement, it would be foolish to jeopardize any major portion of that amount on speculative investment strategies. On the other hand, if you are fortunate enough to have more assets than you will reasonably need, you can afford to speculate, since a loss will not jeopardize your future living style.

MORE TALK WITH WILLIAM GRANT: CONTRARIAN STRATEGIES

I introduced you to an old friend, Bill Grant, when we talked about market timing. Bill was vice-chairman of Smith Barney, chairman of money-manager McKay Shields, and now runs a large fund investing in the health industry. In our conversation, we moved naturally to the topic of speculating in the market, and I asked Grant to share his thoughts with us.

GRANT: There are all kinds of speculation. It's most important to recognize what level of speculation your personality pushes you to and what kind of risk you are capable of taking. To me, speculation is buying and selling of a good or service that has some chance of success with a small possibility of a bonanza. If you accept that, you can ask: Where am I in terms of that definition? You can speculate and recognize an early idea, but most of the great speculators, like scientists or inventors, didn't have a road map. They might have had a concept, and they kept working on the concept. Bill Gates is an example. He had no real idea of the size of the market, but he knew he was going to do something that was going to improve the ability of individuals to function more efficiently and productively.

The important thing is to recognize what kind of a speculator you are. If you want to speculate on options because you think the market is going up, there's nothing wrong with that. But you must decide exactly what you are going to do. Otherwise, if you just keep speculating, the house will take you. It's just a question of how long it will take the house to take you. Just like going to a casino.

The most successful speculators start out as contrarians. They become less of a contrarian as they move up the success ladder, but a successful speculator is a real loner to start. And there are not a lot of them. They are people who like to be alone for an extended period of time. One of the best is Larry Tisch. Larry Tisch always said that like most people, he was not very good at trying to see the future. What he espoused was the need to define the risk on the downside and know where the bottom is. So, if he had a concept that nobody else had, his risk was peanuts, okay? That's why Larry has been such an enormously successful speculator. Larry started out with movie-theater chains. At the industry bottom, who was the biggest buyer in the world of drilling rigs? Larry! Now, of course, they are at a peak, and I haven't talked to him about it, but my guess is he is probably reducing his large drilling industry holdings.

TANOUS: You evoked a memory by using the term "contrarian investing," a popular concept today. My editor, Ellen Coleman, just edited a book on that subject. It occurs to me that you may well be the person who originated that phrase. I first heard it from you back in the sixties. You mentioned Bill Gates. I also think of Michael Dell of Dell Computers and Andy Grove of Intel, two of today's enormous success stories. Are there any clues to finding and understanding that you really found a winner? What do you look for?

GRANT: I would say that you look for an idea in areas where nobody else is working. That's also a dose of contrarianism. Let me give you an example, which comes from my background as a director of SmithKline. In the United States, you can't practice medicine without laboratory tests. Yet, these laboratories are very unpopular investments today. There are two large public companies in the field. One is Laboratory Corporation of America, which is down maybe 90% from its high. The other is Quest, which was spun out of Corning Glass. Nobody likes these companies because the government has been after them and, fairly or unfairly, they have been knocked down. But the practice of medicine can't live without them. So why are they unpopular? A spate of lawsuits against the pharmaceutical companies that own these lab companies or the labs themselves have scared investors. From a speculative viewpoint, these companies are now very interesting. For one thing, they've had the worst of everything hit them and, two, they've got themselves down to a survival mode. Now despite all the pressure on them, we are starting to see little bits of evidence, some of it anecdotal, that things are turning around. Anecdotal evidence is always the beginning of a great idea. But where are the stocks? Still way down here. Nobody likes them. No analysts write them up.

TANOUS: Which stocks are we talking about?

GRANT: Labco (Laboratory Corporation of America) and Quest Diagnostics. A speculator recognizes anecdotal evidence of a turn, and, if you follow the Larry Tisch rule, you'll know what your downside is. In this case, the stocks are already on the floor and don't have any friends in the world. If you can recognize and extrapolate the anecdotal evidence, you have an attractive risk reward ratio.

TANOUS: Are you willing to go on record with this?

GRANT: Yeah. No problem. Remember, I have no downside on it!

TANOUS: Okay. Laboratory Corporation of America Holdings (LH) is now 2½ and Quest Diagnostics (DGX) is selling around 20. Both stocks are listed on the New York Stock Exchange.

GRANT: Anyway, that's a good example. Some people have no conceptual ability to recognize a piece of anecdotal evidence. In my opinion, every successful speculator understands what to do with a good piece of anecdotal evidence. Looking back at my peculiar career as a research analyst, research director, my involvement in hedge funds,

Now let's look at the other rules you should apply to speculative investment strategies.

SPECULATIVE STOCKS

For this purpose, we will define speculative stocks as stocks of companies that are quite small, usually under $100 million in market capitalization, but where there is a reason to believe that the company has a proprietary product or a fresh approach to an industry that will lead to explosive growth. Most of the time, these ideas will not emanate from large brokerage firms, so the source of an idea is unlikely to be your broker. The major firms generally do not want to recommend highly speculative small stocks. The first reason is obvious. They don't want to risk the wrath (and possible lawsuits) of clients who have lost a lot of money on speculative recommendations made by their brokers. The second reason is purely one of self-interest. The large firms can't generate enough commission business in very small companies to make the exercise worthwhile. The small companies have a very small "float," or number of shares outstanding, so they are very difficult to buy in quantity.

The key to investing in speculative stocks is to realize that the odds are against you. So you must do whatever you can to move the odds in your favor. Here are some guidelines:

investment banking, and as a venture capitalist, it all comes back to taking anecdotal evidence and pushing it through to its logical end.

A successful speculator is a contrarian. Otherwise, the opportunity wouldn't be there. He—or she—understands what most people don't, that the enemy of speculation is the time clock (which is always running against him), not just on the cost of money he put in, but also the cost of his personal effort. Time is running against him because more and more people are going to figure out what he's doing over time, so your odds start to run against you.

This is something we are very conscious of in the venture-capital business. We want to get performance for our clients, and as soon as we take their money down, our clock is ticking. We never know what the future holds.

Invest in companies that are in industries you understand. For example, if you are a doctor, you are in a far better position to understand a new medical product, be it a drug or a medical device, than is a non-medically trained investor. Put your knowledge to use and move the odds in your favor. Don't buy into stories you don't understand. Many investors will recognize this dictum as vintage Peter Lynch. Peter is the one who popularized the notion of looking for great companies in your own backyard.

Investigate. Yes, you've heard this before. But in the case of speculative stocks, this is crucial. Just because a golfing buddy or a friend at the beauty salon purports to have some inside information on TechnoHypo, don't throw caution aside. Do your own independent research before putting up your money. I can't tell you how many great stories I hear in the course of an average month. I assure you, every one of them is tempting. You want to own them all! If I don't have time to investigate, I don't buy.

One of the most successful practitioners of this investment discipline is Michael Price, the legendary manager of the Mutual Series funds. In *Investment Gurus*, I recounted the story of Price's extensive research into the prospects for an unknown metal, Tantalum, which was fueled by his curiosity about an acquisition that had taken place that he didn't quite understand. His research led to huge profits for his fund shareholders. This was nothing more than old-fashioned detective work by a dedicated practitioner.

How do you go about investigating a story you've heard about an exciting new company? Use your resources to find someone in the same industry you can ask. For example, if a story that tempts you involves the computer industry, talk to someone in the industry or impose on a friend to ask someone. Now is the time to call in favors. It's your money that's at stake.

Develop a relationship with a quality regional broker. As I mentioned earlier, if your regular broker works for a large national firm, he or she is unlikely to recommend small speculative stocks. However, small regional brokers often know more about these stocks, because they have the ability to follow small companies that are located in their area. Moreover, their proximity to companies in their own backyard will give them a decided advantage when it comes to learning about important developments. Finally, since these broker-age firms are quite small, they don't have to worry about having thousands of brokers recommending the same thinly traded stock (something a large firm would have to worry about). Some of the top small-cap mutual-fund managers in the country use small regional brokers to get ideas. Scott Johnston of Sterling Johnston nurtures his relationship with regional brokers in far-flung corners of the country, hoping to latch on to an exciting new idea before it becomes part of the Wall Street mainstream. You may not want to establish accounts with multiple regional brokers, but you can certainly start with one, perhaps even a broker who covers small companies in the region where you live.

SELLING SHORT

As we pointed out earlier, the principal danger of selling short is that your losses are theoretically unlimited. Somehow, that goes against the grain. Let me share a personal story with you. Some years ago, some friends approached me about becoming a "name" at Lloyd's of London. Many of my wealthy friends had done so, includ-ing some pretty astute and well-known individuals. To do so was relatively simple. You joined a syndicate under the leadership of the world-famous insurance company. You didn't even have to put up any money! You got your bank to issue a letter of credit (at the time it was only $250,000), and, after a couple of years, you got a return on your noninvestment of 20% to 30% each year. Many of my friends had invested one or more millions of dollars and were living the good life off their Lloyd's of London earnings. Of course, to be considered was a privilege; you had to be recommended by one or more existing names before they would consider letting you in on this license to steal.

Oh, there was one little added feature of this wonderful investment opportunity. You had to personally guarantee your share of any syndicate against losses. *Personally guarantee*, I asked? *Meaning every cent of your net worth was on the line?* Yes, theoretically, but Lloyds had been in existence for over 300 years and there had never been a situation where investors were out more than the amount they originally put up. In fact, there were never any instances of losses of principal over any extended period of time. So the personal liability clause was, you realize, some quirk of British law, which Lloyd's had to follow not because they wanted to, you understand, but because they had to. A detail, really.

Now the idea of signing on to any investment that puts your entire net worth on the line should a problem arise is not something anyone should do. I am certain you agree. I declined the opportunity. Perhaps you remember what happened. In the early 1990s, Lloyd's suffered the effects of a string of earlier disasters ranging from a slew of asbestos claims, earthquakes, and hurricanes to the Exxon Valdez oil spill. Names in the United States were called on not only for the letters of credit they had put up (in some of my friends' cases this amounted to millions of dollars), but for several million dollars more. That personal liability clause they had innocently signed was now being invoked. Two of my friends were literally wiped out. Years of lawsuits followed. All in all, it was a tremendous headache, and the end result was financial catastrophe for most of the American names.

I recount this story to make an extremely important point to you. Never, never agree to an investment that invokes your personal liability or otherwise subjects you to unlimited losses. Short selling does that *unless* at the time of the short sale, you decide on the maximum loss you are willing to take and place an order to cover your short position at a higher price. For example, if you decide that TechnoHypo is overpriced at 10 and you sell it short at that price, you might decide that 2 points is the maximum loss you are willing to take. You place an order to buy back the shares at, say, 12. In this case, your loss is limited to about 2 points per share. If you want to gamble on a stock going down in price, consider buying puts on the stock if they are available. With puts, your potential loss is limited to the cost of the puts that you bought.

OPTIONS

Speculating in options, as we discussed earlier, is risky because most of the time we run out of time. But if you have a strong belief that a stock, or the market, is going to move up or down, you may decide to go for it. Let's say you have been following a stock and you believe that the next earnings announcement will be higher than expected. You expect that the stock will move higher as soon as the earnings are announced. Your conviction is such that you are willing to bet on it. You want to buy call options on the stock. Here are some guidelines to follow to execute your strategy:

Buy options that are "in the money" or close to being in the money. This means that the strike price, or the price at which you can exercise the option, is close to the price currently prevailing in the market. For example, if a stock is selling at 40, there may be options on it with strike prices that range from 20 to 60. Obviously, you will make more money, and take a much greater risk, buying "out of the money" options; that is, options with an exercise price well above the current price, such as 50. I don't recommend it. If you stick with options that are in the money, you have a much greater chance of some residual value at the end of the contract. Let's say you buy options with a strike price of 40 and the current price is around 40, you have a better chance that those options will be worth something even if the stock moves only a little bit. Your risk, in this case, is the stock price, and the "premium" you paid for the options. That premium might be as little as 10% of the stock price, depending on how long your options have to go before they expire.

Buy options with expiration dates at least six months out.   You can buy options with just a few months to run, and you may be tempted to do just that if you are betting on a particular event like an earnings announcement, but, here again, you will be better off going longer. You may well be right about the earnings; the higher-than-

expected earnings come through just as you had brilliantly antici-
pated. Only the stock doesn't react right away. That happens. At this
point, time is your enemy. Make time your friend by buying longer
options than you might want to buy initially. Of course, the longer
options will cost you more money, but that is insurance that may
well be worth the price. (A newer type of option, called LEAPS,
offers you the right to buy a stock for periods of a year or longer.
Check them out.)

Here are some additional tips for trading in options:

**If you have a strong hunch about the short-term direction of the
market, bet on it.**   You will find out soon enough if your hunches
have any profit-making potential. If you lose more than you gain on
your hunches, face the fact that your hunches are not going to do
you any good and stop. If you make money more often than not,
continue to play those hunches, but heed this important caveat: *Do
not increase the amount of your bet just because you have been right
in the past.* One thing I am sure of is, when you decide to double
or triple your bet on the next hunch, that's the one that will lose you
money very painfully.

Most traders bet on the market by buying OEX options on the
S&P 100. Now a new type of option traded on the Chicago Board of
Option Exchange (CBOE) offers investors the opportunity to trade
the Dow Jones Industrial Average. These options are listed in *The
Wall Street Journal* and they offer a wide variety of expirations and
strike prices. If you make money more often than not, you are on to
something. If you don't, analyze what you did wrong. As in the
other points, perhaps you just ran out of time by buying options that
expired. There are moments in time when most of us will develop
strong feelings on market trends, and if we are right often enough,
this can be a good source of profits.

I confess that I do this myself from time to time. When the market declined 554 points on October 27, 1997, I was certain there
would be a rally. The following morning, I expected that the market
would open down, continuing the downward momentum of the
previous day, which was one of the largest point declines in market
history. But I also expected the market to turn, given the good economic and corporate earning news that continued to pour out of the
financial press. So at about 11 A.M. on October 28, when the market
was down another 100 points, I bought OEX calls at 14. The market

started turning at noon and soon a buying rout occurred. By the end of that day, the options had reached 38. I had made nearly three times on my money.

Now if I could give you a prescription for doing this all the time, nothing would make me happier. There are no such prescriptions. Those among you who have trading instincts will know when to act on these beliefs. The trick is to be prepared and be decisive and, above all, not to speculate over your head or beyond the limits that you should have established as part of your investment program. Personally, I develop feelings as strong as in the preceding example about three or four times a year. Your experience may be different, and time and experience will tell you when to heed the signal.

Set limits. There is a good chance that when you buy options, you are going to lose 100% of your investment on many trades. This is emotionally tough to take. Many traders justify their purchases of options, and the losses they sometimes generate, by limiting the percentage of funds they use to buy options. For example, if you limit your option purchases to 3% of your total portfolio value, a total loss in your options portfolio would result in only a 3% loss for your entire portfolio. That is easier to get your arms around.

Reassess. If you are inclined to speculate in options, try this strategy. Keep track of your profits and losses for a six-month period. After that time, assess your results. Did you lose money? Did you make money? Did you break even? If you wish, continue for another six months and review your results again after that time. If you have lost money in both periods, I suggest you seriously consider abandoning the strategy. If you broke even, consider whether or not the exercise was worth your time and effort, and if you wish, go for another six months. If you made a lot of money, consider writing a book!

PRIVATE PLACEMENTS

You are likely to be offered private placements from one of two sources. The first is an investment firm that is raising money for a privately held company. More than likely, this will be a small brokerage firm, although the larger firms are increasingly expanding into this business. However, it is not likely you will be approached by a large firm to invest in a private offering if you cannot invest at least $100,000. A small firm may have lower investment requirements.

The second source is a friend, or nephew of a friend, or your own nephew, who wants you to invest in his or her brand new business. Most of the time, you are better off passing on these offerings, but sometimes you may want to invest either because the idea appeals to you or because you figure if you don't, your brother may never speak to you again.

If you invest in a family business, or a startup that has been offered to you, you will, of course, investigate to be sure that in your own judgment the business has a decent chance of succeeding. Once that has been established to your satisfaction, be sure that you are protected by a shareholders' agreement. The key to investing in a privately held company is the shareholders' agreement. A shareholders' agreement is designed to protect the interests of minority shareholders in a privately held company. There is a good chance that if you invest in a private company, you are going to be a minority shareholder. The genius you are backing is going to own the majority of the stock, and you and your fellow investors will be minority shareholders.

Now you may be offered a position on the board of directors, which is flattering and also useful. It will entitle you to know what is going on at the company on a periodic basis, but that still doesn't give you the protection you need. The problem is that since the genius who runs the company owns the majority of the shares, he or she can pretty much decide to do anything he or she wants to do. Remember that the shareholders of a company elect the board of directors. So even though you are on the board, you really serve at the pleasure of the person with the controlling stock interest, who can call a special shareholders' meeting pretty much any time and kick you unceremoniously off the board should you become a pain in the neck.

A shareholders' agreement solves some of these problems. For example, you might include a provision that requires two thirds shareholder (not just board) approval for certain levels of capital expenditures and other major decisions. A lawyer can help you with the details, but no agreement will protect you against *all* contingencies. Just keep this in mind should you ever decide to invest in a private company.

IPOs

For all practical purposes, there are two kinds of IPOs: the hot issues, and all the others. The hot issues are those where the demand for the stock greatly exceeds the supply. Even if you have a very good relationship with your broker, chances are you will get far fewer shares than you really want in a hot issue. These deals are "allotted," meaning the brokers get a small amount of stock to distribute, based (generally) on their overall volume of business. In turn, the broker will favor his or her best clients with the allotted stock. Here are the guidelines to follow on IPOs:

Read the prospectus.   Of course you've heard this before. At the least, read the summary at the beginning of the prospectus. Learn what you can about the business. If it is a company you want to own, find out first if the offering will be a hot issue.

Don't buy a hot issue in the aftermarket on the day of the offering. These issues generally go to high premiums right after the issue is released, as the unrequited demand for stock results in a frenzy of buying on the offering day. Let your calmer self prevail. Buy the stock when the furor dies down.

If a broker calls to offer you an IPO, don't buy it.   The fact that the broker is calling you is a possible sign that the issue is cold and likely difficult to place. If the company is one you want to own, there is a good chance that it will trade lower after the public offering. The broker makes more money on the initial offering, so he or she will want you to buy it then. Don't.

COMMODITIES

Here the key is simple: Unless you are a farmer or a currency expert, *don't do it.* If you insist on speculating in commodities, seek advice elsewhere.

HEDGE FUNDS

Hedge funds are becoming more accessible to more investors. Many of the large investment firms are packaging hedge-fund products for investors with lower minimums than has previously been the case. Investors who want to invest as little as $50,000 now have an opportunity to do so. Hedge funds can actually make sense for investors with high risk tolerance, particularly you Reds and Blues.

A new opportunity to invest in hedge funds is being offered by Wall Street firms in the form of "funds of hedge funds," offering investors not one, but a combination of hedge funds. There are advantages and disadvantages to this approach. The principal advantage is that it offers access to hedge funds that most investors could not afford since individual fund minimums are generally very high ($100,000 to $1 million typically). It also offers the advantage of diversification, but this advantage works only if the diversification is done intelligently.

Consider this. If you buy a hedge fund managed by some hotshot with a terrific record, you need to understand the risk. Let's say this fund is subject to interest-rate risk because the manager invests in fixed income instruments. To offset that risk, you might want to own a completely different type of fund, say one that has exposure to oil prices. These risks will offer good diversification because they tend not to be correlated, and, in fact, have offsetting risk characteristics. (A fund with interest-rate exposure might not do well in a rising interest-rate environment, but a fund with oil-industry exposure might do well in that environment because interest rates usually rise as inflation expectations rise. When inflation expectations are rising, commodity prices, like oil, tend to go up, too.) These are not perfect hedges, but anything you can do to offset risk helps, particularly in the volatile areas of hedge funds.

My point is that a fund of hedge funds that is diversified *intelligently* (and that's the key word) might be able to offer offsetting risk characteristics. If you consider such a fund, ask pointed questions about how the different hedge-fund managers are chosen. If they are chosen just because they have good records, with no attention paid to their risk features, move on.

The biggest disadvantage to funds of hedge funds is that they tend to be fee heavy. You probably know that the standard hedge-fund charge is 1% of assets under management plus 20% of the profits. Okay. But the funds of funds guys also want a piece of the action, and they will charge an additional 10% or 20% in some cases. It takes some great performance to justify these fees. If they can deliver, they will deserve it, but it is appropriate to be skeptical.

In general, I prefer that small investors invest in a combination of hedge funds rather than just one, simply because the risk characteristics of hedge funds are high and diversification can keep you out of trouble.

A TALK WITH VICTOR NIEDERHOFFER: ON SPECULATING

Victor Niederhoffer has experienced the extremes of investment success, from the heights of enormous profits and uncannily accurate
calls, to the depths of investment despair, a total wipeout. His views are
worth heeding.

TANOUS: You say that the only newspaper you read is the *National
Enquirer*, you don't own a television, and you don't like books that are
less than 100 years old, but your book, *The Education of a Speculator*,
was a best-seller. When I talk to people who want to be part-time speculators, I can't help thinking about this quote from your book: "I do not
have the natural flair or wisdom of some traders or the research skill of
others, but I excel in concentration and focus." Does that mean that someone who isn't prepared to devote full time to speculating shouldn't do it?

NIEDERHOFFER: Speculation is endemic to all aspects of life. Like
it or not, you have to speculate. Whether it's buying or selling a house,
purchasing an inventory for a business, deciding whether or not to
invest in stocks or bonds, or how much income to put into retirement,
these are decisions where the outcome is uncertain. There is a variable
reward at stake, and your breaking point, or stopping point, is a certain
number of intervals below or above the initial starting point.

TANOUS: What determines the stopping point?

NIEDERHOFFER: There is a point of maximum loss that you can
take. That is the bottom level. The top level is the point at which you
are prepared to call it a day because your profits are high enough.

TANOUS: There is a very good example of that in your book where
you describe your success in investing in gold. You started with a
$40,000 initial stake, which you ran up to $22 million. A staggering success story! You went on to explain that you had a mental stop-loss limit
of $11 million so that the worst you could do would be to come out
ahead $11 million. As I recall, it didn't work out that way. What caused
it to change?

NIEDERHOFFER: A slip between the cup and the lip. Many people
who gamble are accustomed to saying, well, I'm going to go to Vegas
with a thousand dollars to burn, and if I lose that I'll call it day. I've had
some fun, and that's the price I'm willing to pay. They're not accustomed
to stopping when they have a certain gain so they have an asymmetric

reward and risk. Worse, many people have a kind of system where they sell the equivalent of a premium on options. That results in a very limited amount of gain, but they risk an unlimited amount of loss. That's one of the big mistakes people make. They have a stopping point based only upon loss. They don't have a stopping point based on gain. They should.

TANOUS: That is sound advice, although I recall that you wound up losing 95% of the $22 million gain. Do you think that the success of your book resulted in your getting more publicity than you should have following the sudden demise of your funds in October 1997?

NIEDERHOFFER: Everybody loves a loser, you know. "There but for the grace of God go I."

TANOUS: That part may be a natural instinct. I don't mean to pick on you, since what happened to you has also happened to others, but what is it about futures trading that makes it so appealing and creates such risks that you as an individual still want to do this?

NIEDERHOFFER: Well, I've been successful for a long time, and I've always believed that the only way to make money is to take quite a bit of risk. I like to emphasize my losses, because it keeps me humble and it also informs anybody who wishes to be associated with me about the risks that I am subject to. I've also found that going against the grain is the key to speculative success. In many markets, going against the grain can have a high winning probability, but it can have a large tail with a small probability of a huge loss. For many years I had an extraordinary return, and I hope to have that kind of return in the future.

TANOUS: Victor, in this book we are introducing a psychological element to investing for nonprofessional investors. You've been around a while, and I'd like you to comment on the psychology of investing. For example, despite your recent bad experience, I am fascinated by your willingness to take positions—sometimes against your own advice—where the risk of being wrong is potentially a wipeout.

NIEDERHOFFER: Most of the time markets move frequently to ferret out the point of maximum pain to force you out, and then they reverse and go back to their normal level. The market has an uncanny sense of finding your point of maximum pain and punishing the fearful and the cowardly while rewarding those who have courage and financial resources. If every time the market moved against you, you became fearful and got out, you would have extraordinarily negative returns. Of course, this has to be quantified. This isn't a psychological thing. The basic question of speculation is whether under certain conditions, prices tend to jiggle about and reverse themselves, but at other extraordinary times they tend to move to new equilibriums and forge momentous trends. The quantitative question of speculation is how to ascertain which of those particular states one is in and how to manage one's risk during that particular process.

TANOUS: If in a particular speculation, you analyze all of the possibilities from best case to worst case, and worst case is a small chance of being completely wiped out, might it still be worth doing because the chance of total loss, although present, is tiny?

NIEDERHOFFER: A person who uses a hedge should always put survival above everything, and a person who believes that he or she wants to live and last a normal lifetime has to take account of the probability of ruin and should put a particularly high cost factor on ruin. Survival is essential.

If you're talking about my particular situation, I believe that the positions that I was involved in had very good *a priori* chances of resulting in profits relative to the risk. Those positions had made a tremendous fortune for my customers in the past. This was something that I had consistently been involved in over the previous year and a half and ultimately ended up making my customers a lot more than they lost.

TANOUS: This seems like a good time to ask you to share some advice for investors who may be tempted to speculate on their own.

NIEDERHOFFER: I find it somewhat ironic that you would be asking me for advice. To many people, my guidance is somewhat doubtful, to say the least. One always has to be humble in speculating, especially after a time of disaster such as I've been exposed to. But with those caveats in mind, I think the key to successful speculation is to have some systematic reason for believing that one will be able to get the edge and to have it quantified in some scientific fashion. That is what we are taught in our science classes, and that has been the fruit of the scientific revolution and the age of reason.

TANOUS: So you need a system or a discipline.

NIEDERHOFFER: Well, my checker's mentor had an expression: "You should always have a system, even if it's a bad system." It gives one strength and it prevents one from being exposed to the psychological biases and improper decision making. There are movements in markets that induce one to have a visceral reaction to events, and that's the wrong way. A systematic edge can be a piece of knowledge or an insight that others haven't taken into account. It might also be some systematic conclusion concerning excesses and when they'll be resolved or a knowledge of liquidity situations and how they will work out in the marketplace. But it should be a systematic and quantitative reason for believing that one has an ability to profit. And one should take into account the transaction costs, the spreads, and the starting capital relative to the parameter of when you will be satisfied with the gain or when you are going to call it quits.

TANOUS: But speculating is intellectual. It's not a hunch.

NIEDERHOFFER: What's called for is a systematic hypothesis capable of being verified by empirical evidence. A speculator must have a proper base of operations in terms of starting capital relative to stopping points on both sides, given the uncertainty of the outcomes. That's the fundamental speculative issue that all investors should take into account in their activities if they are going to have any chance of success.

TANOUS: Is there another Niederhoffer book in the offing?

NIEDERHOFFER: I'm in a learning and seeking-of-knowledge phase, not in a proselytizing phase right now. I'm trying to gain knowledge, not impart knowledge, as is appropriate for me at a time like this.

TANOUS: Anything you would like to add?

NIEDERHOFFER: I think speculation is a noble vocation that arises in every aspect of life. It uses every ability or lack thereof a person has. It encompasses every subject one has mastered. Every aspect of good character or bad character manifests itself within it. Speculators provide a magnificent function in the grand scheme of things by preventing gluts and shortages and by helping to provide the proper allocation of resources in society. It's a very noble vocation, and it is absolutely essential to the quality of life that one enjoys in modern civilizations.

TANOUS: One of the things you point out in your book is that there is a tendency often observed in athletes that one tends to do better after a defeat. Is it safe to predict that Victor Niederhoffer will come back?

NIEDERHOFFER: One has to be resilient and be prepared. I've done a lot of losing before. I have six kids, and I have every reason to hope that I'll be able to cover their multitudinous financial requirements of life in the future. Many times during my athletic career I heard the halcyon cry: "Niederhoffer is dead. He's gone." My answer then was always that the racket will do the talking. In the future, my results will do the talking.

KEY POINTS

Here is what I would like you to remember from this Master Key:

- ### SPECULATE INTELLIGENTLY

  If you must speculate, do so intelligently with your eyes wide open and your mind fully engaged.

- ### LIMIT YOUR RISK

  Never risk more than the amount you put up.

- ### NEVER ACCEPT PERSONAL LIABILITY

  Never invest in anything that puts your personal assets at risk.

- ### USE OPTIONS JUDICIOUSLY

  If you bet with options, be prepared to lose the amount you put up, no more, no less.

- ### AVOID COMMODITIES

  Stay away from commodities unless you are a currency expert or a seasoned farmer.

- ### DIVERSIFY HEDGE-FUND EXPOSURE

  If you choose to invest in hedge funds, try to diversify by investing in more than one to spread the risk.

- ### TARGET BOTH GAINS AND LOSSES

  When speculating, follow Niederhoffer's advice: Set limits on your losses *and* your gains. Sell when your maximum level of pain is reached and take profits when your expected gain has been achieved.

MASTER KEY 5
STAY ALERT; AVOID "DUMB" MISTAKES

View tips cautiously. They usually end up costing you a ton of money.
TODD RABOLD, WACHOVIA ASSET MANAGEMENT

Don't be afraid to sell a loser.
PAUL JACKSON, PAUL J. JACKSON & ASSOCIATES

Marry a very wealthy spouse.
JOE JOSHI, SYSTEMATIC FINANCIAL MANAGEMENT, L.P.

When you think about it, half of the process of building wealth involves making the right investment decisions. The other half involves avoiding dumb mistakes that will cause you to lose what you made. For that reason, one of the most important Master Keys to investment success is learning how to avoid mistakes that can unravel your gains and set you back one, two, three years or more in your plan for wealth.

We asked the money managers we surveyed how important various factors were to investment success. Avoiding dumb mistakes was cited by 68% of the managers as "very important," the highest category of importance. We call them dumb mistakes because most of us think of mistakes as dumb. If they had been smart decisions in the first place, they probably wouldn't wind up being mistakes.

There are few situations in the world of investing that are as frustrating as losing money for the wrong reason. On occasion, every serious investor knows that he or she will lose money. If the stock market, and most stocks, went up in a symmetrical straight line, everybody would be a genius at investing because there would be few surprises and even less risk. There are periods when investors need to batten down the hatches and ride out the storm. We know that sooner or later, the storm will pass and we will continue on our road to the creation of more wealth. After all, volatility and risk are the price we pay to get the returns we expect out of the stock market.

SIX FUNDAMENTAL ERRORS

But an investment loss that is the result of a fundamental error is different. These are the errors we seek to avoid or, at the least, having made a particular mistake once, we vow not to repeat it. As part of our investment training, we must train ourselves to be alert to those things that lead to potential mistakes. In this chapter, we look at some examples of investment mistakes and discover how to avoid those pitfalls.

HUBRIS

My dictionary defines hubris as "wanton insolence or arrogance resulting from excessive pride." When it comes to investing, hubris tends to rear its head after some successful investment strategies we employ pan out and we make a considerable profit. The danger is obvious. We begin to think we are the next Warren Buffett. We think we're invincible. Our sense of judgment and sense of the market is superb. We just know when something is about to happen, a merger, a stock split, and a favorable earnings announcement. (Now part of this may be true. Some of us are, frankly, better investors than others.) Golds and Blues may be particularly susceptible to hubris (especially now that you know that almost all of the great money managers are in one of these categories). What's more, you Blues may be especially susceptible since you handle risk well, and the combination of this trait and a few successful trading events can be dangerous. Reds also have affinity for risk and should tune their psyches to the danger of excessive pride.

Think hard about your investment success and try to do what the academics constantly do—ask yourself, was it skill or luck that accounted for your recent wizardry. If you don't know, play it safe. In fact, if you do know, play it safe. Either way, there is nothing wrong with being lucky. Just don't let it go to your head.

The point here is *if you have a string of investment successes*, do not *change your overall investment strategy*. The temptation is to double up on your next idea since you have been proven so right in the recent past. That's a big mistake. If you do that, you are setting yourself up for a big loss.

Another antidote to hubris is doing some old-fashioned homework before you invest. As Donald Yacktman (Yacktman Asset Management) says, "The biggest mistake for a long-term investor is not knowing enough about the business being purchased. There is no substitute for knowledge."

Anybody disagree?

EXCESSIVE ANXIETY

This is the opposite of hubris. Some investors worry not too little, but too much. They look at their portfolios every day and fret that the market has gone down or gone up. Either event is a cause for anxiety. If the market goes down, they worry that they have lost money. If the market goes up, they worry that they will not be able to hold on to the gains. All personality groups are susceptible to anxiety, although the Golds, whose sense of responsibility is so ingrained in their personalities, may be most susceptible.

If you are prone to anxiety attacks when it comes to the market, the best thing to do is discipline yourself *not* to look at the market every day. Instead, establish and force yourself to follow a procedure to review your portfolio and holdings and make judgments at specific set intervals. In the investment advisory business, reviews are typically done quarterly. That's because the industry has determined that a review every three months or so is all that is needed to examine and evaluate the performance of a long-term portfolio. If you can discipline yourself to dispel short-term anxiety by ignoring your long-term portfolio in between review sessions, you stand a much greater chance of success. Treat your portfolio like a plant that will die from too much attention and overwatering. As a matter of fact, pretend it is a cactus. You'll know what to do.

OVERTRADING

No doubt, you are aware that excessive trading tends to hurt investment performance. Trading is expensive, whether you do it or your manager or mutual fund engages in it. Some managers are very good at trading but no portfolio should be composed of managers who are predominantly heavy traders.

A TALK WITH SUSAN BYRNE: ON DUMB MISTAKES (AND HOW TO AVOID THEM)

I invited a well-known mutual-fund manager to recount her experiences both in terms of avoiding mistakes and otherwise investing intelligently. I picked someone who was not only very successful, but who had to endure her own share of adversity on the path to success. Susan Byrne is president of Westwood Management in Dallas, which she founded in 1983. She is the manager of the Westwood Equity Fund and the Westwood Balanced Fund, both of which have enjoyed superior returns.

TANOUS: Susan, your background as a money manager is not very typical. You started your career as a secretary, did not finish college, and had a young family to raise, most of which suggests a great many obstacles to a successful career. It also tells me that you likely know something about avoiding mistakes.

BYRNE: I probably do. The idea of avoiding mistakes is part of the approach we take here. I didn't always look at my background with great pride. I was embarrassed about it for a time and felt inferior to a lot of the people I worked with and for. I imagined that they knew a lot more than I did, and, therefore, they might be better than I. It took me a few years to realize that there was more to it than that.

TANOUS: Can you relate your experience to that of an investor facing the challenges of the stock market?

BYRNE: When I was starting out, my first five years in the business were the years 1970 to 1975. I saw quite brilliant people lose huge amounts of money. [*The stock market declined about 40% in 1973-1974, one of the worst declines in history.*] I watched how painful it was for them and their clients, so my first experience in the business was not to see money made, but to see money lost. People's outlook on life tends to be colored by their early experiences. So I became very concerned about avoiding losses.

TANOUS: I think that most investors can readily identify with that. Most of them are not professionals, and they have to invest their own money. Sooner or later, they realize it's tough to do.

BYRNE: One of the things that was difficult for me—although looking back it was almost a blessing—was that since I didn't have a highly structured view of the way business should be, I was able to observe it as it was. I didn't have to worry about things not fitting in to what I had learned. I was swimming upstream, not coming from a privileged background, and not being male (there were very few women in the business at the time). I remember people being irritated because I kept asking a lot of questions (which might irritate me today!).

In my early experience, I observed professionals analyzing and applying valuations rigorously, and they were losing money. So it wasn't that they were getting the formulas wrong. For example, over the last 20 years Polaroid has sold at a historical relationship to the S&P 500 of 100% to 150% of the market multiple [*price earnings ratio*]. The stock is now selling at 98% of the market multiple; therefore it is cheap; therefore buy it. Of course, the math was correct, and this was the way valuation was done at the "nifty fifty" research boutique where I was working at the time. So as a young person, while I could learn the formulas and do the math, it was clear to me that that was not relevant to what was going on with the stock prices. Just going by the numbers was a mistake. [*This approach based on the "math" doesn't allow for the fact that the company's fundamentals or competitive position may have deteriorated, as indeed they did at Polaroid.*]

I became rather obsessed with why something that had made sense to a lot of people for a long time all of a sudden doesn't make sense any more. What is the message? It made me, as a research analyst and as a portfolio manager, very interested in the forest. I left the trees to people on Wall Street. When I wanted to have a discourse on trees I could call them up. But when I wanted to think about portfolio risk and where I could lose money, I always went to the forest.

The important job of a portfolio manager is to ask the right questions. What is the most important determinant of profitability in a particular company or industry? What is the one thing that says that the sales of Coca-Cola are worth three times the sales of Alcoa?

TANOUS: What's the answer?

BYRNE: How people feel about it! People have a feeling about Coca-Cola, and right now the Coca-Cola investment thesis is based on its ability to grow in a stable, unvolatile, uninterrupted way, come rain or come shine. I think that's the most important determinant of its price-earnings multiple. But if there is a question anywhere down the road about the company's ability to sustain the growth, then there will be a question about the valuation of that industry or company. The corollary to asking the right question is only do what you understand.

TANOUS: This goes back to the theme of avoiding mistakes. One way to avoid some mistakes is to invest only in things you understand.

BYRNE: I think hubris is really the enemy. The bible says "pride preceedeth the fall." I think that's still meaningful. Hubris leads to huge mistakes in investing. You need a discipline that forces you to say, I'm not going to do that because I don't understand it. That may not be an easy thing to say out loud, but I think it's worth gobs of mental health, especially in a bull market.

TANOUS: Does that mean that an investor shouldn't invest in high tech?

BYRNE: Not necessarily. For instance, in my case, I have a lot of trouble understanding the airline business. I understand the basics. They have planes and leverage and I understand the finance, but I don't understand the variables that are going to bring about surprisingly good earnings. I don't know how to put a computer together or take it apart, but I can and did understand that the direct-sales model that Dell uses made sense to me.

TANOUS: Good point. What are some of the other mistakes that an investor should avoid, particularly those who aren't going to spend full time at it?

BYRNE: First of all, and I know this thought has been popularized by Peter Lynch, look around and see what is going on. We talk to everybody we can about what people are buying, what their kids like, who went to what place to eat. Then we ask, gee, who owns that? Or, gee,

The problem with trading is that we tend to sell our good stocks too early and our bad ones too late (another casualty, perhaps, of misguided efforts to time the market). If you have spent the requisite amount of time on the all-important key of asset allocation of the portfolio, you will spend less time worrying about trading individual stocks. It is much better to worry about whether or not the computer industry is overrepresented in your portfolio than to worry about whether or not IBM is too high.

are they making money doing that? Or, gosh, does that make sense? When I was a young person, I used to think I could trade options in my IRA and make a lot of quick money since I didn't have to pay taxes on it. Instead, I lost it. I would argue today that to speculate in options is a terrible idea. You not only have to be right on the stock, which is hard enough, but you also have to be right on the timing. I find that combination nearly impossible.

TANOUS: That's certainly a good example of a mistake to avoid.

BYRNE: Take the example of people who have done well buying Nike. If they have kids and they were paying attention and listening, they might have caught a real anti-Nike mood coming on about a year ago. Teenagers wouldn't be caught dead in Nikes because it was just too much. So kids started wearing Adidas retro things so that nobody would confuse them with the upper-middle-class Nike kids. If you could see that coming you might have realized that that would translate into a sales backlash at a company that had been growing really fast.

TANOUS: Is there any other advice you can offer for avoiding mistakes?

BYRNE: If you are investing for capital appreciation and you own a company that is a market leader, keep the company and don't worry about the stock. As long as the company is a good company and the business that they're in is still growing, don't worry about the stock in the short run. Just sit back, and it will come back, just like Wal-Mart, which did nothing for about three years and now has practically doubled in six months. You tend to get those kinds of moves in good growth companies. Buy them and let them grow over time. Don't let the government become your partner by selling them.

Another problem with trading is that it costs money, sometimes lots of money. Remember that if you are dealing with a broker, it is likely that his or her income is derived from the commissions earned on trading stocks and bonds and other financial instruments. So the more trading you do, the richer your broker will be. This puts the broker in an ethically difficult position. The broker knows, or ought to know, that more trading is not likely to result in a higher overall return. Since most brokers are honest folks, my conclusion is that they delude themselves early on to believe that while more trading is generally bad, in the case of the trades they are recommending, more trading is actually good. Remember: You know better.

The problem of overtrading doesn't apply only to stocks. Overtrading in mutual funds is a growing problem. That isn't so surprising when you think about it. The financial press has over-dosed on mutual funds, and just about every magazine on the planet now has its own annual mutual-fund rating issue. So when your favorite magazine comes out with its ten "can't-miss" mutual-fund rankings, you might be tempted to sell the underachieving funds you hold and buy the new stars. The problem, of course, is that six months from now, another ten funds will emerge as sure winners, and your most recent purchases will be relegated to the bottom of the heap.

Mutual-fund holders should focus on the asset allocation of their portfolio of mutual funds and review the performance attributes of their individual funds annually. Overtrading in mutual funds based on short-term performance will almost guarantee inferior investment results.

STOCK TIPS

At times, tips are almost irresistible. One of your friends who works for a pharmaceutical company tells you about a new product at another company—not his—that will revolutionize the medical profession. It is the single most likely discovery to lead to a cure of (a) AIDS, (b) heart failure, or (c) the common cold. Considering the source of the information, you have just got to be interested in what your friend is saying. He is not touting his own company's product, since he is an executive of a competing pharmaceutical company, and he knows this business cold. Here's a real chance to get in on the ground floor.

There's a good chance that this story, or a close variation thereof, is part of your own experience. It happens to almost all of us. For the most part, these investments turn out not only badly, but disas-trously. Yes, a very few will get lucky on information like this. (A very few people will also win the Publishers Clearing House grand prize. It's one thing to risk a first-class stamp; it's quite another to invest a considerable amount of money with about the same odds of success.) Skepticism in situations like these is your best friend.

Ask yourself, how did I get so lucky to get this information before anyone else? Is it because I have a friend in the business? Is he the only one who knows about this great development? Chances are that he is not. This is where it's worth recalling the Efficient Market Hypothesis. It holds that everything that is publicly known about a company is reflected in the price of its stock. While this is not always true, it is highly unlikely that you and a couple of buddies are the only ones to know about a major new discovery that is not yet reflected in the price of that company's stock. I mean, the president, twelve vice presidents, secretaries, account executives, and so forth don't have any friends? Nobody else knows or talked about this story? I don't think so.

If you are going to listen to stock tips, limit the amount of money you will devote to this activity. When you lose it all, learn your lesson and stop. If you make millions of dollars, call me and we'll write a book together.

PLAYING CATCH-UP

We all know what playing catch-up is. In football, when a team is behind by three touchdowns at the start of the fourth quarter, the only realistic hope of winning the game is to throw long bombs and hope for a few miracles. At this stage of the game, catching up by running three or four yards at a time will not get you there before you run out of time. The problem with throwing a lot of long passes, however, is that there's a real good chance that they either won't be caught or worse, the other team will intercept the ball.

Investors sometime engage in a game of catch-up. If they perceive that their performance isn't what it should have been, they will consciously or unconsciously ratchet up the risk of their investments in an attempt to score big and bring the portfolio returns back to where they think they ought to be.

Big mistake.

The key difference in playing catch-up in the last quarter of a football game and playing catch-up with your portfolio is that you are not in the fourth quarter! You are not about to run out of time. So why are you going to expose yourself to considerably higher risk to earn a higher return *quickly*? There is a better than even chance that the extra risk will turn on you and produce even worse returns in the short run.

If you are not satisfied with the returns your portfolio is yielding, first check the asset allocation. Are you diversified the way you want to be in different classes of stocks and bonds, small and large, domestic and international? If so, are your investment components performing as they ought to be? If you have chosen mutual funds, are they performing according to the appropriate benchmarks you compare them against? Is the overall risk of your portfolio in line with your personal risk tolerance?

Many of these questions will be answered for you when we talk about creating your personal investment program where your personal risk tolerance and investment attitudes will contribute to the asset allocation that is right for you. If your portfolio reflects your personal desires and investment attitudes, you will never need to play catch-up.

UNLIMITED LOSS—THE WORST MISTAKE

Have you ever had the nightmare where you are on top of a building or a mountain and you fall off, and you keep falling and falling and screaming at the top of your lungs waiting for the inevitable impact? Only the impact never comes. You wake up in a cold sweat.

The investment parallel to that nightmare is called *unlimited losses*. You keep falling and falling, only you don't wake up. You end up penniless instead. This is the dumbest mistake you can make. It has a way of creeping up on you and grabbing you by the throat when you are not paying attention. So, *en garde*. Our best defense against this towering mistake is to be prepared. You want to reach a point where as soon as you are exposed to any situation that could lead to unlimited losses, the experience provokes a Pavlovian reaction, a chill down your spine, an immediate spike of adrenaline that tells you to get the hell out of there, *fast*.

Lest you think that experienced professionals like me are impervious to dumb mistakes such as this, well, it is time for "true confessions." A number of years ago, some friends in Florida invited me to join in an opportunity to buy an apartment complex. This was an unusual deal in that we didn't even have to put up any money. The bank would lend us the full amount since we were fortunate enough to be able to buy this complex below its appraised value. I knew these fellows pretty well; they were astute real-estate investors, so I agreed to join them. After all, no money down! We formed a partnership, and the transaction promptly closed. We had become the owners of a small apartment complex in beautiful, sunny Florida.

At first, we had no trouble leasing the units, and the income we received easily covered our loan payments. We were essentially letting the property pay for itself. Over time, however, the neighborhood changed and both the property and the general area became considerably less desirable. I left the management of the property to my friends since they were in the real-estate business and lived in Florida. I pretty much forgot about it. At tax time, I received some reports that I turned over to my accountant, and that was about all the attention I paid to this investment.

Seven years had passed when I got a call from one of my original partners. Frankly, I had to struggle to remember who was calling me (I hadn't heard from any of them in years, but a bell went off and I took the call). My friend of old told me he had some bad news. Remember that apartment complex we all bought in Florida? Well, the property had become a virtual slum. No one wanted to live there—at least no one who had any intention of paying any rent—and the bank was foreclosing. Frankly, at this point, I didn't really care. I hadn't put up any money so as far as I was concerned, the bank was more than welcome to my share. Alas, he told me, there was more to it than that. Since the property had sunk in value well below the amount the bank originally lent us, our friendly bankers were coming after us for the balance, a considerable sum. The problem, you see, was that we formed a partnership to buy the property and, as partners, we were each liable jointly and severally, a legal term which means that if any of the partners default, the rest of us are liable for that amount, too. To make a bad situation even worse, two of the original partners were broke. In other words, the investment I had made years ago that had cost me nothing was about to cost me a lot. We negotiated with the bank and agreed on a sum that was less than they wanted and considerably more than I wanted to pay. But we settled.

The lesson here is that even though I was an experienced financial person, I let my guard down and made a dumb mistake. I don't like talking about it much but it taught me a valuable lesson. I share it with you because it is something you can learn from as well. Know the extent of your liability in any investment you make of any kind. If necessary, spend the money to have a lawyer look at it, and tell the lawyer what your concern is. This, too, is important. If you don't, the lawyer may well assume you know you are personally responsible for the investment. You have been forewarned.

Some of the most common ways to lose all of your money before you realize it are these:

- *Short-selling.* When you sell short (by borrowing stock to sell and repaying with stock you hope to buy back at a lower price) your goal is to make money when a stock goes down, instead of up. But in short sales, the losses are potentially unlimited. If you borrow stock, which instead of going down, goes up, you will some day have to buy that stock back to replace the stock you borrowed. But what if the stock has gone up two, three . . . ten, or twenty times! Chances are, you are heading to bankruptcy. Is it worth it?

- *Commodities.* Some commodity transactions also offer you the opportunity to lose an unlimited amount of money. I have suggested throughout this book that you not engage in commodity trading unless you are a professional with profound knowledge of the commodity you are trading. The risk is not worth it.

- *Personal liability.* Some types of investment require that you personally sign for the investment, which means that you are personally liable for any losses that are incurred. This often happens (as I learned the hard way) in the case of real-estate transactions. For example, when you buy a house or a piece of property and take out a mortgage, normally you are not personally liable for the loan beyond the value of the property. If you default on your payments, the bank takes the property back. If the property is worth less than the amount they lent you, it's their tough luck. That's why bankers now often ask borrowers to personally sign for the loan. That means if you default, they can get not only the property you bought, but they also can come after you for any other assets you may have to satisfy their claim.

Now, if you are in the real-estate business, you may not have any choice but to guarantee your loans. It is increasingly becoming a part of the game. If you are not in the business, however, do not guarantee any investment that you do not control. Here again, your losses can wind up being a great deal more than your investment, especially if you put up only a fraction of the cost of the property as a down payment. Better to learn from my costly experience than your own.

NOT LEARNING FROM EXPERIENCE

Here's a secret you may already know: To avoid making dumb mistakes of your own, pay attention to the dumb mistakes of others and don't do them. There are plenty of kind souls out there who will share their misfortunes with you if you are willing to buy them a drink or otherwise be a good listener. Take advantage of it.

KEY POINTS

We learn almost instinctively that success comes from making the right decisions. Later in life, we start to appreciate that success is both a combination of making the right decisions and avoiding the decisions that turn out to be mistakes. The combination of these two traits is called judgment. So it is in our investment lives. Most of us are capable of making enough right decisions to make money in the stock market. It requires some intelligence, some application, and some discipline. The difference between those who succeed and grow rich and those who don't is often the difference between those who make a lot of mistakes in their investments and those who don't. If you develop a radar for dumb investment mistakes, you will greatly enhance your capacity for investment wealth.

For starters, put these on your radar screen:

- HUBRIS

   Don't let investment success go to your head. Your next investment decision might be costlier than you could imagine.

- EXCESSIVE ANXIETY

   If you have a tendency to worry too much about your investments, discipline yourself not to look at the financial pages every day. Review your investment holdings quarterly and make rational decisions accordingly.

- OVERTRADING

  Trading can be fun. Most of the time it is very costly. Don't trade stocks unless you plan to do it for a living. That old saw "buy for the long term" has merit.

- STOCK TIPS

  The chance of your making a lot of money on a stock tip is about the same as winning the lottery or the Publishers Clearing House sweepstakes. It's less costly to do the latter. Investing a dollar on a ticket or a first-class stamp on a sweepstakes is a lot more sensible than risking a portion of your life savings.

- UNLIMITED LIABILITY

  The phrase should make you run for the hills. Never risk a loss that exceeds your investment or your expectation. Always assume that the worst-case scenario has a reasonable chance of occurring. Can you live with the consequences? No matter what the investment, it is not worth the risk of financial ruin.

- LEARN FROM THE EXPERIENCE OF OTHERS

  People are funny. Many of them will be willing to share their worst experiences with you if you ask them in the right way. If you say that you want to learn from their experience, the teacher/mentor instinct will emerge. Approach someone you respect and tell him or her candidly that you want to hear about his or her worst investment mistake so that you might learn from the experience. Then pull up a chair. You may be there for a while.

- MARKET TIMING

  We did not include market timing in this chapter because market timing is such a bad mistake it is the subject of a chapter all its own.

MASTER KEY 6
HAVE FAITH

The epistle of James, Chapter 1, Verse 5, reads, "If any of you lacks wisdom, let him ask of God, who gives liberally and without reproach, and it will be given to him." This promise has been activated by the people of this firm since our formation.

THOMAS G. FOX
PRESIDENT AND CEO, TREND CAPITAL MANAGEMENT

I suspect that you have not often seen a discussion of faith in a book about investing. Neither have I. So I think I owe you a little explanation of why we are delving into this subject here.

When I was doing the research for my previous book, *Investment Gurus*, I interviewed a cross section of the truly great money managers. I used a number of different criteria to select the best and sought to discover what it was about these superstars that contributed to their stellar performance. Many of the traits I found were not surprising. For example, we learned that *all* of the great managers shared a strong single-mindedness about their work and were very focused and disciplined. No real surprise there.

There was one trait that, while not universal among the managers, occurred much more often than I might have expected. To my surprise, I found that many of the great managers were also very religious. I decided not to comment on that fact in *Investment Gurus*, but it fascinated me and I tucked it away as information to use at a later date. That date soon came. As I prepared the survey for this book, I decided to ask about religious beliefs. Once again, I found that many of the managers were either religious in a traditional sense or had a keen sense of a higher being as most of us would understand it. What's more, 58% of the respondents said they regularly attend religious services. This is higher than the population as a whole. (A study done by the Catholic Church found that only 44%

of Americans were regular churchgoers.) When we asked, "Do you believe that faith or involvement with religion plays a significant role in managing money?" 35% answered positively. These figures are high enough to warrant our attention.

What does this mean to you and me as investors? I suspect that this is a question each of us will have to decide for himself or herself. First, let's see what a cross section of these managers said about this subject and then ponder if there are any conclusions to be drawn.

- "Conviction is important. 'Faith' is defined (by me) as being willing to believe in something that is 'unprovable.' Investing is believing in things not yet proven!" (Thomas E. McGowan, Lynch & Mayer, Inc.)

- "Faith dictates character, which dictates actions." (Thomas J. Condon, Provident Investment Counsel)

- "The unalterable moral truths that are communicated through sacred scripture set the foundation upon which any business should be built." (Thomas G. Fox, Trend Capital Management)

Resonating through these comments is a deep sense of faith *in something*, not necessarily organized religion as we know it, but in some ephemeral, perhaps even mystical, quality that many of these managers are convinced contribute in one way or another to their investment success.

T. Scott Wittman of Vantage Investment Advisors is typical of many responses: "Religious faith is something that affects all aspects of your life. It provides perspective that is very helpful in dealing with the inevitable ups and downs of managing money."

Some of the managers we surveyed likened faith to the importance of ethics in the business and an appreciation of right and wrong.

- "A manager's fiduciary responsibility is to act prudently and with the highest level of personal integrity. The Bible charges us to 'add to faith, wisdom, knowledge, perseverance, godliness, kindness, self-control (discipline), and love.' These attributes will better equip the manager to successfully serve the client and meet their investment objectives." (James C. Wadsworth, Mellon Bank Corp.)

- "One should know the difference between right and wrong, honesty and dishonesty, and have the conviction to stick with one's beliefs." (Bernard R. Horn, Jr., Polaris Capital Management)

- "Managing money can be very lonely and demoralizing at times. Having the ability to speak with a greater power can be comforting and uplifting." (Craig T. Johnson, Leonetti and Associates)

Remember that these voices are those of managers at the top of their form, individuals whose performance and talent rank them above their peers, many of whom admit openly that faith and spirituality affect the way they conduct their business lives. Some, like Gerald T. Kennedy of Kennedy Capital Management, relate religious beliefs directly to the money-management process: "I believe that the discipline of strong religious beliefs carries over into the strong discipline and perseverance needed to remain with a good strategy even through difficult times." Others view the relationship in a more general sense. "You need to believe in something greater than yourself and/or public opinion," says Ron Muhlenkamp of Muhlenkamp & Company. Jack Darrell, of Darrell & King, adds on the subject of religion in investing that "I believe it helps me accept adversity as part of life which helps lead to rational decisions. When things are going well I try to be thankful as I realize that the major events are beyond my control."

Here is a straightforward response from Joe Joshi of Systematic Financial Management: "I believe that good investors are quite optimistic about the future. In my case, optimism flows from my strong religious commitments."

Carl W. Hafele of National Asset Management links faith to character when he comments that "having a strong faith is often a characteristic seen in a well-rounded individual. Well-rounded individuals are most likely to make better decisions in a business where level-headedness is essential."

Not all managers agreed. Many checked the box that said they did not believe that religion played a role in their investing life. Paul Jackson of Paul J. Jackson & Associates said, "I think it is important to have some religious convictions, but it plays no role in my managing of money."

A TALK WITH FOSTER FRIESS: ON FAITH AND INVESTING

To get a deeper perspective on the role faith may play in managing money, I went to Foster Friess, the legendary manager of the Brandywine Fund ($9 billion in assets; ten-year annualized return, through 1997, 20.25%). The role faith plays in Foster's daily life is unusually deep, and his comments are intriguing.

TANOUS: When I was doing the research for *Investment Gurus*, I was struck by how often the subject of faith and investing came up. In fact, you were the one who started me down this path. For this book, I surveyed 100 top money managers, and 58% of my respondents—all top money managers— said that they regularly attend church services. What's more, 35% answered yes to the question: *Do you believe that faith or involvement with religion plays a significant role in managing money?* I confess I don't know what to make of it. Why do you think so many answered yes to that question?

FRIESS: I'm surprised it wasn't more.

TANOUS: Then let's try to zero in on how the faith helps some people manage money. I'm trying to find out if there is a nexus between faith in God and faith in one's own investment judgment.

FRIESS: Let's see if I can get at it this way. In our business, you can have very high-energy-level people, but there's a vast difference between having that high energy emanate from someone who is *called* versus someone who's driven. Do you remember the movie *Chariots of Fire?* One guy was driven by self-aggrandizement; the other to glorify God. We are all exposed by our nature to pride and ego, and we have to deal with it. Judaism tells us that pride is a destructive force, and it certainly is in the stock market. For example, people who use their investment performance to measure their value as people have a much more difficult time selling a stock if it's going against them than those who are secure about who they are. Because of their relationship to God or however they define that security, they don't constantly have to be proving themselves.

TANOUS: So, you think faith contributes to well-roundedness?

FRIESS: Well, throughout the generations, Peter, people said that human beings have a physical aspect, a mental aspect, and a spiritual aspect. In my own life, at one point I spent a lot of time on my physical attributes, like improving my golf game, lifting weights, watching my diet, and so forth. Then I spent time on my mental ability, learning Spanish, or becoming more adept at reading the footnotes in an annual report, understanding the difference between financing leasing and operating leasing, and the impact on earnings of FIFO versus LIFO inventory accounting. I remained ignorant of my spiritual side, but my ignorance didn't prevent me from suffering the consequences of my disobedience to them.

TANOUS: What was the catalyst to get you from one state to the other?

FRIESS: In my late thirties, I was making over $100,000 a year. I thought I'd died and gone to heaven; I'd never dreamed I'd be making that much money. I grew up in a small village in Wisconsin where the richest guys in town were the Mobil gas station owner and the undertaker. Making that kind of money just blew my mind. I had everything I'd dreamed of. I had a beautiful wife, four great kids who were going to the right schools, nice cars, and I lived in the right part of town. Suddenly, it wasn't very satisfying anymore. My wife and I were having difficulties. My kids and I weren't getting along.

Then our fourth child, Michael, developed spinal meningitis. It left him profoundly deaf. That had a dramatic impact on my life. Michael is fine; he's part of the firm; researches stocks and is maybe the world's first FAA-certified deaf helicopter pilot! I come from a line of self-willed people. They believed that if you put in the extra effort, you could achieve anything in your control. The key is being *in control*. With Michael, at age seven months, so ill, my life's myth of self-sufficiency burst. This trauma, together with my bad marriage and unhappy family life and complete boredom with my work, reached a pinnacle.

Just then, a friend called and said he had just come into several million dollars that he wanted to invest. I hadn't seen Bill for about 18 months, but I had known him for about 20 years. I knew that he had been depressed and probably drinking a little too much. When we met, I couldn't believe the transformation. He was excited about life; he was purposeful; and he was happy. He had stopped drinking. He said he had invited Christ into his life and pulled out one of these religious pamphlets. At that time I hated those little pamphlets, but knowing that he might be laying three million bucks in my lap, I took them. They had a remarkable impact, and I came to accept Christ.

TANOUS: Foster, I'd like you to share how, on a daily basis, your faith and experience help you with investment decisions.

FRIESS: One example might be the realization that nobody's perfect. I've been diagnosed and recognize myself as a recovering perfectionist. There's a difference between excellence and perfectionism. The Christian message rejects the notion that I must become perfect in order for me to be acceptable to God. Therefore, if I can feel good about who I am, with all my flaws and imperfections, it gives me a greater capacity to embrace people in that same spirit. So when brokers screw up and give me bad ideas, I'm more inclined to say, "Hey, we're big boys. We bought the stock, we did our research, and we lost money. We all make mistakes; so let's brush ourselves off and find another idea." My pre-Christian reaction was to blame the broker, hold him accountable, and berate him. That's one example.

TANOUS: What about ordinary investors, people who are not professionals? They don't have access to the sources of information you do. The top brokers on Wall Street don't call them with ideas. How does faith help them when investing on their own?

FRIESS: I think their faith may help them trust somebody else who has those resources. When people develop faith, they develop the capacity to trust others; they give up having to be self-reliant. Does that make sense?

TANOUS: It does, but the bottom line seems to be, "use your faith to find a manager instead of doing it yourself."

FRIESS: I think faith will also help those people who choose to manage their money themselves. It depends on what you have faith in. When you ask people about faith, many say they have faith in themselves. I also think the ability to admit mistakes is important. In my life, before I could become a Christian, I had to recognize a need to be rescued from my own sinfulness. God calls us to eliminate pride from our lives. At Brandywine, it manifests itself like this: When we write a report saying that we've had a very good quarter, we never say we're proud of the quarter, we say we're *grateful* for the quarter.

TANOUS: Good point. It occurs to me that the Book of Job is about man's faith in God being tested. Isn't it true that investors and money managers are tested every day? Is there a parallel here?

FRIESS: Money management is not unlike athletics. We're tested all the time. I think you're on to something, Peter, and I hope it will be helpful as well to people who are struggling with the purpose of life. Why are we here? Is it for self-aggrandizement, or is it to be used to fulfill the need of others? At Brandywine, we get terrific excitement from knowing that if we've done well for the Nobel Foundation [*one of Foster Friess' clients*], they can give better prizes to scientists. Or if we've done well for an orphanage, the kids can have a better meal.

TANOUS: To conclude, Foster, can you give any advice to investors that embodies your strong faith?

FRIESS: The experience I have is so far-reaching in terms of making us better husbands, better fathers, better citizens, but to relate it specifically to investment success, I'd say that faith takes some of the emotional roller coaster out of it. God brings you down off the mountaintop when you get a little arrogant, and He brings you up from the valley when you think you're really screwing up. I think it offers a balance to one's emotional life by taking the roller-coaster ride out. It offers you the chance to look at adversity with a different perspective.

TANOUS: Can you give me an example?

FRIESS: There are so many! For instance, we got hit on a number of our companies because of events in Asia. In James 1:2-3, we are challenged to be grateful for the adversity that comes into our lives because it will build perseverance. What's come out of this is that we are building a network of over 20 contacts all over Asia, in Hong Kong, Korea, and Japan. We're also going to develop a network in Europe and in South America. Getting back to the perfectionism-and-excellence idea, and the difference between the two. Perfectionism abhors error. It tries to eradicate and destroy it. Excellence embraces error; it builds on it and transforms it. Now when something goes askew, we no longer call it a mistake or a screw-up, we call it an adjustment opportunity.

TANOUS: We'll remember that.

Among other managers in the survey who chose to comment on this subject, I was struck by those among them who say that they are not deeply religious, or not religious at all, but who identify with the more religious managers in that they draw similar conclusions on lifestyle issues. Rob Arnott of First Quadrant spoke for many when he said of money managers, "Those who are not religious (I'm not) still need a deeply rooted ethical sense to serve as a rudder for personal and business behavior." Scott Johnston of Sterling Johnston Capital Management said that he didn't think that religion played a significant role in terms of the specifics of managing money, but added, "A key personality trait that leads to success is optimism in the face of adversity (such as a bear market). Knowing that there is a higher power or God that is looking out for you and is on your side at all times, that He loves you, helps immensely."

Scott's point about optimism is well taken. For many people, the inner motivation that leads some to faith leads others to self-confidence. Optimists are believers; they live to fight another day. Among the MoneyQ types, many enjoy varying degrees of self-confidence, but Gold Conservators are not as likely as others to be great optimists. They are vulnerable to self-doubt, which leads them to be more conservative in their investment approach. There is a danger lurking here. Other MoneyQ types who use faith in God or themselves inappropriately will have to be very careful about taking unwarranted investment risks. Perhaps you can identify with this type of reasoning: *I'm going to buy this stock because I have a real good feeling about it. I just know this company is going to do well! The Lord (or my own keen judgment) will not let me down.* Beware overconfidence, which borders on hubris! Faith cannot replace hard work and good judgment.

What can we as investors derive from this? Obviously, we are dealing with a subject you did not expect to find in an investment book. Believe me, I didn't expect to be writing about it, either. So what do we make of it? Speaking for myself, I was very taken by the importance of faith to so many of these highly successful investment professionals and found it difficult to ignore. Now, I don't know your particular take on religion and faith and the role it plays in your life. Chances are, if your MoneyQ profile is Gold or Green, there is a good chance that religion will play an important part of every aspect of your life. You Golds and Greens may find it quite easy to identify with the money managers quoted in this chapter. Faith may well be an important Master Key in your own life, investing and otherwise.

For the rest of us, we need to avoid the temptation to dismiss these practitioners as a bunch of Bible-thumping holy rollers. There is something here for everyone. Let's assume you are not particularly religious or perhaps not religious at all. Nevertheless, you probably believe in (have faith in) something. At the least, you must surely believe in yourself. For you, faith may be a firm belief in yourself and your ability to do what you set out to do, to accomplish any reasonable goal you set for yourself. Investing is one of these goals.

One of the goals in *The Wealth Equation* is to demonstrate to you that your own mastery of the techniques of investing and your psychological self-awareness will lead you to intelligent and, above all, rational decisions on how to invest your assets to ensure your future wealth. Indeed, it is your faith in yourself that will be the harbinger of your ultimate success. You will not be fooled by silly investment schemes, get-rich-quick plans, and other investment noise that infiltrate the media. Your keen sense of self and your innate intelligence will guide you to correct decisions. Your understanding of your personal MoneyQ temperament, along with your judgment and know-how, will steer you to the correct mix of investment strategies. The information you find in *The Wealth Equation* is but your guide. Your ultimate success will depend on the faith you have in your ability to distinguish reality from fantasy and judgment from wishful thinking. *The Wealth Equation* will help you do that, at least as far as your investment life is concerned. It is the tool. The rest is up to you. And you can do it.

For those among you who consider faith in the more traditional sense, you will no doubt recognize the supreme power of the almighty in His effect on our daily lives. If you believe in a personal God, you will speak to Him and you will feel His guidance. I suggest you ask not for specific investment advice; there is no indication that divine intervention has helped any investment professional in the specifics of selecting investment vehicles. Instead, pray for the wisdom to make the right choices yourself, then use your own instincts and skills to select the investments that you believe are right for you. There is a wealth of information that has been gleaned over the years from finance academics and investment practitioners. *The Wealth Equation* puts the best of this knowledge at your fingertips so that you can master your own wealth formula. Our role is to weave the components in such a way as to make wealth natural for you, a wealth that derives from the right combination of your personality, skills, and learning.

As I am sure you can see, this chapter means different things to different people. The key points in this chapter will inevitably be your own. I believe that no matter what your level of belief, there is something here from which every one of us can learn.

I will conclude with this elegant observation from William H. Fissell of Fissell Laidlaw & Co., Inc.: "I do not think that prayer makes stocks go up, but it may keep you from going down."

KEY POINTS

- **FAITH MEANS DIFFERENT THINGS TO DIFFERENT PEOPLE.**

  Faith in something is essential for all of us. For some, like Foster Friess, it takes the form of a deeply felt religious devotion. For others, it may be faith in one's talents, the ability to rebound from adversity, or the spirit of optimism that keeps us motivated. Find yours.

- **FAITH, IF ONLY IN ONESELF, WILL HELP US IN EVERY HUMAN ENDEAVOR.**

  Use your faith in yourself to master the art of investing. What you need to know is in your hands now.

MASTER KEY 7
ALLOCATE WISELY

Select an asset allocation strategy that is appropriate for your age, wealth, risk tolerance, and income, and stick to it.

GLENN C. WEIRICK
WESTCAP INVESTORS

Asset allocation refers to the way our portfolios are put together. A portfolio with all of its assets in stocks is considered a 100% equity portfolio. Many portfolios contain both stocks and bonds. Usually this is done to reduce volatility and risk. It is a throwback to the old days of money management, when a crusty old trust officer at the stately local bank would sit across the mahogany desk from his (yes, it was always a male in those days) wealthy clients and dispense advice. With his thumbs in the small pockets of his vest, the trust officer would lean back and decide that your portfolio ought to be invested 60% in blue-chip stocks and 40% in solid government and corporate bonds.

Remember, in the old days you bought stocks for different reasons from the way you do today. Long ago, stocks actually had dividend yields that were higher than the yields on safe U.S. government bonds. This was largely because stocks were riskier, and, therefore, they were supposed to pay more than bonds, which were relatively risk-free. That all changed with time. In more recent history, stocks were chosen not because of their dividends, but because they were supposed to go up in price, and most of the time they did. Even later, we became familiar with the concept of *total return*, which holds that your investment gain is a combination of your dividend and interest earnings *plus* the appreciation in the value of your stocks.

The world changes, and our financial world is no exception. Bonds used to be considered the ballast of a portfolio, that area of investment that would mitigate the volatility of stocks, providing steady, unexciting but assured income. Bonds had coupons attached with dates on them. Twice a year, when the date came along, you sent the coupon in and got a check for the interest owed to you. That's where the term "coupon clippers" (referring to people whose principal talent and line of work was clipping and sending in their bond coupons every six months) comes from.

But in the 1970s, all that started to change. The advent of world-wide bond trading combined with the scourge of inflation we experienced in the United States permanently changed the character of bonds and their role in portfolios. The prime rate soared past 20% and U.S. government bonds were offered with an interest coupon of 14%. Imagine.

Now, I suspect you know how bonds work, but here's a quick reminder. If you buy a long-term bond, say the Treasury's so-called long bond, you are buying a piece of paper that won't get paid back for 30 years. The interest rate on that bond will be a function of whatever the bond market says it ought to be at the time the bond is issued. If the interest rate is too low, nobody will buy it. If it is too high, a lot of people will buy it, but then the Treasury will have given money away by offering a yield higher than was necessary.

You probably know that interest rates determine bond prices. If the interest rate goes down, your bond price goes up and vice versa. Since interest rates fluctuate a lot more today then they did years ago, we have come to realize that bonds can be as volatile, and as risky, as stocks. This is particularly true for long-term bonds, those that don't get paid back for 20 or 30 years, since you are stuck with the interest rate they pay until they mature. I bring this up because in the old days, fluctuations in interest rates were very rare. By comparison, 1994 was one of the worst years in bond-market history. It is said that more money was lost in the bond market in 1994 than was lost in the stock market crash of October 1987.

Portfolio managers still buy bonds, but they do so now for one of two reasons. First, for safety. But if they want to use bonds the old fashioned way, to reduce risk and volatility, they tend to use short- to intermediate-term bonds. That's because short-term bonds don't fluctuate as much as long-term bonds. If your bond has only a few years to run, the interest rate isn't as great a concern since you are going to get your money back much sooner than if you bought those 30-year issues.

The second reason a portfolio manager might buy bonds is to make money. In this case, the manager is making an *interest-rate bet*. If the manager thinks that interest rates are going down, there's money to be made in long-term bonds. Remember, the bond price will go up if interest rates go down, because the manager will own a bond with an interest rate higher than the currently prevailing rate, so it is worth more. As a result, your astute portfolio manager has the advantage of a potential capital gain since his bond will now sell for a higher price in the market, to reflect the lower yield now prevailing.

DIVVYING UP YOUR ASSETS

If you or your investment adviser decides that you ought to have some money in bonds, the question is how much? The decision of how much to put into bonds versus stocks is an asset-allocation decision, and a very important one to boot. But it isn't the only asset-allocation decision. Other decisions affecting asset allocation involve how much money the manager (or you) allocates to small-cap versus large-cap stocks, how much to growth versus value stocks, and increasingly these days, how much money you decide to invest abroad.

All these decisions fall under the umbrella of asset allocation. So your next question may well be, how important is asset allocation anyway? The answer is that it is *very* important. In fact, while most money managers tend to stick to one style, many of the managers we interviewed had advice for individuals on the subject of asset allocation. Glenn C. Weirick of Westcap Investors said, "Select a seasoned investment counselor who matches your risk tolerance and is compatible with your personal philosophy. Have a well-diversified portfolio." For long-term growth, however, almost all of the managers advocate that your portfolio be heavily concentrated in equities because that's where the growth is. "It is important to emphasize a consistent overweighing of stocks versus bonds or cash for the long term," adds Fred Kuehndorf of Deutsche Morgan Grenfell.

You may be familiar with the now famous study by Gary Brinson, Randolph Hood, and Gil Beebower on asset allocation.

Gary Brinson, an academic and money manager, and his colleagues wondered what accounted for the difference in investment performance among different pension plans. (If you look at some of the major pension funds in the United States, you find that their returns are very different from one another.) Could it be that one pension fund was luckier than the others? Did one group make better market-timing decisions, thereby avoiding serious market declines that plagued the other funds? Or did one fund have an unusually good stock picker with a talent for picking stock market winners? Brinson and friends were determined to find out what accounted for the difference in performance of these pension funds, whose long-term objectives were pretty much the same.

To that end, they studied 91 U.S. pension plans to try to determine what factors contributed to their investment returns. (Their findings were first published in the July–August 1986 edition of the *Financial Analysts Journal* and were updated and published again in 1991.)

They found a bombshell.

Was it stock picking that determined investment performance? No. Was it superior market timing? No. What Brinson and Beebower found was that 93.6% of the differences in performance of these funds could be explained by one factor: asset allocation. In other words, having Peter Lynch or Warren Buffett as your stock picker would be awfully nice, but much more important was the initial decision of *how much of your assets you would put in stocks.* When you think about it, that makes sense. Even if you have the greatest stock picker in the world on your team, it's not going to do you much good if you only give her a third of your assets to work with. In a rising market, even a mediocre stock picker might outperform your investment results if the mediocre guy had two thirds of his portfolio in stocks and you didn't.

I want to make sure I have made this clear. Suppose you have a portfolio of $1 million. You've got Peter Lynch and Warren Buffett (or their equivalents) on your stock-picking team. You decide to give the Lynch-Buffett team $400,000 of your money to manage. Because this is a conservative fund, and you are a conservative person, you put the rest in bonds.

Lynch and Buffett do not disappoint. Over a period of years, they return an annualized 25% on their investment. The bonds do what they are supposed to do and give you 5%. Let's see—that's

25% on $400,000, or $100,000 per year plus the bond portfolio's return of 5% on $600,000, or $30,000, for a total average annual return of $130,000.

Now suppose that another fund isn't lucky enough to have Peter Lynch and Warren Buffett on their investment committee. Instead, they are going to let the market do the work and buy an index fund. Fortunately, in both cases, the market is doing well. Over a period of years, the market's return is 20% a year. That's not as good as the Lynch-Buffett team's return of 25%, but such is life on Wall Street. The difference here is that the manager of this portfolio is a real believer in equities. She decides to put 75% of the portfolio in stocks and 25% in those safe bonds. In this case, the return on the stock portfolio was 20% on $750,000, or $150,000, plus 5% on $250,000, or $12,500 for a total annual return of $162,500.

Thus, the portfolio with the Lynch-Buffett investment team did not do as well as the portfolio with a bread-and-butter index fund for one principal reason: The manager of the Lynch-Buffett investment team decided to play it safe and gave the dynamic investment duo only 40% of the portfolio to invest. That was a costly decision. But it clearly exemplifies the findings of Brinson and Beebower. It was the asset-allocation decision that was the most important factor in determining your investment result, not the fact that you had the greatest investment minds on your team.

As you might expect, the popularity of the Brinson, Beebower study in the investment advisory community caused a great deal of discomfort on Wall Street. Think about it. If the asset-allocation decision is all that matters (or at least 93% of what matters in investment performance), then why are we spending so much time on investment research and stockbrokers selling stories to get orders? Why do we spend millions of dollars each year subscribing to investment newsletters or watching *Wall Street Week* on PBS every Friday evening? Why do brokerage firms lie in panic every October, waiting for *Institutional Investor* magazine's all-star research-analyst list to come out to learn which Wall Street research analysts have been voted best in each category based on the recommendations they make to their clients? Riding on the results of this famous survey are the jobs of analysts and research directors. Even today, an analyst who makes the all-star team can expect a nice little bonus of $1 million or more at Christmas time. Those not on the list might do well to look over their shoulders.

A TALK WITH GARY BRINSON: ON ALLOCATION

What's a struggling investor to believe? I thought about that and decided to do what I know you would want me to do. I went to the source. I called up Gary Brinson and had a nice chat with him. My colleague, Peter Forbes, joined me in the discussion.

TANOUS: Gary, thanks for talking to me and sharing our conversation with the readers of this book. Your original study on asset allocation was updated recently, and the findings were similar. As I was writing this chapter, it struck me as intuitive that if you have Peter Lynch managing the equity portion of your portfolio and you made the dumb decision in a bull market to put only 30 percent of your portfolio in equities, then your performance is going to suffer compared to a mediocre manager who has 80 percent of the portfolio in equities.

BRINSON: Peter, what you just said succinctly captures the whole issue of asset allocation. That is precisely the point.

TANOUS: Then you have to wonder why people consider it such a revelation. For example, a recent *Wall Street Journal* article made it very clear that the findings in your study are used by just about every financial consultant around in telling their clients what is important. To what extent do you think your findings are misused?

BRINSON: One of the things that has troubled me about some of the commentaries on the studies is that people sometimes conclude that active management doesn't have any value. Nowhere in either of the two articles did we ever say that. Nor do we agree with the statement that the data present themselves that way. So I guess in response to your question, we've been a little perplexed that people have chosen to draw that line of inference from the articles.

TANOUS: I understand that, but to the financial-planner types, or the Wall Street community, the message seems pretty clear: Picking stocks is far less important than the asset-allocation decision. If that interpretation is correct, are we spending too much time in the wrong place?

BRINSON: It could be, particularly for the individual investor. Most of the commentary that investors hear doesn't focus enough on the importance of the decision to be invested—or not invested—in particular asset classes. They get too caught up in the minutiae of well, gee, did I have the best U.S. equity portfolio. The questions to ask are: what about all the other asset classes and how much weight did I assign to the United States [*versus foreign stocks*]?

FORBES: To me, the 64-dollar question on asset allocation is where do we draw the line between asset allocation and market timing?

BRINSON: I wrote a paper on that seven or eight years ago. What I tried to point out—and somebody could say this is largely semantics— is that asset allocation (in my mind) examines forward-looking (expected) returns and makes decisions accordingly. Market timing is different in that it tries to forecast how a particular market is going to change; that is, is the market going to go up or is the market going to go down? An example I could contribute goes back to 1981 when, in the U.S. bond market, if you bought just a zero-coupon treasury bond you could get a forward return with no risk of 14 percent. So one could say from an asset-allocation standpoint that that was a number that you could put your hands on. That's a forward return known with near certainty. You could compare and contrast that with other forward-looking returns and you could build your asset allocation from that set of judgments. That's different from saying I think the bond market will go up or down. It's basically looking at those forward returns, not trying to guess whether the market itself is going to go up or down.

TANOUS: And in the case of the bonds you just mentioned, with the added comfort of the certainty of that return.

BRINSON: Right. And if you do that in risk-return space, [*taking into account the risk you are taking for the return you are getting*] as you should, that ought to lead you toward putting together a certain profile or array of asset classes that meet whatever specific risk agenda the investor desires, whether you use one of those fancy optimizers or whether you use just common sense. [*Here's the point. If you knew for sure that you could earn an interest rate of 14% with absolutely no risk, wouldn't you want to take it? You are "looking forward" at the prospect of earning a U.S. government guaranteed return of 14%. Do you want it?*]

TANOUS: This leads to another question. Do you change your asset allocation because your personal circumstances change or because market conditions change?

BRINSON: Market conditions do play a role. On occasion, markets will get into a condition where the forward-looking returns fall outside of any kind of equilibrium setting. I got into a lot of trouble in the late '80s when our portfolios didn't own any Japanese equities. We felt, at the time, that the market had priced itself so high that the forward-looking returns were then so inferior to what we could see in other equity and bond markets around the world that it just didn't make any sense. [*At the time, most portfolio managers were heavily weighted in Japan and the market paid them handsomely by going up at a dizzying rate. Portfolio managers who were not heavily invested in Japan saw their investment performance suffer, since the other markets were not doing nearly as well*]. We would argue that periodically forward-looking returns might change in such a fashion that you would want to change your asset-allocation weights.

TANOUS: So this becomes a portfolio-management decision. Aren't you saying that the change in asset allocation you were just talking about is basically the result of a perception looking forward that the Japanese market is too expensive?

BRINSON: Right. It's a judgment that the then forward-looking returns are going to be inferior to what they should be in normal circumstances. Therefore, one would not want to hold a normal position in Japan at that time. [*Gary Brinson's point about the Japanese market's high valuation in the '80s is well taken and should serve as an important historical example. The Nikkei 225 index reached a peak of 38,995 on December 29, 1989. That same index was trading below 14,000 in September 1998, having declined over 60% from its level of nearly nine years earlier. Thus, a manager who was prescient enough to avoid the Japanese-market euphoria missed the tremendous decline that ensued.*]

FORBES: Gary, is there an optimum amount of time for the asset allocation and your other findings to work?

BRINSON: Tough question. I've often said that if you are looking at anything less than three to five years, you're looking at noise more than anything else. The problem with setting an absolute time frame is that you need a time frame during which markets go through their normal cycle or their normal behavior pattern. If you look at anything over a time period that is unidirectional, you're probably going to fool yourself and draw incorrect conclusions from that.

TANOUS: In the context of asset allocation, what advice would you give the average investor who wants to build wealth in the equity markets?

BRINSON: If you're willing to take an equity-type risk, you should look at it from a global perspective and not restrict yourself to equities. For example, emerging-market debt has equity-like risk characteristics, but it's not correlated with equities. Some people say, well, I don't want to put emerging-market debt into my portfolio because it's too risky. But the point they're missing is that it doesn't matter in and of itself that it's risky, what matters is that it doesn't change the risk of your aggregate portfolio. At the average-investor level, that still tends to be the biggest problem he or she faces. They look at a specific investment in terms of its specific risk, and they don't ask the right question, which is what does that risk look like *after* I put it into my portfolio. Many investors are now familiar with these charts that show that if you add risky assets to a portfolio, it can actually reduce the risk of the aggregate portfolio. That's not an intuitive concept for the man or woman on the street. [*In fact, many academic studies have demonstrated that with the right kind of diversification, or asset allocation, you can include some risky stocks, or a risky fund, in your portfolio because it offers potentially above-average returns. However, the risk of your total portfolio won't be affected, or might even improve, because your portfolio contains other stocks or funds whose risk characteristics offset the risk of the ones you just bought.*]

TANOUS: Here's my last question, Gary. Your asset allocation study is now over ten years old. Are you surprised at how widely accepted and quoted it has become or at the use to which it's been put in the investment community?

BRINSON: Well, I suppose I was a little surprised. It got a lot of academic attention when it came out in the '80s, but not much general attention. In another vein, I'm not overly surprised that, with the passage of time, people will grab on to things that do matter. As you said, the intuition of thoughtful people is such that they act on what rings true to them. It does make sense to spend some time thinking about this asset-allocation issue, and to realize that it is going to have a profound effect on the return and the risk profile of their portfolio over time.

But wait a minute. If, according to the study, only 4.6% of investment returns are a result of stock picking, why should we care about Wall Street research at all?

Wall Street was not about to take this assault lying down. The long sharp knives quickly came out. Counter studies appeared, and continue to appear, woefully decrying the Brinson, Beebower results. Others, in a spirit of generosity, claim that the research was okay, but that most of the investment community has simply misinterpreted it.

In fact, there are different ways to interpret this information. Some advisers take these findings to extremes and say that you should devote all of your investment energies and acumen to the asset-allocation decision and not worry about what stocks to buy. That's not too smart. The asset-allocation decision is, in my opinion, derivative. It is not a decision you make in the abstract. Rather, it is a function of a set of circumstances that are personal to you as an individual. With your own MoneyQ profile, you will, in fact, have the ability to assess the kind of investor you really are. Are you a Gold Trustee? Your investment plan will be different from a Red Realist, *even if your investment objectives and risk profiles seem to be the same.* For the first time, you will have the power to construct a portfolio that is tailored to you as a human being. Asset allocation is one of the means we will use to get there. Yes, asset allocation is the most important determinant of investment results, but it is not the only one. The right asset allocation will not make up for lousy investment decisions within that asset allocation.

ASSET ALLOCATION AND ACTIVE MANAGEMENT

Despite the near universal acceptance of his study on asset allocation, Gary Brinson insists on pointing out that his study should not have led investors to believe that they should abandon active management; that is, finding the best managers of portfolios or mutual funds to invest their money. A number of professionals have interpreted his study to mean that you should buy only index funds since stock selection accounts for such a small percentage of performance attributes, but that is an erroneous interpretation of the study. Once you get the asset allocation right, there is nothing wrong with trying to pick the best managers to manage that portion of the asset allocation at which they excel.

Finally, here's Gary's most important point, and it goes right to the heart of asset allocation: You should not shun a risky asset class just because it is risky. Why? Because you should not consider risk in a vacuum. By that I mean that you should consider risk in the context of your entire portfolio, not the risk of the individual components. After all, it is really the portfolio risk that matters, not what each segment has done. Gary Brinson even pointed out that a risky asset class could contribute to lessening the overall risk in a portfolio. These are important lessons to observe.

When you get to the asset allocations for your individual MoneyQ profile, chances are that one or more of the proposed allocations will have an asset class that is riskier than others, small cap stocks, for example. The percentage allocated to the riskier asset class will be a function of your personal risk tolerance and time objective. The reason that a riskier asset class is there at all is to enhance the long-term return of the particular portfolio, since riskier asset classes offer higher rewards. The allocation is a carefully orchestrated process by which the right balance of risk and return is measured to achieve an optimum portfolio balance.

ONE BASKET VS. MANY

Although asset allocation is understandably one of the great disciplines of top *investors*, it is the one discipline that is not universally practiced by the majority of great managers. Most great managers are specialists; they tend to be great growth managers, great value managers, or top small-cap managers, and so on. Although great managers do not universally practice asset allocation, it is safe to say that most of the greats agree it is something we need to do. For investors, this is a crucial point. In fact, in our manager survey, 86% of the top managers indicated that asset allocation in a portfolio was either very important or somewhat important. Michelle Clayman's (New Amsterdam Partners) comments are typical, "Be a long-term investor, save as much as you can, and determine your investment goals and income needs. Base your asset allocation on balancing these objectives to produce an asset-allocation framework that produces the required return at the lowest risk." That's good advice.

Indeed, in our survey, risk tolerance is cited most often as one of the key factors in investment decision making; specifically, in answer to the question, what are the most important issues in determining an investment approach and what factors must people consider? Of 13 possible responses, the one that topped the list was risk tolerance based on individual personality.

Okay. I can hear your logical question: If these very successful managers don't practice asset allocation, why should I? After all, the successful managers all have track records any one of us would be satisfied with, so why bother with asset allocation?

Here's why. If all we had to do were to pick investment performance by looking back, the answer would be easy. Just pick the manager with the greatest record and give him or her all your money. Right? You know it isn't that simple. Great performance records notwithstanding, most of us are not clairvoyant, and we are not real good at predicting the future. That's where asset allocation comes in. The principal reason for asset allocation is our lack of success as fortune-tellers and mystics. So what we do is hedge our bets. We might not want to bet our entire portfolio on one type of stock, or for that matter, on one manager. Instead, we seek to diversify our investments among several different styles to increase our chances of superior performance. That's not to say that some investors won't be fortunate enough to put all their eggs in one lucky basket with one successful manager, but that is not what I recommend you do. Rather, let's try to find several exceptional practitioners and bet on a bunch of them, not just one. All the evidence shows that, especially in the long term, this is a more intelligent way to go about it.

Although most managers are specialists, there are a number of managers who not only believe in asset allocation, they practice it in one form or another. For the most part, these managers do not diversify by style (value, growth) or by size (large cap, mid cap, small cap), but by balancing their portfolios with bonds or cash, just as those crusty old trust officers used to do in the old days.

What's even more interesting is that an increasing number of professionals do it differently these days. Here's an example from a manager I like, Arthur Zaske, of Zaske, Sarafa and Associates. Art and his partners have a lot in common. They all were raised in Michigan, where their firm is located, and came from working-class backgrounds. They knew what it was like to work with their hands, and that instilled in them a profound respect for the value of money. The firm has had its ups and downs, but they remain one of the top-performing management teams in the country. Zaske points out that he continues to "seek out employees who have worked with their hands. That includes simple hard labor, or sports, and extends to such things as typing and filing." He believes that this type of background contributes to a philosophy where the client's money is treated more carefully and there is a stronger commitment to work.

What Art Zaske practices is called tactical asset allocation. "In my research," he says, "I came upon a concept called variable-weighted balanced-fund management, now renamed tactical asset allocation. It made sense to me that the percentages of stocks and bonds should not always be the same, so I adopted this style for portfolio structure."

ASSET ALLOCATION AND MARKET TIMING

Other managers practice some form of this type of asset allocation. Is it market timing in disguise? That question can provoke a heated discussion in investment circles. After all, if you decide to put more of your portfolio into safe bonds for a period of time, aren't you simply saying that you think the stock market is headed for a dive? Not necessarily. While tactical asset allocators may on occasion allow some form of market apprehension to enter into their decision-making process, I do not believe that market timing drives their decisions. Many managers resort to cash or bonds when they can't find anything to buy they really like. This makes sense since they tend to stick to a particular style, and in market environments they may not be able to find any stocks to buy that suit their particular style and that they consider reasonably priced. I believe that in such instances allocation is an acceptable alternative to market timing. I can go on arguing about this if you wish, but maybe we can leave it at this: Some managers are disciplined enough to stop buying stocks whenever they find it hard or even impossible to find stocks that meet their rigid criteria for investment. These guys are likely to be successful tactical asset allocators. I'm not so sure about the others.

They used to say that giving money to a real-estate developer was the moral equivalent of giving liquor to an alcoholic. That's because, given the cash, a real-estate developer will always find some excuse to build something, no matter what the real-estate-market environment may dictate. So it is with some money managers. Give them some money, and they will find something to buy. Those managers do not follow a disciplined enough style to warrant following.

KEY POINTS

Here are the points I want you to remember from this chapter:

- ## ASSET ALLOCATION IS REALLY, REALLY IMPORTANT

  The Brinson, Beebower study got it right. Your portfolio's performance is primarily dependent on the allocation decisions you make; that is, how much of your money goes into stocks, then what kinds of stock; how much into bonds and what kinds of bonds; how much into the international markets; and so forth. The other decisions are important, but less so.

- ## WORRY ABOUT THE RISK OF YOUR ENTIRE PORTFOLIO, NOT THE RISK OF ITS COMPONENTS

  Remember, it is the overall return and risk of your portfolio that matters, not how each individual segment has performed. You can actually reduce risk by diversifying intelligently even if you include risky asset classes in your mix. The point is that with proper diversification, your risky asset class will be offset by a different asset class in your portfolio whose risk does not correlate with the first asset class. In this context, consider international diversification. The U.S. markets today represent only a fraction of the total equity markets in the world. As a result, you can add to your diversification strategy by considering foreign markets.

- ## BEWARE OF LONG TRENDS IN THE MARKET

  A long trend, whether bullish or bearish, is likely to lull us into complacency. Bullish trends, like the one we have been in for more than 15 years, can lead us to relax our guard and not pay enough attention to our portfolio. Conversely, a bearish trend may convince us not to be invested at all. Stay alert and act accordingly. Learn the principles that work over time—we will keep drumming them into your head—and practice them relentlessly.

PART THREE

THE
SOLUTION

COMPLETING THE EQUATION: CUSTOMIZING YOUR PLAN

In the final phase of *The Wealth Equation*, we invite you to complete MoneyQ2, a short questionnaire, which addresses important questions about your age, risk tolerance, and investment time frame. Once you have completed the six questions, you will be able to determine which of the five specially designed portfolios in your MoneyQ group is most appropriate for you. The five choices are:

Conservative

Conservative/Moderate

Moderate

Moderate/Aggressive

Aggressive

Please complete MoneyQ2 on pages 172–173.

MoneyQ2

Answer the six questions. Add up your points. Score your results to determine your MoneyQ2 portfolio level.

1. I am _____ years old.

Points	Answer	Points	Answer
1	Over 60 years old	4	31–40 years old
2	51–60 years old	5	30 years old or under
3	41–50 years old		

2. Which do you consider the most appropriate time horizon for your investments? When will you need access to your money?

Points	Answer	Points	Answer
1	Less than 3 years	4	11–15 years
2	3–6 years	5	More than 15 years
3	7–10 years		

3. Overall, how would you characterize your investment objectives for this portfolio?

Points	Answer
1	Income oriented, preservation of capital
2	Income with some growth
3	Growth with some income
4	Mainly growth
5	Aggressive growth

4. I am a long-term investor who expects to do well over the next five to ten years or longer. The final result is more important to me than daily, monthly, or annual fluctuations in the value of my account.

Points	Answer
1	Totally disagree
2	Willing to accept some fluctuations, but not much loss of principal
3	Can accept a moderate amount of annual volatility, but not loss of significant principal
4	Would accept an occasional loss year if the final results were good
5	Totally agree

5. How much could you stand losing in a down market?

Points	Answer
0	0%. In addition, I expect at least 4% each year.
1	0%
2	5% loss
3	10% loss
4	10%–15% loss
5	More than 15% loss

6. With respect to this portfolio, please indicate your attitude toward investment volatility.

Points	Answer
1	I cannot accept any loss of principal on amount invested.
2	I am more concerned with preserving capital than maximizing the growth of my capital, and I can tolerate infrequent, moderate downturns through a market cycle.
3	My main objective is growth of capital. I have limited income needs and I can tolerate negative returns for brief periods.
4	I seek higher returns, and I understand that pursuing those higher returns means that I may have to endure several quarters of negative returns through difficult phases in a market cycle.
5	My main objective is maximizing long-term growth of capital, and I can tolerate more than one year of negative returns through the inevitable poor performance cycles in the market.

Total _____

MONEYQ2 SCORE

Add up your score from your answers to the six questions. Your total score indicates your MoneyQ2 portfolio level on the key below:

8 or below:	Conservative
9–14	Conservative/Moderate
15–20	Moderate
21–26	Moderate/Aggressive
27 and above	Aggressive

You may now insert your MoneyQ profile in the box below.
Example:

Color: Blue

Type: Strategist

Portfolio: Moderate/Aggressive

```
┌─────────────────────────────────────────────────┐
│                                                   │
│          MY PERSONAL MONEYQ PROFILE:              │
│                                                   │
│   COLOR:         _____            │
│                                                   │
│   TYPE:          _____            │
│                                                   │
│   PORTFOLIO:    _____             │
│                                                   │
└─────────────────────────────────────────────────┘
```

In the next section, I introduce you to the custom-designed portfolios and explain how they were devised. Please read this section carefully. It is very important to understanding how your portfolio was created and why it will work for you.

YOUR PERSONAL ASSET ALLOCATION

IMPORTANT: Read this section before proceeding to your personal asset allocation

We are now ready to create your personal asset allocation, the one specifically designed for your individual MoneyQ Profile. Coupled with the knowledge you have acquired from the 7 Master Keys, you are now ready to embark on a serious investment program, one that is ideally suited for you—from both a psychological and a financial point of view. Achieving investment success isn't easy, but your knowledge of the investment keys and disciplines that are considered important by the top money managers in the country should reinforce your confidence in your personal investment strategy and provide the backbone needed to weather the inevitable storms that you will encounter along the way. Remember, if it were very easy to achieve investment success, everybody you know would be rich. You have come a long way toward achieving the goal that eludes so many others. You now have an intelligently crafted plan and an understanding of how and why it will work.

To prepare these allocations, I enlisted the aid of a bright young colleague, Gregory H. Leekley, of TeamVest, LLC, in Charlotte, North Carolina. Leekley is an investment consultant with experience beyond his years. Along with his smart and talented assistant, Jennifer Schmitt, Greg formulated the charts and data you will find in this chapter, enduring capricious change requests as well as exhortations and threats from yours truly to get the work done on time. I expect you will be pleased with the results.

Before you turn to your personal asset allocation, here are a few things you should know and understand.

For each color profile, there are five *separate* portfolios. MoneyQ1 determined your MoneyQ profile based on your psychological needs. MoneyQ2 further refines your asset-allocation strategy into categories by investment objectives ranging from Conservative to Aggressive based on your financial needs, time horizon, and attitudes toward risk. This, in turn, leads to an asset allocation that is right for you. Thus, your individual asset allocation, based on your MoneyQ profile, includes certain features and investment alternatives that are specifically designed for your specific needs. Your portfolio choice, among the five offered, is based on your risk tolerance, age, and investment time horizon, according to your answers to MoneyQ2. Since some of your answers to the MoneyQ profiles may have been borderline—I'm sure you hesitated more than once before you answered some of the questions—I want you to look at the portfolio choice that is just above and just below the one you selected. You may well be equally or more comfortable with one of these other choices. For example, if your MoneyQ profile is Gold Trustee, and your MoneyQ2 indicated that your portfolio choice was the Growth and Income (Moderate) allocation, have a look as well at the Income and Growth (Conservative/Moderate) allocation and also consider the Growth (Moderate/Aggressive) allocation (for the Gold Trustee). These are the portfolios that are just below and above the one indicated by your MoneyQ2 response. Any of the three may be acceptable; choose the one with which you are *most* comfortable.

HOW TO USE YOUR PERSONAL ALLOCATION

When you turn to your MoneyQ allocation, you will find your five portfolio choices laid out by the three major asset classes, cash, bonds, and stocks. Within these asset allocations is your style allocation; that is, large-growth stocks, large-value stocks, small-growth stocks, international stocks, and so on. Finally, for each investor we provided specific mutual-fund recommendations, or, for some portfolios, a "self-managed" allocation, which will include stocks you pick yourself, since your profile indicates you have a desire and a potential talent for doing so. The recommended funds are not, of course, the only funds you may select. There are other funds with the same style characteristics that can be substituted for the ones we have used. Your financial adviser may have other suggestions. Just be sure that the style is consistent with your overall portfolio objectives. In other words, if your portfolio includes the Scudder Small Cap Value Fund and you want to replace it with another fund, be sure to replace it with another fund that also invests in small-cap value stocks. That way, the integrity of the asset allocation is preserved.

Allocation Strategies   You will also notice that there are two overall allocation strategies. Allocation I is the purest. It is the one that most closely tracks the performance characteristics of your chosen profile and allocation. To do this you must invest in as many as nine or ten separate funds. Some of you may not want to do that or may not be starting with enough money to allocate among ten funds. As an alternative, we offer Allocation II. It is designed to replicate the performance of Allocation I with fewer funds. Allocation II is not as "pure" as Allocation I, but it comes pretty close and should do the job if you do not want to invest in as many funds as you will find in Allocation I.

Important Note   I don't mean to belabor the obvious, but I do want to remind you that although we are recommending specific mutual funds for your portfolio based on our analysis of the style, performance history, and methodology of these chosen funds, you should carefully do your own research or consult your own adviser before making final fund selections. Circumstances change. Fund managers come and go. Countless events occur that may cause you to question a particular fund selection, and you should do precisely that. I have no reason to believe that these funds will not continue to deliver good performance, but given the unpredictability of changing conditions, you should review these recommendations, and once you create your investment portfolio, conduct a semi-annual "checkup" of your holdings to make sure all the elements that led to your decisions are still there.

Volatility   The next chart in your allocation displays some of the volatility characteristics of your chosen portfolio. I included this chart because I want you to understand the nature of the risk you are taking with a specific allocation. To be blunt, I want to make sure that you don't select the most aggressive allocation just because its long-term performance characteristics look better. To make this point, I selected a particularly active period in stock market history, from early 1987 through the end of 1992. This period includes the 1987 October stock market crash. In order to keep the chart clear, I included the performance characteristics of only three of the five portfolios, the most aggressive, the most conservative, and the middle, or moderate, case. In cases where a particular fund in the allocation did not have a performance history back to 1987, I used the appropriate market indexes as a proxy for the past performance.

Below the chart, you will find a short description. As you will see, in all cases the most aggressive portfolio is also the most volatile, delivering larger losses and larger gains, depending on how the market is doing at any particular time. That's something to keep in mind, especially if you are tempted to deviate from your individual portfolio choice.

Growth of $10,000   This chart shows how your portfolio would have grown had you invested $10,000 beginning April 1993. You will find a dollar amount on the chart showing what your initial $10,000 investment would have been worth after five years (March 1998) for each of the five portfolios in your color category. These results are based on the performance of the specific funds in your Fund Allocation I portfolio. When a fund did not have a long enough history, we substituted the performance of that fund's peer group, as defined by Morningstar, for the missing period. It's important to note that this particular period in market history includes some exceptionally good years, so it would be unwise to extrapolate this performance indefinitely into the future. The next charts give a more realistic view of what is likely to happen.

Probable Range of Returns—One Year   This chart will give you a solid grasp of the range of performance of your portfolio looking forward for *any given year*. Rather than assume that the funds would achieve *extraordinary* returns in the future, we used the historic performance characteristics of the particular investment style and asset class to make this range of returns as realistic as possible . This gives the data much more statistical validity. Now, the ranges of returns we display show the possible returns in 90% of the cases, which, for our purposes, is a very high probability. The fattest part of the balloon indicates the most frequent range of return while the narrow part indicates less frequent ranges of returns. The line near the middle of the balloon is the average, or expected return, indicating that's what you might expect 50% of the time. The probabilities change as we move up or down, from greater-than-average returns to lower-than-average returns. As you will see, in any given year, that range can be pretty great. The range will narrow considerably over a longer time period, as you will see in the next chart.

Probable Range of Returns—20 Years   If we look at the more conservative allocations, you will see that the range of returns over 20 years is much tighter than the range for the more aggressive allocations. This is, of course, what we want. Conservative investors want predictability. More aggressive investors are willing to bet that their returns will be higher than average, knowing that they are assuming the risk of a greater loss. Again, these ranges statistically represent the returns you can expect in 90% of market environments. So barring any unforeseen major catastrophe, like the Great Depression of the '30s, you can reasonably expect that your asset allocation will produce returns in the range we have indicated over that period of time. I want to emphasize that to make this projection as accurate as possible, we did not rely on the performance of a single fund in each category. Rather, we took more traditional performance characteristics of the particular asset classes and investment styles of stocks or bonds. This should provide more reasonable and conservative expectations than relying on the expected performance of just one or even a few managers.

REVIEWING YOUR CUSTOM-DESIGNED PORTFOLIO

The time to see your chosen portfolio is at hand. Following is a list of all the MoneyQ profiles. Go to the page for your profile to review your personal asset-allocation strategy.

COLOR	TYPE	PLAN
GOLD	TRUSTEE	Page 180
GOLD	CONSERVATOR	Page 187
RED	TACTICIAN	Page 194
RED	REALIST	Page 201
BLUE	STRATEGIST	Page 208
BLUE	INNOVATOR	Page 215
GREEN	MENTOR	Page 222
GREEN	ADVOCATE	Page 229

GOLD TRUSTEE

FINANCIAL ORIENTATION
(reported rankings against other types)

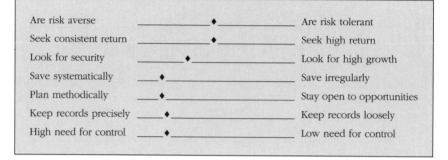

Are risk averse	♦	Are risk tolerant
Seek consistent return	♦	Seek high return
Look for security	♦	Look for high growth
Save systematically	♦	Save irregularly
Plan methodically	♦	Stay open to opportunities
Keep records precisely	♦	Keep records loosely
High need for control	♦	Low need for control

YOUR PORTFOLIO

Your long-term portfolio reflects the characteristics that are important to you and a diversification of funds with which you will be comfortable over a long period of time. You understand the pernicious characteristics of risk, and you want to avoid them as much as possible. Your mutual-fund selections are neither very risky nor very conservative—they are middle-of-the-road, a good blend of funds and managers with good risk-adjusted performance characteristics. Note the use of the Vanguard Index fund, which will ensure market-like performance for that portion of your portfolio. The fixed-income portion features primarily short-term-bond funds whose performance is not likely to be affected by changes in long-term interest rates. We did not include any high-yield ("junk") bonds in the portfolio, as it is unlikely that you would be comfortable with this riskier type of fixed-income investment.

The fund choices for your portfolio are all names you will likely recognize, established leaders in their field who have stood the test of time. This portfolio reflects many of the characteristics that you value, including its relative predictability, its low volatility, and managers who rank in the upper echelon among their peers.

Gold Trustee
Portfolios by Investment Objective
and Time Horizon

Objective:	Income	Income & Growth	Growth & Income	Growth	Aggressive Growth

Asset Allocation	Conservative	Conservative/ Moderate	Moderate	Moderate/ Aggressive	Aggressive
☐ Cash	20	20	15	10	5
▨ Bonds	60	50	35	20	5
■ Equity	20	30	50	70	90
Total Portfolio	100%	100%	100%	100%	100%

Investment Style Allocation	Conservative	Conservative/ Moderate	Moderate	Moderate/ Aggressive	Aggressive
Money Market	20	20	15	10	5
Short-Term Bond	20	20	15	10	0
Intermediate-Term Bond	20	15	10	5	5
Non-US Bond	20	15	10	5	0
Large Value	4	6	10	14	18
Large Growth	4	6	10	14	18
Small Value	2	3	5	7	9
Small Growth	2	3	5	7	9
Non-US Equity	4	6	10	14	18
Emerging Markets	2	3	5	7	9
Real Estate	2	3	5	7	9
Total Portfolio	100%	100%	100%	100%	100%

Gold Trustee
(continued)

Objective:	Income	Income & Growth	Growth & Income	Growth	Aggressive Growth
Fund Allocation I	Conservative	Conservative/ Moderate	Moderate	Moderate/ Aggressive	Aggressive
Your Money Market	20	20	15	10	5
PimCo Low Duration	20	20	15	10	0
PimCo Total Return	20	15	10	5	5
Goldman Sachs Global Income	20	15	10	5	0
Vanguard Index 500	8	12	20	28	36
Scudder Small Cap Value	2	3	5	7	9
Franklin Small Cap Growth	2	3	5	7	9
T. Rowe Price International Stock	4	6	10	14	18
Templeton Developing Markets	2	3	5	7	9
Cohen & Steers Real Estate	2	3	5	7	9
Total Portfolio	100%	100%	100%	100%	100%

Fund Allocation II	Conservative	Conservative/ Moderate	Moderate	Moderate/ Aggressive	Aggressive
Your Money Market	20	20	15	10	5
PimCo Low Duration	60	50	35	20	5
Vanguard Index 500	10	14	23	31	40
Nations Managed Small Cap Index	4	6	12	16	20
T. Rowe Price International Stock	6	10	15	23	30
Total Portfolio	100%	100%	100%	100%	100%

VOLATILITY

The chart shows how your portfolio would have behaved during a particularly active period of the market. Of the five possible allocations, we have plotted the most conservative, the middle, and the most aggressive of the allocations to demonstrate their different return and risk features. Note that had you invested in the most aggressive portfolio in early 1987, you would have suffered a considerable loss (–20%) at the time of the October 1987 crash. On the other hand, had you been invested in the most conservative allocation, you would hardly have felt the ups and downs of the market during this turbulent period. Of course, as you know by now, risk comes with its own reward (if you plan right) as you will see in the chart on the next page.

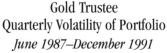

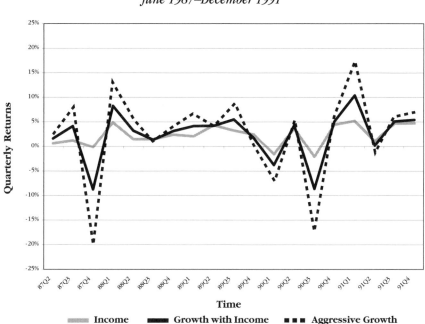

Gold Trustee
Quarterly Volatility of Portfolio
June 1987–December 1991

GROWTH OF $10,000

This chart shouldn't surprise you. Over the five-year period ending March 1998, the portfolio with the riskiest profile performed best, and the least risky portfolio performed worst. That's the way it should be. Bear in mind, however, that we are looking at a particularly good chunk of stock-market history here. It is also possible that during five poor years, the most conservative portfolio would have outperformed the riskiest one.

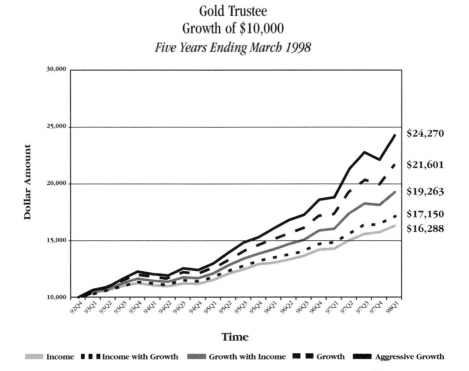

Gold Trustee
Growth of $10,000
Five Years Ending March 1998

PROBABLE RANGES OF RETURN—ONE YEAR

This chart shows at a glance what the probable range of returns is for your chosen portfolio (from most conservative to most aggressive) over any given one-year period. This range of probabilities covers 90% of the cases. If you look at the extremes, there is about a 5% chance that if you chose the moderate (Growth & Income) portfolio, your $10,000 would grow to $12,826, and an equal 5% chance that it would decline to $8,978 (*or* there is a 95% chance that you will do better than $8,978). The expected return (50% probability) is that your $10,000 will grow to $10,731 in a given year. Look at your chosen allocation and imagine the possibilities, then turn to the chart on the next page.

Probability Ranges of the Growth/Loss of $10,000 Invested over 1-Year Time Periods

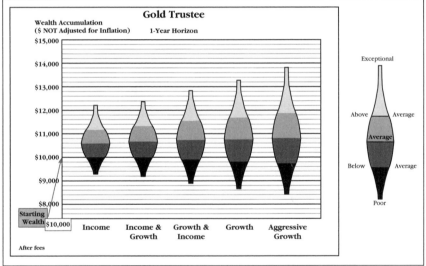

Graph courtesy Lockwood Advisors, Inc.

Expected Wealth Accumulation/Loss by Market Condition

Market Condition	Income	Income & Growth	Growth & Income	Growth	Aggressive Growth	%tile Rank	Market Condition/ Scenario Interpretation
Exceptional	$12,195	$12,359	$12,826	$13,298	$13,792	5%	Top 5% of all Markets
Above Average	$11,254	$11,332	$11,545	$11,753	$11,966	25%	Top 25% of all Markets
Average	**$10,643**	**$10,671**	**$10,731**	**$10,788**	**$10,842**	**50%**	**Average Markets—50%**
Below Average	$10,066	$10,047	$9,975	$9,901	$9,824	75%	75% of Markets Are Higher
Poor	$9,288	$9,213	$8,978	$8,751	$8,523	95%	95% of Markets Are Higher

PROBABLE RANGES OF RETURN—20 YEARS

If you consider your $10,000 investment over a 20-year span, here is what your portfolio might look like at different degrees of probability. In the middle case (Growth & Income), your most probable portfolio value after 20 years will be $45,836. The expected range is as high as $101,983 in a particularly good market environment and as low as $20,601 should the market environment be unusually bad. You can easily see how these numbers would be dramatically higher if you added only a little to your portfolio every year over the 20-year period. Overall, these allocations conform to your MoneyQ profile and comfort level at different degrees of risk tolerance.

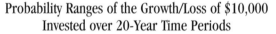

Probability Ranges of the Growth/Loss of $10,000 Invested over 20-Year Time Periods

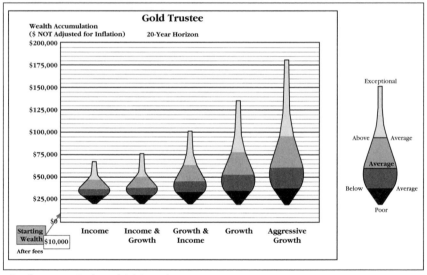

Graph courtesy Lockwood Advisors, Inc.

Expected Wealth Accumulation/Loss by Market Condition

Market Condition	Income	Income & Growth	Growth & Income	Growth	Aggressive Growth	%tile Rank	Market Condition/ Scenario Interpretation
Exceptional	$68,293	$76,279	$101,983	$135,865	$181,996	5%	Top 5% of all Markets
Above Average	$47,650	$51,728	$63,611	$78,043	$96,111	25%	Top 25% of all Markets
Average	**$37,113**	**$39,501**	**$45,836**	**$53,109**	**$61,695**	**50%**	**Average Markets—50%**
Below Average	$28,906	$30,164	$33,027	$36,141	$39,603	75%	75% of Markets Are Higher
Poor	$20,169	$20,455	$20,601	$20,760	$20,914	95%	95% of Markets Are Higher

GOLD CONSERVATOR

FINANCIAL ORIENTATION
(reported rankings against other types)

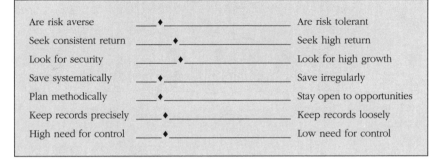

Are risk averse	Are risk tolerant
Seek consistent return	Seek high return
Look for security	Look for high growth
Save systematically	Save irregularly
Plan methodically	Stay open to opportunities
Keep records precisely	Keep records loosely
High need for control	Low need for control

YOUR PORTFOLIO

Your portfolio is designed to reflect your MoneyQ profile and the other characteristics that are important to you as an investor and as an individual. To begin, you recognize that you are a very conservative investor. You know what risk is, and you want as little of it as possible. One way to assuage your concerns about the market is to create a portfolio that offers as much consistency in returns as possible. We have taken that into account in constructing your asset allocation. Note that your allocation includes a fairly heavy tilt toward bonds, although we are emphasizing short- to intermediate-term-bond funds to avoid the potential volatility that comes with long-term-bond investments. Your portfolio also has a value stock tilt, a further effort to reduce volatility. You should have some international exposure, and we have accomplished this with an international fund with low volatility. In order to include some high-growth funds, we have included very small allocations to developing markets and real estate.

Gold Conservator
Portfolios by Investment Objective
and Time Horizon

Objective:	Income	Income & Growth	Growth & Income	Growth	Aggressive Growth

Asset Allocation	Conservative	Conservative/ Moderate	Moderate	Moderate/ Aggressive	Aggressive
☐ Cash	20	20	15	10	5
▨ Bonds	60	50	35	20	5
■ Equity	20	30	50	70	90
Total Portfolio	100%	100%	100%	100%	100%

Investment Style Allocation	Conservative	Conservative/ Moderate	Moderate	Moderate/ Aggressive	Aggressive
Money Market	20	20	15	10	5
Short-Term Bond	30	30	20	10	5
Intermediate-Term Bond	30	20	15	10	0
Large Value	5	6	11	16	21
Large Growth	3	5	8	11	14
Small Value	3	5	8	11	14
Small Growth	1	2	3	4	5
Non-US Equity	4	6	10	14	18
Emerging Markets	2	3	5	7	9
Real Estate	2	3	5	7	9
Total Portfolio	100%	100%	100%	100%	100%

Gold Conservator
(continued)

Objective:	Income	Income & Growth	Growth & Income	Growth	Aggressive Growth

Fund Allocation I	Conservative	Conservative/ Moderate	Moderate	Moderate/ Aggressive	Aggressive
Your Money Market	20	20	15	10	5
PimCo Low Duration	30	30	20	10	5
PimCo Total Return	30	20	15	10	0
T. Rowe Price Equity-Income	5	6	11	16	21
Vanguard US Growth	3	5	8	11	14
Scudder Small-Cap Value	3	5	8	11	14
Franklin Small-Cap Growth	1	2	3	4	5
SOGEN Overseas	4	6	10	14	18
Templeton Developing Markets	2	3	5	7	9
Cohen & Steers Real Estate	2	3	5	7	9
Total Portfolio	100%	100%	100%	100%	100%

Fund Allocation II	Conservative	Conservative/ Moderate	Moderate	Moderate/ Aggressive	Aggressive
Your Money Market	20	20	15	10	5
PimCo Low Duration	60	50	35	20	5
Mutual Beacon	10	13	23	32	41
Brandywine Blue	4	7	12	16	20
SOGEN Overseas	6	10	15	22	29
Total Portfolio	100%	100%	100%	100%	100%

VOLATILITY

The chart shows how your portfolio would have behaved during a particularly active period of the market. Of the five possible allocations, we have plotted the most conservative, the middle, and the most aggressive of the allocations to demonstrate their different return and risk features. Note that had you invested in the most aggressive portfolio in early 1987, you would have suffered a considerable loss, nearly 20%, at the time of the October 1987 crash. On the other hand, had you been invested in the most conservative allocation, you would hardly have felt the ups and downs of the market during this turbulent period. *A note of caution:* Given your profile, it is highly unlikely that you would choose the Aggressive Growth allocation among your five portfolio choices. While your aggressive portfolio is less aggressive than the aggressive portfolios in all of the other groups, it does not seem likely that it will be appropriate for most of you.

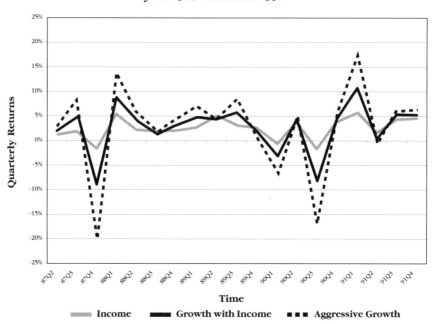

Gold Conservator
Quarterly Volatility of Portfolio
June 1987–December 1991

GROWTH OF $10,000

This chart shouldn't surprise you. Over the five-year period ending March 1998, the portfolio with the riskiest profile performed best, and the least risky portfolio performed worst. That's the way it should be. Bear in mind, however, that we are looking at a particularly good chunk of stock-market history here. It is also possible that during five poor years, the most conservative portfolio would have outperformed the riskiest one.

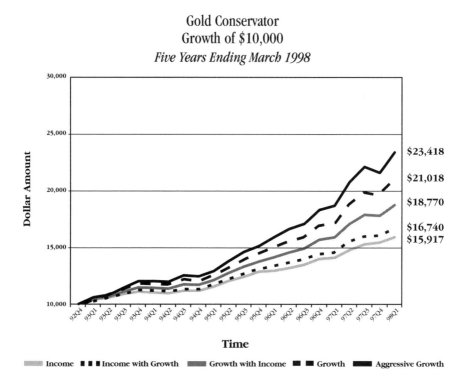

Gold Conservator
Growth of $10,000
Five Years Ending March 1998

PROBABLE RANGES OF RETURN—ONE YEAR

This chart shows at a glance what the probable range of returns is for your chosen portfolio (from most conservative to most aggressive) over any given one-year period. This range of probabilities covers 90% of the cases. If you look at the extremes, there is about a 5% chance that if you chose the moderate (Growth & Income) portfolio, your $10,000 would grow to $12,655, and an equal 5% chance that it would decline to $9,112 (*or* there is a 95% chance that you will do better than $9,112). The expected return (50% probability) is that your $10,000 will grow to $10,738 in a given year. Look at your chosen allocation and imagine the possibilities, then turn to the chart on the next page.

Probability Ranges of the Growth/Loss of $10,000 Invested over 1-Year Time Periods

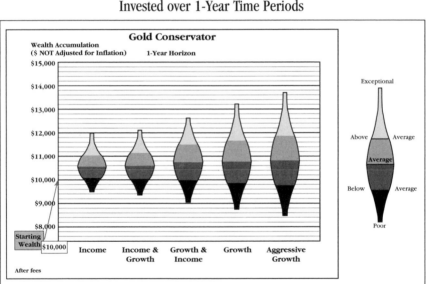

Graph courtesy Lockwood Advisors, Inc.

Expected Wealth Accumulation/Loss by Market Condition

Market Condition	Income	Income & Growth	Growth & Income	Growth	Aggressive Growth	%tile Rank	Market Condition/ Scenario Interpretation
Exceptional	$11,889	$12,122	$12,655	$13,195	$13,725	5%	Top 5% of all Markets
Above Average	$11,138	$11,245	$11,486	$11,722	$11,947	25%	Top 25% of all Markets
Average	**$10,645**	**$10,674**	**$10,738**	**$10,797**	**$10,850**	**50%**	**Average Markets—50%**
Below Average	$10,174	$10,132	$10,039	$9,945	$9,854	75%	75% of Markets Are Higher
Poor	$9,531	$9,399	$9,112	$8,835	$8,577	95%	95% of Markets Are Higher

PROBABLE RANGES OF RETURN—20 YEARS

If you consider your $10,000 investment over a 20-year span, here is what your portfolio might look like at different degrees of probability. In the middle case (Growth & Income), your most probable portfolio value after 20 years will be $45,675. The expected range is as high as $95,374 in a particularly good market environment and as low as $21, 874 should the market environment be unusually bad. You can easily see how these numbers would be dramatically higher if you added only a little to your portfolio every year over the 20-year period. Overall, these allocations conform to your MoneyQ profile and comfort level at different degrees of risk tolerance. You can see how these expected returns play out for whichever portfolio you chose.

Probability Ranges of the Growth/Loss of $10,000 Invested over 20-Year Time Periods

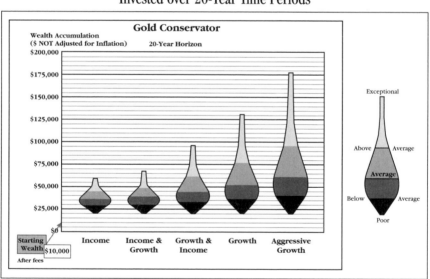

Graph courtesy Lockwood Advisors, Inc.

Expected Wealth Accumulation/Loss by Market Condition

Market Condition	Income	Income & Growth	Growth & Income	Growth	Aggressive Growth	%tile Rank	Market Condition/ Scenario Interpretation
Exceptional	$59,780	$68,953	$95,374	$131,328	$178,461	5%	Top 5% of all Markets
Above Average	$44,637	$49,264	$61,760	$77,206	$95,670	25%	Top 25% of all Markets
Average	**$36,443**	**$39,007**	**$45,675**	**$53,391**	**$62,056**	**50%**	**Average Markets—50%**
Below Average	$29,753	$30,885	$33,779	$36,922	$40,252	75%	75% of Markets Are Higher
Poor	$22,216	$22,066	$21,874	$21,706	$21,578	95%	95% of Markets Are Higher

RED TACTICIAN

FINANCIAL ORIENTATION
(reported rankings against other types)

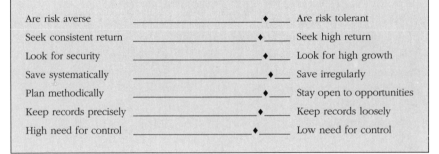

Are risk averse	Are risk tolerant
Seek consistent return	Seek high return
Look for security	Look for high growth
Save systematically	Save irregularly
Plan methodically	Stay open to opportunities
Keep records precisely	Keep records loosely
High need for control	Low need for control

YOUR PORTFOLIO

Your portfolio reflects your resourceful nature and your fearless approach to investing and life in general. You get a thrill from investing and take the investment process seriously. Your portfolio, however, reflects a dichotomy in your approach; that is, you consider yourself an aggressive investor, and while your tolerance for risk is high, you feel losses acutely. In preparing your allocation, we have set aside up to 20% for you to manage yourself, with ideas you will have generated and researched and that you are prepared to follow. We have also allocated a small amount to emerging markets and high-yield bonds. If your circumstances allow, you may be a candidate for hedge-fund investments for a limited amount of your risk capital. Note that there is no cash allocation in the portfolio because, frankly, if there were, you might be likely to take it out and spend it. This risk is lessened somewhat if cash assets are invested in a fund.

Red Tactician
Portfolios by Investment Objective and Time Horizon

Objective:	Income	Income & Growth	Growth & Income	Growth	Aggressive Growth

Asset Allocation	Conservative	Conservative/ Moderate	Moderate	Moderate/ Aggressive	Aggressive
☐ Cash	0	0	0	0	0
▨ Bonds	80	60	40	20	0
■ Equity	20	40	60	80	100
Total Portfolio	100%	100%	100%	100%	100%

Investment Style Allocation	Conservative	Conservative/ Moderate	Moderate	Moderate/ Aggressive	Aggressive
Short-Term Bond	40	30	20	5	0
Intermediate-Term Bond	20	10	10	5	0
High-Yield Bond	10	10	5	5	0
Non-US Bond	10	10	5	5	0
Large Value	3	6	10	13	16
Large Growth	3	6	10	13	16
Small Value	2	5	7	10	12
Small Growth	2	5	7	10	12
Non-US Equity	3	6	10	13	16
Emerging Markets	2	4	6	6	8
Self-Managed	5	8	10	15	20
Total Portfolio	100%	100%	100%	100%	100%

Red Tactician
(continued)

Objective:	Income	Income & Growth	Growth & Income	Growth	Aggressive Growth

Fund Allocation I	Conservative	Conservative/ Moderate	Moderate	Moderate/ Aggressive	Aggressive
PimCo Low Duration	40	30	20	5	0
Hotchkis & Wiley Total Return	20	10	10	5	0
Fidelity Spartan High Income	10	10	5	5	0
PimCo Foreign Bond	10	10	5	5	0
Davis NY Venture	3	6	10	13	16
Montag & Caldwell Growth	3	6	10	13	16
Scudder Small Cap Value	2	5	7	10	12
TIP: Turner Small Cap	2	5	7	10	12
Harbor International Growth	3	6	10	13	16
Templeton Developing Markets	2	4	6	6	8
Self-Managed	5	8	10	15	20
Total Portfolio	100%	100%	100%	100%	100%

Fund Allocation II	Conservative	Conservative/ Moderate	Moderate	Moderate/ Aggressive	Aggressive
PimCo Low Duration	40	30	20	5	0
Hotchkis & Wiley Total Return	40	30	20	15	0
T. Rowe Price Blue Chip Growth	6	12	20	26	32
Baron Asset	4	10	15	20	24
Harbor International Growth	5	9	15	19	24
Self-Managed	5	9	10	15	20
Total Portfolio	100%	100%	100%	100%	100%

VOLATILITY

The chart shows how your portfolio would have behaved during a particularly active period of the market. Of the five possible allocations, we have plotted the most conservative, the middle, and the most aggressive of the allocations to demonstrate their different return and risk features. Note that had you invested in the most aggressive portfolio in early 1987, you would have suffered a loss of nearly 25% at the time of the October 1987 crash and you also would have endured another large decline in 1990. Given your profile, it is likely that you would have remained invested throughout these periods. On the other hand, had you been invested in the most conservative allocation, you would hardly have felt the ups and downs of the market during this turbulent period. Of course, as you know by now, risk comes with its own reward (if you plan right) as you will see in the chart on the next page.

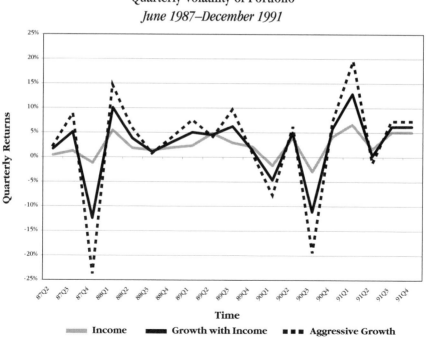

Red Tactician
Quarterly Volatility of Portfolio
June 1987–December 1991

GROWTH OF $10,000

This chart shouldn't surprise you. Over the five-year period ending March 1998, the portfolio with the riskiest profile performed best, and the least risky portfolio performed worst. That's the way it should be. Bear in mind, however, that we are looking at a particularly good chunk of stock-market history here. It is also possible that during five poor years, the most conservative portfolio would have outperformed the riskiest one.

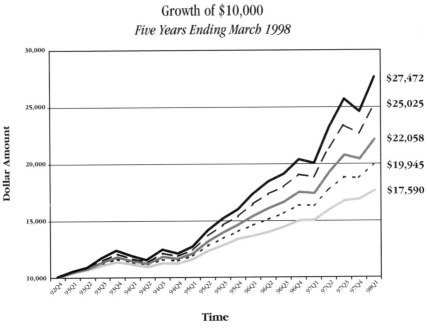

Red Tactician
Growth of $10,000
Five Years Ending March 1998

PROBABLE RANGES OF RETURN—ONE YEAR

This chart shows at a glance what the probable range of returns is for your chosen portfolio (from most conservative to most aggressive) over any given one-year period. This range of probabilities covers 90% of the cases. If you look at the extremes, there is about a 5% chance that if you chose the moderate (Growth & Income) portfolio, your $10,000 might grow to $13,229, and an equal 5% chance that it would decline to $8,790 (*or* there is a 95% chance that you will do better than $8,790). The expected return (50% probability) is that your $10,000 will grow to $10,783 in a given year. Look at your chosen allocation and imagine the possibilities, then turn to the chart on the next page.

Probability Ranges of the Growth/Loss of $10,000 Invested over 1-Year Time Periods

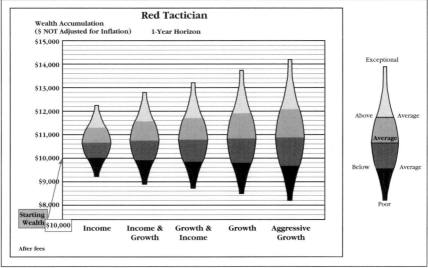

Graph courtesy Lockwood Advisors, Inc.

Expected Wealth Accumulation/Loss by Market Condition

Market Condition	Income	Income & Growth	Growth & Income	Growth	Aggressive Growth	%tile Rank	Market Condition/ Scenario Interpretation
Exceptional	$12,284	$12,799	$13,229	$13,772	$14,194	5%	Top 5% of all Markets
Above Average	$11,305	$11,532	$11,726	$11,952	$12,133	25%	Top 25% of all Markets
Average	**$10,671**	**$10,727**	**$10,783**	**$10,832**	**$10,881**	**50%**	**Average Markets—50%**
Below Average	$10,072	$9,978	$9,917	$9,817	$9,758	75%	75% of Markets Are Higher
Poor	$9,269	$8,991	$8,790	$8,520	$8,342	95%	95% of Markets Are Higher

PROBABLE RANGES OF RETURN—20 YEARS

If you consider your $10,000 investment over a 20-year span, here is what your portfolio might look like at different degrees of probability. In the middle case (Growth & Income), your most probable portfolio value after 20 years will be $52,328. The expected range is as high as $130,990 in a particularly good market environment and as low as $20,904 should the market environment be unusually bad. You can easily see how these numbers would be dramatically higher if you added only a little to your portfolio every year over the 20-year period. Overall, these allocations conform to your MoneyQ profile and comfort level at different degrees of risk tolerance.

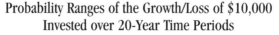

Probability Ranges of the Growth/Loss of $10,000 Invested over 20-Year Time Periods

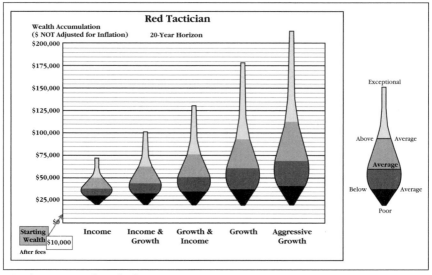

Graph courtesy Lockwood Advisors, Inc.

Expected Wealth Accumulation/Loss by Market Condition

Market Condition	Income	Income & Growth	Growth & Income	Growth	Aggressive Growth	%tile Rank	Market Condition/ Scenario Interpretation
Exceptional	$73,799	$100,262	$130,990	$178,260	$229,317	5%	Top 5% of all Markets
Above Average	$50,853	$62,825	$76,215	$94,284	$113,211	25%	Top 25% of all Markets
Average	**$39,267**	**$45,414**	**$52,328**	**$60,587**	**$69,350**	**50%**	**Average Markets—50%**
Below Average	$30,321	$32,828	$35,928	$38,934	$42,482	75%	75% of Markets Are Higher
Poor	$20,894	$20,570	$20,904	$20,592	$20,973	95%	95% of Markets Are Higher

RED REALIST

FINANCIAL ORIENTATION
(reported rankings against other types)

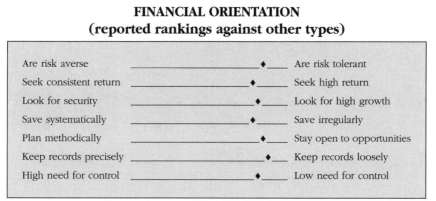

Are risk averse	Are risk tolerant
Seek consistent return	Seek high return
Look for security	Look for high growth
Save systematically	Save irregularly
Plan methodically	Stay open to opportunities
Keep records precisely	Keep records loosely
High need for control	Low need for control

YOUR PORTFOLIO

You may not know Latin, but chances are you know what *carpe diem* means. Indeed, you "seize the day," both in life and in your investment program. You have a relatively high tolerance for risk, and a relatively low tolerance for planning and budgeting, knowing that others are available to do these chores for you. In your investment program, you are open to new ideas. Your portfolio reflects this openness, and you will find some nontraditional choices, such as the Davis NY Venture Fund and the Templeton Developing Markets Fund. Should an opportunity arise for a real-estate investment, your abilities in this area suggest that you should consider it, after having done your own analysis. Since anxiety is an emotion you want to avoid, you might consider one of the lower-risk portfolios featured in your color-profile choices. Note that there is no cash allocation in the portfolio because, frankly, if there were, you might be likely to take it out and spend it. This risk is lessened somewhat if cash assets are invested in a fund.

Red Realist
Portfolios by Investment Objective
and Time Horizon

Objective:	Income	Income & Growth	Growth & Income	Growth	Aggressive Growth

Asset Allocation	Conservative	Conservative/ Moderate	Moderate	Moderate/ Aggressive	Aggressive
☐ Cash	0	0	0	0	0
▨ Bonds	80	60	40	20	0
■ Equity	20	40	60	80	100
Total Portfolio	100%	100%	100%	100%	100%

Investment Style Allocation	Conservative	Conservative/ Moderate	Moderate	Moderate/ Aggressive	Aggressive
Short-Term Bond	40	30	20	5	0
Intermediate-Term Bond	20	10	10	5	0
High-Yield Bond	10	10	5	5	0
Non-US Bond	10	10	5	5	0
Large Value	4	8	12	16	20
Large Growth	4	8	12	16	20
Small Value	2	5	7	10	12
Small Growth	2	3	5	6	8
Non-US Equity	2	5	7	10	12
Emerging Markets	2	3	5	6	8
Self-Managed	4	8	12	16	20
Total Portfolio	100%	100%	100%	100%	100%

Red Realist
(continued)

Objective:	Income	Income & Growth	Growth & Income	Growth	Aggressive Growth

Fund Allocation I	Conservative	Conservative/ Moderate	Moderate	Moderate/ Aggressive	Aggressive
PimCo Low Duration	40	30	20	5	0
Hotchkis & Wiley Total Return	20	10	10	5	0
Fidelity Spartan High Income	10	10	5	5	0
PimCo Foreign Bond	10	10	5	5	0
Davis NY Venture	4	8	12	16	20
Montag & Caldwell Growth	4	8	12	16	20
Scudder Small Cap Value	2	5	7	10	12
Nicholas-Applegate Mini-Cap Growth	2	3	5	6	8
Harbor International Growth	2	5	7	10	12
Templeton Developing Markets	2	3	5	6	8
Self-Managed	4	8	12	16	20
Total Portfolio	100%	100%	100%	100%	100%

Fund Allocation II	Conservative	Conservative/ Moderate	Moderate	Moderate/ Aggressive	Aggressive
PimCo Low Duration	40	30	20	5	0
Hotchkis & Wiley Total Return	40	30	20	15	0
T. Rowe Price Blue Chip Growth	8	16	24	32	40
Longleaf Partners Small Cap	4	8	12	16	20
Harbor International Growth	4	8	12	16	20
Self-Managed	4	8	12	16	20
Total Portfolio	100%	100%	100%	100%	100%

VOLATILITY

The chart shows how your portfolio would have behaved during a particularly active period of the market. Of the five possible allocations, we have plotted the most conservative, the middle, and the most aggressive of the allocations to demonstrate their different return and risk features. Note that had you invested in the most aggressive portfolio in early 1987, you would have suffered a loss of more than 20% at the time of the October 1987 crash, and you also would have endured another large decline in 1990. Given your profile, it is likely that you would have remained invested throughout these periods. On the other hand, had you been invested in the most conservative allocation, you would hardly have felt the ups and downs of the market during this turbulent period. Of course, as you know by now, risk comes with its own reward (if you plan right) as you will see in the chart on the next page.

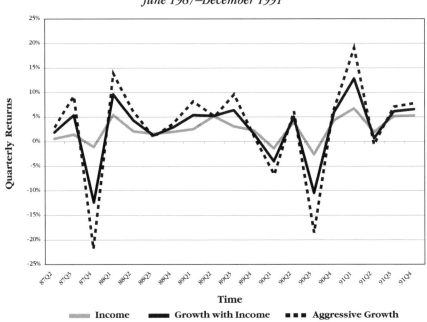

Red Realist
Quarterly Volatility of Portfolio
June 1987–December 1991

GROWTH OF $10,000

This chart shouldn't surprise you. Over the five-year period ending March 1998, the portfolio with the riskiest profile performed best, and the least risky portfolio performed worst. That's the way it should be. Bear in mind, however, that we are looking at a particularly good chunk of stock-market history here. It is also possible that during five poor years, the most conservative portfolio would have outperformed the riskiest one.

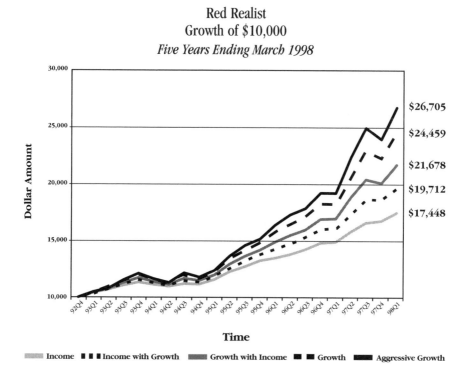

Red Realist
Growth of $10,000
Five Years Ending March 1998

PROBABLE RANGES OF RETURN—ONE YEAR

This chart shows at a glance what the probable range of returns is for your chosen portfolio (from most conservative to most aggressive) over any given one-year period. This range of probabilities covers 90% of the cases. If you look at the extremes, there is about a 5% chance that if you chose the moderate (Growth & Income) portfolio, your $10,000 might grow to $13,181, and an equal 5% chance that it would decline to $8,827 (*or* there is a 95% chance that you will do better than $8,827). The expected return (50% probability) is that your $10,000 will grow to $10,786 in a given year. Look at your chosen allocation and imagine the possibilities, then turn to the chart on the next page.

Probability Ranges of the Growth/Loss of $10,000 Invested over 1-Year Time Periods

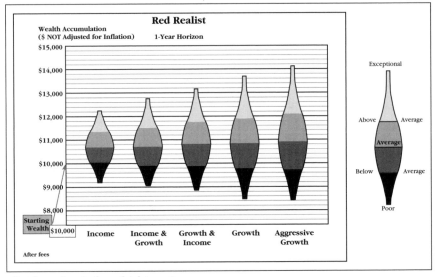

Graph courtesy Lockwood Advisors, Inc.

Expected Wealth Accumulation/Loss by Market Condition

Market Condition	Income	Income & Growth	Growth & Income	Growth	Aggressive Growth	%tile Rank	Market Condition/ Scenario Interpretation
Exceptional	$12,269	$12,767	$13,181	$13,707	$14,111	5%	Top 5% of all Markets
Above Average	$11,299	$11,522	$11,710	$11,932	$12,108	25%	Top 25% of all Markets
Average	**$10,671**	**$10,729**	**$10,786**	**$10,837**	**$10,888**	**50%**	**Average Markets—50%**
Below Average	$10,078	$9,991	$9,936	$9,843	$9,790	75%	75% of Markets Are Higher
Poor	$9,282	$9,016	$8,827	$8,568	$8,400	95%	95% of Markets Are Higher

PROBABLE RANGES OF RETURN—20 YEARS

If you consider your $10,000 investment over a 20-year span, here is what your portfolio might look like at different degrees of probability. In the middle case (Growth & Income), your most probable portfolio value after 20 years will be $52,326. The expected range is as high as $128,682 in a particularly good market environment and as low as $21,278 should the market environment be unusually bad. You can easily see how these numbers would be dramatically higher if you added only a little to your portfolio every year over the 20-year period. Overall, these allocations conform to your MoneyQ profile and comfort level at different degrees of risk tolerance.

Probability Ranges of the Growth/Loss of $10,000 Invested over 20-Year Time Periods

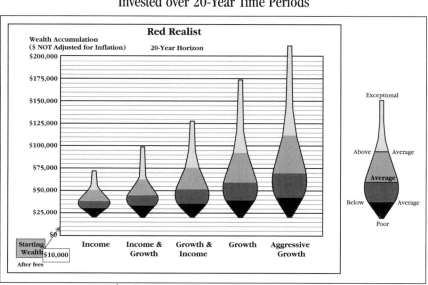

Graph courtesy Lockwood Advisors, Inc.

Expected Wealth Accumulation/Loss by Market Condition

Market Condition	Income	Income & Growth	Growth & Income	Growth	Aggressive Growth	%tile Rank	Market Condition/ Scenario Interpretation
Exceptional	$73,357	$99,071	$128,682	$174,126	$222,754	5%	Top 5% of all Markets
Above Average	$50,727	$62,517	$75,660	$93,383	$111,877	25%	Top 25% of all Markets
Average	**$39,266**	**$45,412**	**$52,326**	**$60,589**	**$69,356**	**50%**	**Average Markets—50%**
Below Average	$30,394	$32,987	$36,189	$39,311	$42,996	75%	75% of Markets Are Higher
Poor	$21,018	$20,816	$21,278	$21,083	$21,595	95%	95% of Markets Are Higher

BLUE STRATEGIST

FINANCIAL ORIENTATION
(reported rankings against other types)

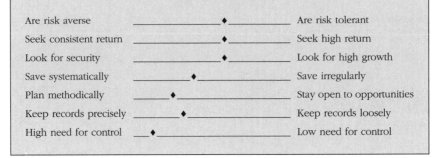

Are risk averse		Are risk tolerant
Seek consistent return		Seek high return
Look for security		Look for high growth
Save systematically		Save irregularly
Plan methodically		Stay open to opportunities
Keep records precisely		Keep records loosely
High need for control		Low need for control

YOUR PORTFOLIO

You are very comfortable with the notion of risk and return, although you wish that risk were not something you had to deal with regularly. As a "big-picture" investor, you are prepared to accept risk in the pursuit of your investment goals. You do not shy away from complex investment strategies, which you will take the time to study and understand. In this way, the risk becomes manageable to you. Drawing on your traits, we have constructed a portfolio that includes some nontraditional investments that offer superior returns over time. You are prepared to accept these strategies as long as they make sense to you. Note that your portfolio selections include foreign stocks, two small-cap funds, a developing-markets fund, and a real-estate investment. Others might shy away from these choices because they do not fit the traditional mold of stock market investing. But not you. You value and understand the principles of intelligent asset allocation, and you are prepared to take sensible risks in strategies you believe in to achieve your long-term investment goals.

Blue Strategist
Portfolios by Investment Objective
and Time Horizon

Objective:	Income	Income & Growth	Growth & Income	Growth	Aggressive Growth

Asset Allocation	Conservative	Conservative/ Moderate	Moderate	Moderate/ Aggressive	Aggressive
☐ Cash	20	15	10	5	0
▓ Bonds	60	45	30	15	0
■ Equity	20	40	60	80	100
Total Portfolio	100%	100%	100%	100%	100%

Investment Style Allocation	Conservative	Conservative/ Moderate	Moderate	Moderate/ Aggressive	Aggressive
Money Market	20	15	10	5	0
Short-Term Bond	30	23	15	8	0
Intermediate-Term Bond	30	22	15	7	0
Large Value	4	8	12	16	20
Large Growth	2	4	6	8	10
Small Value	4	8	12	16	20
Small Growth	2	4	6	8	10
Non-US Equity	3	6	9	12	15
Emerging Markets	3	6	9	12	15
Real Estate*	2	4	6	8	10
Total Portfolio	100%	100%	100%	100%	100%

*Some Blue Strategists have a strong interest in the art of investing. If you are one of them, it is highly recommended that you invest some of the money yourself. To start out, take the real-estate allocation and invest this money yourself in ventures, stocks, or sectors you believe are positioned to outperform over your desired time frame.

Blue Strategist
(continued)

Objective:	Income	Income & Growth	Growth & Income	Growth	Aggressive Growth

Fund Allocation I	Conservative	Conservative/ Moderate	Moderate	Moderate/ Aggressive	Aggressive
Your Money Market	20	15	10	5	0
PimCo Low Duration	30	23	15	8	0
Hotchkis & Wiley Total Return	30	22	15	7	0
T. Rowe Price Equity-Income	4	8	12	16	20
Montag & Caldwell Growth	2	4	6	8	10
Scudder Small Cap Value	4	8	12	16	20
Brazos/JMIC Small Cap Growth	2	4	6	8	10
Hotchkis & Wiley International	3	2	3	4	5
Harbor International Growth		2	3	4	5
Warburg Pincus International Eq Common		2	3	4	5
Templeton Developing Markets	3	6	9	12	15
Security Capital US Real Estate/ Self-Managed	2	4	6	8	10
Total Portfolio	100%	100%	100%	100%	100%

Fund Allocation II	Conservative	Conservative/ Moderate	Moderate	Moderate/ Aggressive	Aggressive
Your Money Market	20	15	10	5	0
Hotchkis & Wiley Total Return	60	45	30	15	0
Gabelli Value	9	18	26	36	44
Brandywine	5	8	14	18	22
Hotchkis & Wiley International	6	14	20	26	34
Total Portfolio	100%	100%	100%	100%	100%

VOLATILITY

The chart shows how your portfolio would have behaved during a particularly active period of the market. Of the five possible allocations, we have plotted the most conservative, the middle, and the most aggressive of the allocations to demonstrate their different return and risk features. Note that had you invested in the most aggressive portfolio in early 1987, you would have suffered a loss of nearly 25% at the time of the October 1987 crash, and you would also have endured another large decline in 1990. Given your profile, it is likely that you would have remained invested throughout these periods. On the other hand, had you been invested in the most conservative allocation, you would hardly have felt the ups and downs of the market during this turbulent period. Of course, as you know by now, risk comes with its own reward (if you plan right) as you will see in the chart on the next page.

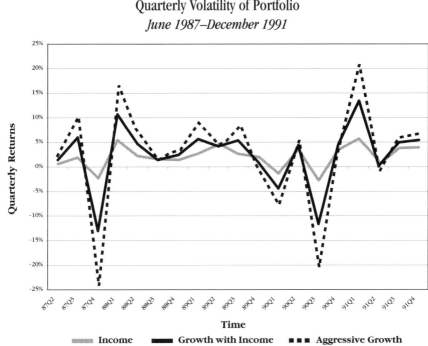

Blue Strategist
Quarterly Volatility of Portfolio
June 1987–December 1991

GROWTH OF $10,000

This chart shouldn't surprise you. Over the five-year period ending March 1998, the portfolio with the riskiest profile performed best, and the least risky portfolio performed worst. That's the way it should be. Bear in mind, however, that we are looking at a particularly good chunk of stock-market history here. It is also possible that during five poor years, the most conservative portfolio would have outperformed the riskiest one.

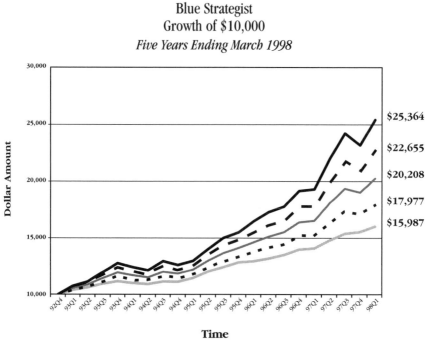

Blue Strategist
Growth of $10,000
Five Years Ending March 1998

PROBABLE RANGES OF RETURN—ONE YEAR

This chart shows at a glance what the probable range of returns is for your chosen portfolio (from most conservative to most aggressive) over any given one-year period. This range of probabilities covers 90% of the cases. If you look at the extremes, there is about a 5% chance that if you chose the moderate (Growth & Income) portfolio, your $10,000 might grow to $13,036, and an equal 5% chance that it would decline to $8,905 (*or* there is a 95% chance that you will do better than $8,905). The expected return (50% probability) is that your $10,000 will grow to $10,774 in a given year. Look at your chosen allocation and imagine the possibilities, then turn to the chart on the next page.

Probability Ranges of the Growth/Loss of $10,000 Invested over 1-Year Time Periods

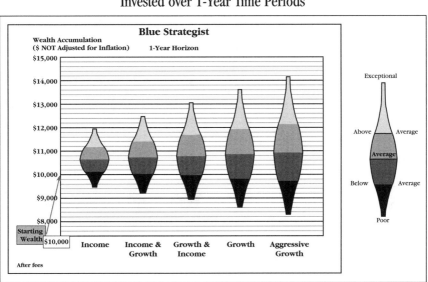

Graph courtesy Lockwood Advisors, Inc.

Expected Wealth Accumulation/Loss by Market Condition

Market Condition	Income	Income & Growth	Growth & Income	Growth	Aggressive Growth	%tile Rank	Market Condition/ Scenario Interpretation
Exceptional	$11,921	$12,473	$13,036	$13,604	$14,181	5%	Top 5% of all Markets
Above Average	$11,151	$11,402	$11,649	$11,890	$12,128	25%	Top 25% of all Markets
Average	**$10,647**	**$10,713**	**$10,774**	**$10,829**	**$10,879**	**50%**	**Average Markets—50%**
Below Average	$10,165	$10,066	$9,965	$9,863	$9,760	75%	75% of Markets Are Higher
Poor	$9,509	$9,202	$8,905	$8,621	$8,346	95%	95% of Markets Are Higher

PROBABLE RANGES OF RETURN—20 YEARS

If you consider your $10,000 investment over a 20-year span, here is what your portfolio might look like at different degrees of probability. In the middle case (Growth & Income), your most probable portfolio value after 20 years will be $50,467. The expected range is as high as $118,658 in a particularly good market environment and as low as $21,464 should the market environment be unusually bad. You can easily see how these numbers would be dramatically higher if you added only a little to your portfolio every year over the 20-year period. Overall, these allocations conform to your MoneyQ profile and comfort level at different degrees of risk tolerance.

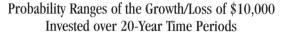

Probability Ranges of the Growth/Loss of $10,000 Invested over 20-Year Time Periods

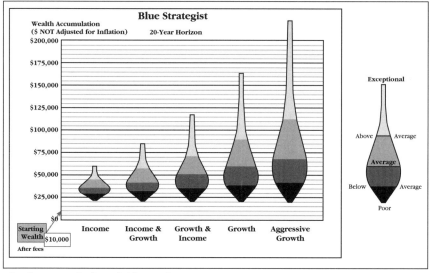

Graph courtesy Lockwood Advisors, Inc.

Expected Wealth Accumulation/Loss by Market Condition

Market Condition	Income	Income & Growth	Growth & Income	Growth	Aggressive Growth	%tile Rank	Market Condition/ Scenario Interpretation
Exceptional	$60,742	$85,018	$118,658	$164,549	$227,579	5%	Top 5% of all Markets
Above Average	$45,060	$56,867	$71,640	$89,876	$112,567	25%	Top 25% of all Markets
Average	**$36,621**	**$43,012**	**$50,467**	**$59,059**	**$69,047**	**50%**	**Average Markets—50%**
Below Average	$29,763	$32,533	$35,551	$38,808	$42,353	75%	75% of Markets Are Higher
Poor	$22,079	$21,761	$21,464	$21,197	$20,949	95%	95% of Markets Are Higher

BLUE INNOVATOR

FINANCIAL ORIENTATION
(reported rankings against other types)

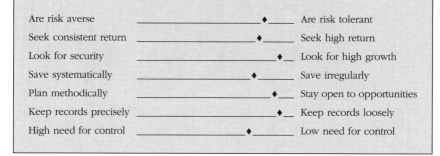

Are risk averse	Are risk tolerant
Seek consistent return	Seek high return
Look for security	Look for high growth
Save systematically	Save irregularly
Plan methodically	Stay open to opportunities
Keep records precisely	Keep records loosely
High need for control	Low need for control

YOUR PORTFOLIO

You are in a rarefied category of investors, those intuitive thinkers who accept high risk after getting their questions about the proposed investment answered to their satisfaction. Interestingly, Blue Innovators are in the same category as most currency traders and many hedge-fund managers. Untested investment theories are attractive to you, if they stand up to the intense scrutiny you will put them through. Your portfolio reflects your investment goals and desires, and you will find a strong bias toward stocks (except in the most conservative allocations), both large cap and small, domestic and international. Managers with an edge to their style who have displayed an ability to achieve superior results will find a home in your asset allocation. The Templeton Developing Markets Fund adds extra zest to the mix. Note that the real-estate allocation can also be used for a self-managed portfolio of your choosing, either in stocks, derivatives, or in an alternative investment such as hedge funds or currencies. As you well know, these are much riskier investments than you might normally expect to find in a long-term growth portfolio, but your temperament and willingness to analyze and accept riskier investments make you a good candidate to invest a reasonable portion of your assets in these high-risk, high-return ventures.

Blue Innovator
Portfolios by Investment Objective
and Time Horizon

Objective:	Income	Income & Growth	Growth & Income	Growth	Aggressive Growth

Asset Allocation	Conservative	Conservative/ Moderate	Moderate	Moderate/ Aggressive	Aggressive
☐ Cash	20	15	10	5	0
▦ Bonds	60	45	30	15	0
■ Equity	20	40	60	80	100
Total Portfolio	100%	100%	100%	100%	100%

Investment Style Allocation	Conservative	Conservative/ Moderate	Moderate	Moderate/ Aggressive	Aggressive
Money Market	20	15	10	5	0
Short-Term Bond	30	23	15	8	0
Intermediate-Term Bond	10	8	5	3	0
High-Yield Bond	10	7	5	2	0
Non-US Bond	10	7	5	2	0
Large Value	3	6	9	12	15
Large Growth	3	6	9	12	15
Small Value	3	6	9	12	15
Small Growth	3	6	9	12	15
Non-US Equity	3	6	9	12	15
Emerging Markets	3	6	9	12	15
Real Estate*	2	4	6	8	10
Total Portfolio	100%	100%	100%	100%	100%

*Some Blue Innovators have a strong interest in the art of investing. If you are one of them, it is highly recommended that you invest some of the money yourself. To start out, take the real-estate allocation and invest this money yourself in ventures, stocks, or sectors you believe are positioned to outperform over your desired time frame.

Blue Innovator
(continued)

Objective:	Income	Income & Growth	Growth & Income	Growth	Aggressive Growth

Fund Allocation I	Conservative	Conservative/ Moderate	Moderate	Moderate/ Aggressive	Aggressive
Your Money Market	20	15	10	5	0
PimCo Low Duration	30	23	15	8	0
Hotchkis & Wiley Total Return	10	8	5	3	0
Fidelity Spartan High Income	10	7	5	2	0
Standish International Fixed Income	10	7	5	2	0
NY Davis Venture	3	6	9	12	15
Montag & Caldwell Growth	3	6	9	12	15
Oakmark Small Cap	3	6	9	12	15
Brazos/JMIC Small Cap Growth Sec	3	6	9	12	15
Hotchkis & Wiley International	3	2	3	4	5
Harbor International Growth		2	3	4	5
Warburg Pincus International Eq Common		2	3	4	5
Templeton Developing Markets	3	6	9	12	15
Security Capital US Real Estate/ Self-Managed	2	4	6	8	10
Total Portfolio	100%	100%	100%	100%	100%

Fund Allocation II	Conservative	Conservative/ Moderate	Moderate	Moderate/ Aggressive	Aggressive
Your Money Market	20	15	10	5	0
Hotchkis & Wiley Total Return	60	45	30	15	0
T. Rowe Price Blue Chip Growth	7	14	20	28	34
T. Rowe Price Small Cap Stock	7	14	20	28	34
Hotchkis & Wiley International	6	12	20	24	32
Total Portfolio	100%	100%	100%	100%	100%

VOLATILITY

The chart shows how your portfolio would have behaved during a particularly active period of the market. Of the five possible allocations, we have plotted the most conservative, the middle, and the most aggressive of the allocations to demonstrate their different return and risk features. Note that had you invested in the most aggressive portfolio in early 1987, you would have suffered a loss of nearly 25% at the time of the October 1987 crash, and you would also have endured another large decline in 1990. Given your profile, it is likely that you would have remained invested throughout these periods. On the other hand, had you been invested in the most conservative allocation, you would hardly have felt the ups and downs of the market during this turbulent period. Of course, as you know by now, risk comes with its own reward (if you plan right) as you will see in the chart on the next page.

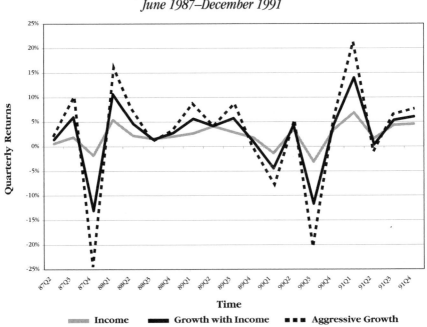

Blue Innovator
Quarterly Volatility of Portfolio
June 1987–December 1991

GROWTH OF $10,000

This chart shouldn't surprise you. Over the five-year period ending March 1998, the portfolio with the riskiest profile performed best, and the least risky portfolio performed worst. That's the way it should be. Bear in mind, however, that we are looking at a particularly good chunk of stock-market history here. It is also possible that during five poor years, the most conservative portfolio would have outperformed the riskiest one.

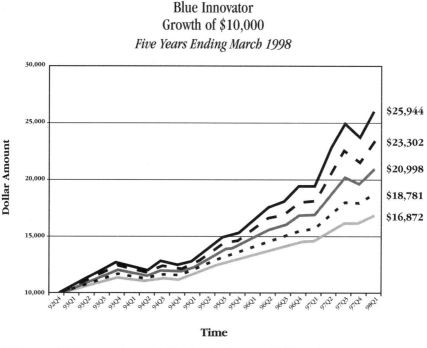

Blue Innovator
Growth of $10,000
Five Years Ending March 1998

Income   ■ ■ ■ Income with Growth   ▓▓▓ Growth with Income   ■■ ■■ Growth   ▬▬ Aggressive Growth

PROBABLE RANGES OF RETURN—ONE YEAR

This chart shows at a glance what the probable range of returns is for your chosen portfolio (from most conservative to most aggressive) over any given one-year period. This range of probabilities covers 90% of the cases. If you look at the extremes, there is about a 5% chance that if you chose the moderate (Growth & Income) portfolio, your $10,000 might grow to $13,168, and an equal 5% chance that it would decline to $8,799 (*or* there is a 95% chance that you will do better than $8,799). The expected return (50% probability) is that your $10,000 would grow to $10,764 in a given year. Look at your chosen allocation and imagine the possibilities, then turn to the chart on the next page.

Probability Ranges of the Growth/Loss of $10,000 Invested over 1-Year Time Periods

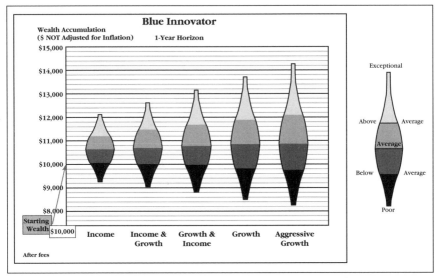

Graph courtesy Lockwood Advisors, Inc.

Expected Wealth Accumulation/Loss by Market Condition

Market Condition	Income	Income & Growth	Growth & Income	Growth	Aggressive Growth	%tile Rank	Market Condition/ Scenario Interpretation
Exceptional	$12,109	$12,624	$13,168	$13,696	$14,252	5%	Top 5% of all Markets
Above Average	$11,220	$11,454	$11,691	$11,917	$12,145	25%	Top 25% of all Markets
Average	**$10,641**	**$10,705**	**$10,764**	**$10,819**	**$10,868**	**50%**	**Average Markets—50%**
Below Average	$10,092	$10,006	$9,911	$9,822	$9,726	75%	75% of Markets Are Higher
Poor	$9,351	$9,078	$8,799	$8,546	$8,288	95%	95% of Markets Are Higher

PROBABLE RANGES OF RETURN—20 YEARS

If you consider your $10,000 investment over a 20-year span, here is what your portfolio might look like at different degrees of probability. In the middle case (Growth & Income), your most probable portfolio value after 20 years will be $50,301. The expected range is as high as $124,285 in a particularly good market environment and as low as $20,358 should the market environment be unusually bad. You can easily see how these numbers would be dramatically higher if you added only a little to your portfolio every year over the 20-year period. Overall, these allocations conform to your MoneyQ profile and comfort level at different degrees of risk tolerance.

Probability Ranges of the Growth/Loss of $10,000 Invested over 20-Year Time Periods

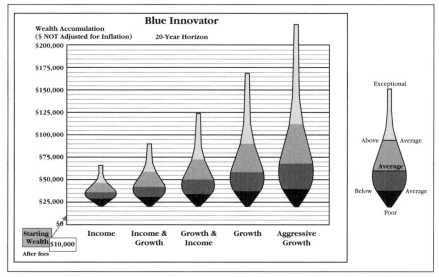

Graph courtesy Lockwood Advisors, Inc.

Expected Wealth Accumulation/Loss by Market Condition

Market Condition	Income	Income & Growth	Growth & Income	Growth	Aggressive Growth	%tile Rank	Market Condition/ Scenario Interpretation
Exceptional	$65,539	$90,047	$124,285	$169,303	$231,704	5%	Top 5% of all Markets
Above Average	$46,571	$58,208	$72,871	$90,581	$112,783	25%	Top 25% of all Markets
Average	**$36,735**	**$42,996**	**$50,301**	**$58,674**	**$68,413**	**50%**	**Average Markets—50%**
Below Average	$28,977	$31,759	$34,721	$38,006	$41,499	75%	75% of Markets Are Higher
Poor	$20,591	$20,530	$20,358	$20,334	$20,200	95%	95% of Markets Are Higher

GREEN MENTOR

FINANCIAL ORIENTATION
(reported rankings against other types)

Are risk averse	——————♦——————	Are risk tolerant
Seek consistent return	————♦——————	Seek high return
Look for security	—————♦—————	Look for high growth
Save systematically	——♦——————	Save irregularly
Plan methodically	——♦——————	Stay open to opportunities
Keep records precisely	————————♦————	Keep records loosely
High need for control	——♦——————	Low need for control

YOUR PORTFOLIO

Unlike some other profiles, money is not important to you *per se*, but rather as a means to an end, including the well-being of your family and the quality of your own life. Managing an investment portfolio is not high on your list of favorite pastimes. Most likely, you will prefer having a trusted adviser, who will explain the investment options to you, and you will be just as happy leaving the choices to him or her. Your portfolio reflects your aversion to high risk and volatility. You will willingly sacrifice a higher return in favor of predictability and lower risk. You find it meaningful to set goals for your investments and measure their progress against the goals you have set.

Your portfolio includes varying amounts of cash (money-market funds) and bonds, depending on the asset allocation you select. In fact, your cash allocation is the highest among color types, given your desire for liquidity. Well-known equity funds have a place in your asset allocation, as do index-type funds with their marketlike returns. Overall, this is a relatively low-volatility portfolio across the five different allocations. You may well be interested in a socially responsible fund. The real-estate allocation may be substituted for such a fund, or, if you prefer, you may substitute one of the other funds so long as its replacement has similar style characteristics; i.e., growth or value, etc.

Green Mentor
Portfolios by Investment Objective and Time Horizon

Objective:	Income	Income & Growth	Growth & Income	Growth	Aggressive Growth

Asset Allocation	Conservative	Conservative/ Moderate	Moderate	Moderate/ Aggressive	Aggressive
☐ Cash	25	25	20	15	5
▨ Bonds	55	45	30	15	5
■ Equity	20	30	50	70	90
Total Portfolio	100%	100%	100%	100%	100%

Investment Style Allocation	Conservative	Conservative/ Moderate	Moderate	Moderate/ Aggressive	Aggressive
Money Market	25	25	20	15	5
Short-Term Bond	40	30	20	10	5
Intermediate-Term Bond	15	15	10	5	0
Large Value	4	6	10	14	18
Large Growth	4	6	10	14	18
Small Value	2	3	5	7	9
Small Growth	2	3	5	7	9
Non-US Equity	4	6	10	14	18
Emerging Markets	2	3	5	7	9
Real Estate	2	3	5	7	9
Total Portfolio	100%	100%	100%	100%	100%

Green Mentor
(continued)

Objective:	Income	Income & Growth	Growth & Income	Growth	Aggressive Growth

Fund Allocation I	Conservative	Conservative/ Moderate	Moderate	Moderate/ Aggressive	Aggressive
Your Money Market	25	25	20	15	5
PimCo Low Duration	40	30	20	10	5
Hotchkis & Wiley Total Return	15	15	10	5	0
T. Rowe Price Equity-Income	4	6	10	14	18
Vanguard US Growth	4	6	10	14	18
Scudder Small Cap Value	2	3	5	7	9
Franklin Small Cap Growth	2	3	5	7	9
Templeton Foreign	4	6	10	14	18
Templeton Developing Markets	2	3	5	7	9
Cohen & Steers Real Estate	2	3	5	7	9
Total Portfolio	100%	100%	100%	100%	100%

Fund Allocation II	Conservative	Conservative/ Moderate	Moderate	Moderate/ Aggressive	Aggressive
Your Money Market	25	25	20	15	5
PimCo Low Duration	55	45	30	15	5
Mutual Beacon	7	10	17	24	30
Brandywine Blue	7	10	17	23	30
Templeton Foreign	6	10	16	23	30
Total Portfolio	100%	100%	100%	100%	100%

VOLATILITY

The chart shows how your portfolio would have behaved during a particularly active period of the market. Of the five possible allocations, we have plotted the most conservative, the middle, and the most aggressive of the allocations to demonstrate their different return and risk features. Note that had you invested in the most aggressive portfolio in early 1987, you would have suffered a loss of over 20% at the time of the October 1987 crash, and you would also have endured another large decline in 1990. Given your profile, it is not likely that you would have been comfortable with that degree of volatility. For this reason, you might be more comfortable with one of the less aggressive of the allocations in your group. For example, had you been invested in the most conservative allocation, you would hardly have felt the ups and downs of the market during this turbulent period. Of course, as you know by now, risk comes with its own reward (if you plan right) as you will see in the chart on the following page.

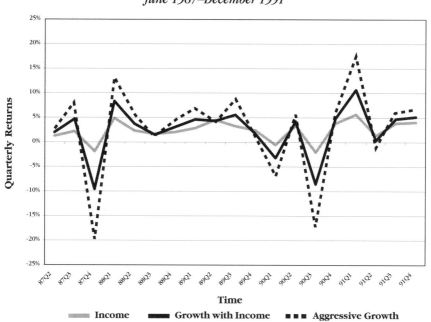

**Green Mentor
Quarterly Volatility of Portfolio**
June 1987–December 1991

GROWTH OF $10,000

This chart shouldn't surprise you. Over the five-year period ending March 1998, the portfolio with the riskiest profile performed best, and the least risky portfolio performed worst. That's the way it should be. Bear in mind, however, that we are looking at a particularly good chunk of stock-market history here. It is also possible that during five poor years, the most conservative portfolio would have outperformed the riskiest one.

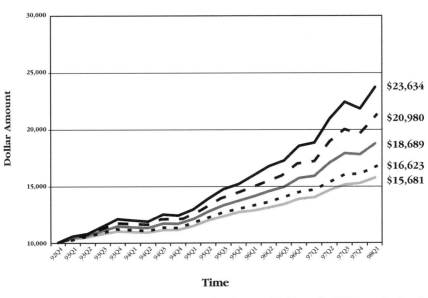

Green Mentor
Growth of $10,000
Five Years Ending March 1998

PROBABLE RANGES OF RETURN—ONE YEAR

This chart shows at a glance what the probable range of returns is for your chosen portfolio (from most conservative to most aggressive) over any given one-year period. This range of probabilities covers 90% of the cases. If you look at the extremes, there is about a 5% chance that if you chose the moderate (Growth & Income) portfolio, your $10,000 might grow to $12,621, and an equal 5% chance that it would decline to $9,116 (*or* there is a 95% chance that you will do better than $9,116). The expected return (50% probability) is that your $10,000 will grow to $10,726 in a given year. Look at your chosen allocation and imagine the possibilities, then turn to the chart on the next page.

Probability Ranges of the Growth/Loss of $10,000 Invested over 1-Year Time Periods

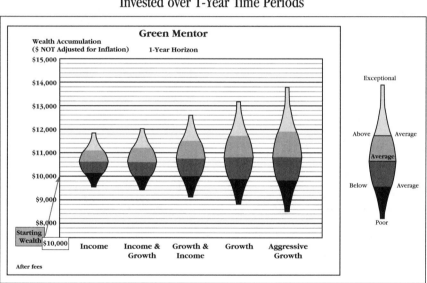

Graph courtesy Lockwood Advisors, Inc.

Expected Wealth Accumulation/Loss by Market Condition

Market Condition	Income	Income & Growth	Growth & Income	Growth	Aggressive Growth	%tile Rank	Market Condition/ Scenario Interpretation
Exceptional	$11,817	$12,075	$12,621	$13,175	$13,775	5%	Top 5% of all Markets
Above Average	$11,102	$11,221	$11,466	$11,706	$11,959	25%	Top 25% of all Markets
Average	**$10,632**	**$10,663**	**$10,726**	**$10,783**	**$10,841**	**50%**	**Average Markets—50%**
Below Average	$10,181	$10,133	$10,034	$9,934	$9,827	75%	75% of Markets Are Higher
Poor	$9,566	$9,416	$9,116	$8,826	$8,531	95%	95% of Markets Are Higher

PROBABLE RANGES OF RETURN—20 YEARS

If you consider your $10,000 investment over a 20-year span, here is what your portfolio might look like at different degrees of probability. In the middle case (Growth & Income), your most probable portfolio value after 20 years will be $44,590. The expected range is as high as $92,463 in a particularly good market environment and as low as $21,503 should the market environment be unusually bad. You can easily see how these numbers would be dramatically higher if you added only a little to your portfolio every year over the 20-year period. Overall, these allocations conform to your MoneyQ profile and comfort level at different degrees of risk tolerance.

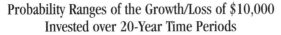

Probability Ranges of the Growth/Loss of $10,000 Invested over 20-Year Time Periods

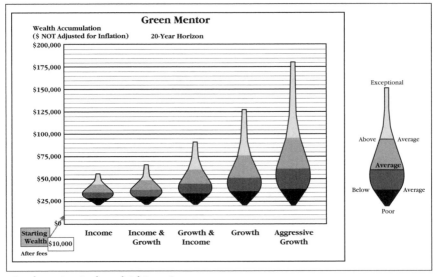

Graph courtesy Lockwood Advisors, Inc.

Expected Wealth Accumulation/Loss by Market Condition

Market Condition	Income	Income & Growth	Growth & Income	Growth	Aggressive Growth	%tile Rank	Market Condition/ Scenario Interpretation
Exceptional	$56,854	$66,572	$92,463	$127,843	$180,372	5%	Top 5% of all Markets
Above Average	$43,004	$47,921	$60,121	$75,211	$95,532	25%	Top 25% of all Markets
Average	**$35,425**	**$38,141**	**$44,590**	**$52,037**	**$61,448**	**50%**	**Average Markets—50%**
Below Average	$29,183	$30,358	$33,071	$36,004	$39,524	75%	75% of Markets Are Higher
Poor	$22,074	$21,853	$21,503	$21,181	$20,934	95%	95% of Markets Are Higher

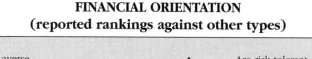

Green Advocate

FINANCIAL ORIENTATION
(reported rankings against other types)

Are risk averse	_____♦_____	Are risk tolerant
Seek consistent return	_____♦_____	Seek high return
Look for security	_____♦_____	Look for high growth
Save systematically	_____♦_____	Save irregularly
Plan methodically	_____♦____	Stay open to opportunities
Keep records precisely	_____♦_	Keep records loosely
High need for control	_____♦_____	Low need for control

YOUR PORTFOLIO

Although you can accept investment risk better than most, you belong to a group that tends to benefit a great deal from a relationship with a trusted financial adviser. You are open to novel investment strategies so long as they are properly explained, and you are able to grasp their nuances. However, you need to be careful since your risk tolerance may be equally inspired by an appetite for risk as it is by an indifference to its consequences. For those reasons, you will want to study your allocation carefully. If you are dealing with a financial adviser, be sure you are placing your trust in him or her for the right reasons and not because the individual happens to be *simpatico.*

Your portfolio includes a balance of stock and bond funds (except in the most aggressive allocation) with a stock allocation covering a variety of funds to achieve a well-diversified investment strategy. Well-known funds are represented to include both growth and value strategies and to offer representation in international markets.

Green Advocate
Portfolios by Investment Objective
and Time Horizon

Objective:	Income	Income & Growth	Growth & Income	Growth	Aggressive Growth

Asset Allocation	Conservative	Conservative/ Moderate	Moderate	Moderate/ Aggressive	Aggressive
☐ Cash	20	15	10	5	0
▨ Bonds	60	45	30	15	0
■ Equity	20	40	60	80	100
Total Portfolio	100%	100%	100%	100%	100%

Investment Style Allocation	Conservative	Conservative/ Moderate	Moderate	Moderate/ Aggressive	Aggressive
Money Market	20	15	10	5	0
Short-Term Bond	20	15	10	5	0
Intermediate-Term Bond	20	15	10	5	0
Non-US Bond	20	15	10	5	0
Large Value	4	8	12	16	20
Large Growth	4	8	12	16	20
Small Value	2	4	6	8	10
Small Growth	2	4	6	8	10
Non-US Equity	4	8	12	16	20
Emerging Markets	2	4	6	8	10
Real Estate	2	4	6	8	10
Total Portfolio	100%	100%	100%	100%	100%

Green Advocate
(continued)

Objective:	Income	Income & Growth	Growth & Income	Growth	Aggressive Growth

Fund Allocation I	Conservative	Conservative/ Moderate	Moderate	Moderate/ Aggressive	Aggressive
Your Money Market	20	15	10	5	0
PimCo Low Duration	20	15	10	5	0
Hotchkis & Wiley Total Return	20	15	10	5	0
Standish International Fixed Income	20	15	10	5	0
T. Rowe Price Equity-Income	4	8	12	16	20
Montag & Caldwell Growth	4	8	12	16	20
Scudder Small Cap Value	2	4	6	8	10
Brazos/JMIC Small Cap Growth Sec	2	4	6	8	10
Hotchkis & Wiley International	4	4	4	6	7
Harbor International Growth		4	4	5	7
Warburg Pincus International Eq Common			4	5	6
Templeton Developing Markets	2	4	6	8	10
Cohen & Steers Real Estate	2	4	6	8	10
Total Portfolio	100%	100%	100%	100%	100%

Fund Allocation II	Conservative	Conservative/ Moderate	Moderate	Moderate/ Aggressive	Aggressive
Your Money Market	20	15	10	5	0
PimCo Low Duration	60	45	30	15	0
Gabelli Value	7	14	20	27	34
Brandywine	7	13	20	27	33
Hotchkis & Wiley International	6	13	20	26	33
Total Portfolio	100%	100%	100%	100%	100%

VOLATILITY

The chart shows how your portfolio would have behaved during a particularly active period of the market. Of the five possible allocations, we have plotted the most conservative, the middle, and the most aggressive of the allocations to demonstrate their different return and risk features. Note that had you invested in the most aggressive portfolio in early 1987, you would have suffered a loss of close to 20% at the time of the October 1987 crash, and you would also have endured another large decline in 1990. Given your profile, it is possible that you would have been comfortable with that degree of volatility throughout these periods. On the other hand, had you been invested in the most conservative allocation, you would hardly have felt the ups and downs of the market during this turbulent period. Of course, as you know by now, risk comes with its own reward (if you plan right) as you will see in the chart on the next page.

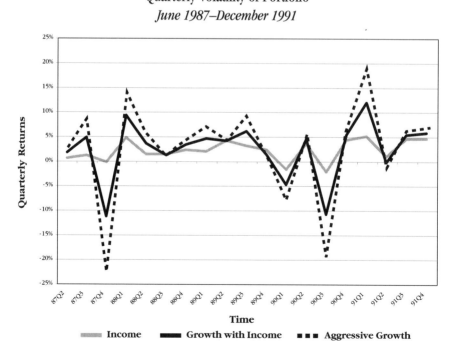

Green Advocate
Quarterly Volatility of Portfolio
June 1987–December 1991

GROWTH OF $10,000

This chart shouldn't surprise you. Over the five-year period ending March 1998, the portfolio with the riskiest profile performed best, and the least risky portfolio performed worst. That's the way it should be. Bear in mind, however, that we are looking at a particularly good chunk of stock-market history here. It is also possible that during five poor years, the most conservative portfolio would have outperformed the riskiest one.

Green Advocate
Growth of $10,000
Five Years Ending March 1998

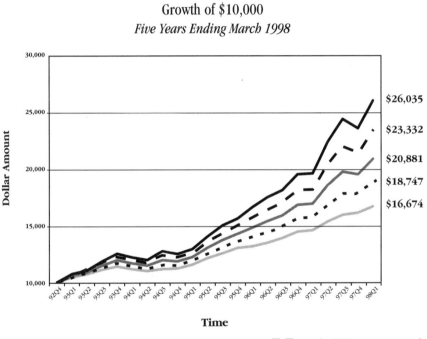

Income   ■ ■ ■ Income with Growth   Growth with Income   ■ ■ Growth   Aggressive Growth

PROBABLE RANGES OF RETURN—ONE YEAR

This chart shows at a glance what the probable range of returns is for your chosen portfolio (from most conservative to most aggressive) over any given one-year period. This range of probabilities covers 90% of the cases. If you look at the extremes, there is about a 5% chance that if you chose the moderate (Growth & Income) portfolio, your $10,000 might grow to $13,131, and an equal 5% chance that it would decline to $8,821 (*or* there is a 95% chance that you will do better than $8,821). The expected return (50% probability) is that your $10,000 would grow to $10,763 in a given year. Look at your chosen allocation and imagine the possibilities, then turn to the chart on the next page.

Probability Ranges of the Growth/Loss of $10,000 Invested over 1-Year Time Periods

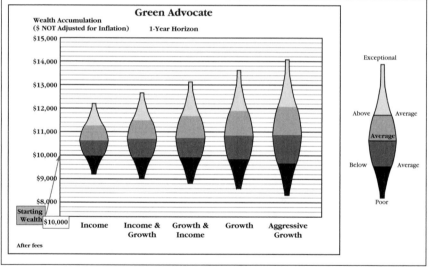

Graph courtesy Lockwood Advisors, Inc.

Expected Wealth Accumulation/Loss by Market Condition

Market Condition	Income	Income & Growth	Growth & Income	Growth	Aggressive Growth	%tile Rank	Market Condition/ Scenario Interpretation
Exceptional	$12,195	$12,661	$13,131	$13,607	$14,086	5%	Top 5% of all Markets
Above Average	$11,254	$11,467	$11,677	$11,883	$12,087	25%	Top 25% of all Markets
Average	**$10,643**	**$10,705**	**$10,763**	**$10,817**	**$10,868**	**50%**	**Average Markets—50%**
Below Average	$10,066	$9,993	$9,920	$9,846	$9,771	75%	75% of Markets Are Higher
Poor	$9,288	$9,051	$8,821	$8,599	$8,384	95%	95% of Markets Are Higher

PROBABLE RANGES OF RETURN—20 YEARS

If you consider your $10,000 investment over a 20-year span, here is what your portfolio might look like at different degrees of probability. In the middle case (Growth & Income), your most probable portfolio value after 20 years will be $49,956. The expected range is as high as $121,973 in a particularly good market environment and as low as $20,461 should the market environment be unusually bad. You can easily see how these numbers would be dramatically higher if you added only a little to your portfolio every year over the 20-year period. Overall, these allocations conform to your MoneyQ profile and comfort level at different degrees of risk tolerance.

Probability Ranges of the Growth/Loss of $10,000 Invested over 20-Year Time Periods

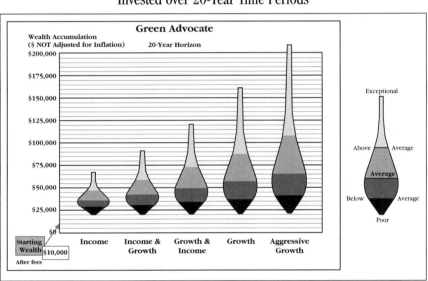

Graph courtesy Lockwood Advisors, Inc.

Expected Wealth Accumulation/Loss by Market Condition

Market Condition	Income	Income & Growth	Growth & Income	Growth	Aggressive Growth	%tile Rank	Market Condition/ Scenario Interpretation
Exceptional	$68,293	$91,431	$121,973	$162,149	$214,800	5%	Top 5% of all Markets
Above Average	$47,650	$58,649	$72,020	$88,238	$107,862	25%	Top 25% of all Markets
Average	**$37,113**	**$43,090**	**$49,956**	**$57,833**	**$66,858**	**50%**	**Average Markets—50%**
Below Average	$28,906	$31,659	$34,652	$37,905	$41,442	75%	75% of Markets Are Higher
Poor	$20,169	$20,308	$20,461	$20,627	$20,810	95%	95% of Markets Are Higher

BEFORE WE PART . . .

We have completed an important journey together, and if you have stayed with me to this point, I have no doubt that investment success is within your reach. Let me be the first to congratulate you on this achievement.

In our concluding few moments, let's go over some of the highlights of our discovery. We all started with a common objective—a desire to achieve true investment success, using the highest level of intelligence available today. There were no naive participants on this journey. Those seeking magic formulas, hot tips, or heretofore-undiscovered secret investment strategies abandoned this group a long time ago. Those who stayed until the end favored reason over hype, intelligent analysis over wishful thinking, and the wisdom of the great money managers over the seductive palaver of investment hucksters. I am proud to include you in this select group.

We began our journey by adopting a fresh approach to investment success, learning how we, as individuals, could use our personality traits to reinforce and enhance our path to investment wealth rather than detracting from it. Indeed, by discovering our MoneyQ profile, we opened the door to an investment program that is tailored to each of us as individuals. This investment approach is unique and rooted in a new area of research incorporating our personality, behavior, and attitudes toward money in addition to the usual concerns most of us have about risk and volatility. Although the research that went into it is complex, the reasoning is quite simple: We are more likely to follow and stick with an investment program that is tailored to our traits, behavioral patterns, and attitude toward money than we are following a program that is generically designed for everybody in our age group.

Of course, the road to wealth begins, but does not end, with our MoneyQ profile. There is knowledge to acquire about investing.

The problem is not a scarcity of knowledge, but too much of it. The subject of investing in stocks is abundantly served by every variety of huckster and buffoon imaginable, all eager to sell you something that, they claim, will accelerate your achievement of wealth. I realize that I often rant and rave to excess on this subject but, as a professional investment consultant, it really upsets me to observe shoddy investment advice promulgated to a willing but unsuspecting public. The problem, you see, is that investors with limited resources, or those who started later in life, are ripe for strategies that will enable them to "catch up" with their peers who started earlier and acquired more wealth. I expect that you know there is no such thing as catching up, unless you win the lottery or otherwise strike it rich through a stroke of luck. The formulas for catching up are inevitably an invitation to take more risk. You know the consequences of doing that.

The 7 Master Keys to investment wealth that we covered in *The Wealth Equation* represent the wisdom of scores of investment professionals who are leaders in their field. Why would you want to listen to anybody else? The principles represented in the 7 Master Keys are time-tested maxims of intelligent investment strategy. The Master Keys combine the wisdom of the successful investment professionals with the findings of the financial academic community to arrive at the most intelligent investment plan you can find, and that, too, is an element to the Wealth Equation. Several of the lessons we learned about investing were drawn from the research of individuals in academia who won the Nobel Prize in economics for their efforts. In my book, that is a group worth listening to, and we did.

By the time we got to Part Three of *The Wealth Equation*, we were ready to introduce you to your personal investment program. The combination of the MoneyQ profile and a deeper understanding of sound investment principles prepared you to accept and implement an intelligent and personally formulated investment strategy. This is the fulfillment of the promise I made to you at the beginning of the book.

Now it is up to you. I will tell you in all candor that if you made it this far, your probability of success is very high. Once your investment portfolio is established and operating, keep the book handy to check back for any advice you may need or might have forgotten.

Some of the funds or managers may change with time, but the investment principles will not. Use them to anchor your own convictions.

So we reach the end of our mission. Wealth through investing is within your reach, and I know you will grab it, hold on, and achieve the riches you surely deserve.

Thanks for making the journey with me. I hope our paths cross again.

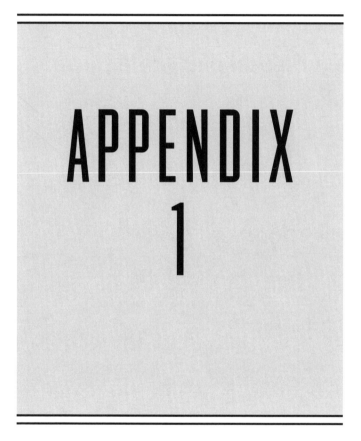

APPENDIX
1

MONEY MANAGER SURVEY

On the following pages, you will find the detailed, question-by-question, responses from the investment managers who were invited to complete the survey. A word of explanation is in order. The survey was conducted in two phases. In the first phase, 65 managers were polled. Phase two involved completing the survey by polling an additional 35 managers, some of whom were polled by phone. In some cases, you will find that the responses apply only to the first sample of 65 respondents, although in most cases, the returns apply to all 100 participants. Statisticians will tell you that a sample of 100 money managers, out of the thousands who are in business, is not a broad enough sample from which to draw sweeping conclusions. They are right, of course, and our purpose is not to attribute these results to a broad cross section of investment managers. Our poll was limited to managers who qualify as being among the top of their peers based primarily on superior performance and longevity. As such, they are in a more rarified class of investment professionals. Our purpose was to discover common traits, disciplines, and interests among this elite group. I did not intend to attribute these results to all portfolio managers in the business.

You will also note that some of the response totals are in parentheses. This is an indication that these particular responses were out of the ordinary, meaning that the response of that particular group was higher than one might expect it to be, and therefore it may warrant a second look. We gave them second looks where we felt it was warranted and discussed those findings in Part One, "The Common Denominators: What Makes Great Managers Great." Another point: You may recall that the vast majority of our managers fell into the Blue and Gold profiles. Hence we emphasize the results from these two groups.

Otherwise, the usual caveats apply. Numbers may not add up due to rounding, some responses may not be applicable for various reasons, some respondents may have left certain questions blank, and so on.

NOTES TO SURVEY:

* = 1 if base is less than 100

[ ] When comparing Blue versus Gold, the number in [ ] is significantly large (at the 90% or higher level of confidence)

UK/NA Unknown/Not Applicable

Columns may not add to 100% because in some cases respondents did not answer or gave more than one answer, and/or as a result of rounding errors.

MoneyQ Profile by Type

	Total (100) %
BLUE	44
GOLD	42
RED	9
GREEN	5

Primary Investment Style

Which of these categories or combinations of categories describes
your primary investment style?

	TOTAL (100) %	BLUE (44) %	GOLD (42) %
Large Cap	54	50	57
Value	47	32	[48]
Mid Cap	41	46	38
Growth @ reasonable price	37	39	36
Growth	33	39	33
Small Cap	27	30	26
Balanced	20	21	17
International	11	9	17
Momentum	4	*	7
Other (Net)	19	[23]	14
Tactical asset allocation	3	5	2
Convertibles	2	5	0
Global	2	*	*
Growth/value	3	0	5
Contrarian	1	0	0
Eclectic	1	0	0
US Macro investing long and short	1	0	*
Equity-style rotation	1	*	0
Equity/income	1	*	0
Socially responsible	*	*	0

Number of Investment Styles Chosen

	TOTAL (100) %	BLUE (44) %	GOLD (42) %
Chose only one style	14	14	12
Chose more than 1	86	86	88
Chose more than 2	55	57	50
Chose more than 3	36	[36]	21
Chose more than 4	19	16	21

Reasons for Choosing Primary Investment Style

Why did you choose your primary investment style? Why does it work for you?

	TOTAL (65) %	BLUE (31) %	GOLD (25) %
Greatest potential for growth/profit/return	26	32	24
Growth/profit balanced with reasonable/ managed risk	24	19	28
Experience based/proven/evolved/it works	25	9	[24]
Has flexibility/differing styles per objectives/ market conditions/business cycle	15	19	12
Research/computer model/analysis based	14	13	16
Long-term time frame/superior returns over time/compounding/buy and hold	14	16	12
Details own approach/specifics	12	7	[20]
Buy strong/growing/good companies/ stock = ownership	9	13	*
Disciplined/logical/rational/objective/ consistent approach	9	*	20
Asset class selection/allocation/ diversified approach	9	16	*
Controls volatility/smoothes ups/downs	8	10	0
Select best equities/stocks	5	0	12
Fits personality/individual	5	3	*
Common sense based/practical approach	5	6	*
Controls/manages/limits risk/acceptable risk level	3	*	*

Investment Orientation

In your investment strategy, what is more important . . . ?

	TOTAL (100) %	BLUE (44) %	GOLD (42) %
Beating the market with higher risk of loss	46	48	55
Preserving capital with market/ submarket returns	44	[46]	29
Other Volunteered Responses			
Beating market with less risk	3	*	8
Preserving capital and beating the market	2	0	*
Depends on circumstances	1	*	0
Making money	1	*	0
DK/NA	3	*	10

Factors Determining Investment Style

What are the most important issues in determining an investment approach? What factors must people consider?

MENTIONED BY 5% OR MORE	TOTAL (65) %	BLUE (31) %	GOLD (25) %
Risk tolerance/personality	42	36	52
Specific/clear goals/objectives	23	29	16
Logic/rationale for actions/common sense	22	26	20
Have long time frame/patience/buy and hold	22	13	[32]
Good research/know reasons why/analysis	22	19	24
Good earnings/growth/revenue/ gains history and potential	19	13	24
Systematic/disciplined approach/strategy to meet goals	14	19	*
Personal situation/age/time frame	12	16	*
Well-established approach/worked in the past/can be repeated	11	10	*
Downside potential/loss/risk	11	16	0
Balance of risk and reward	11	10	12
Asset allocation/diversified holdings	11	7	[20]
Well managed/good companies/ good track record	9	*	16
Be consistent/stay the course/ stick to plan/style	9	13	8
Stocks/equities/assets selected	9	*	16
Performance vs. benchmarks/ reevaluation/adjustment	6	10	*
Sell discipline	5	10	0
Preservation of capital	5	*	*
Franchise/industry characteristics/ trends/understand business	5	7	*

Competitive Frame

Do you think of yourself as primarily competing against . . . ?

	TOTAL (100) %	BLUE (44) %	GOLD (42) %
An appropriate benchmark	60	64	57
The market	46	39	48
Your peers	45	[52]	36
Yourself	43	48	41
Other			
Absolute return	3	*	*
Client objectives/goals	2	5	0
Risk-free returns	2	0	0
Russell 2000 Growth Index	1	*	0
Treasury bonds/bills	1	*	0

Motivations for Investment Activities

How important are each of these factors in motivating you in your investment activities?

	TOTAL (100) %	BLUE (44) %	GOLD (42) %
"Very Important"			
Achieving investors' goals	96	[100]	93
Personal reputation	58	[64]	55
Beating the market	49	41	[60]
Avoiding failure	44	50	41
Own living standard	17	18	18
Other	6	9	5
Absolute return			
Challenge			
Doing the right thing right			
Love what I do			
Making money			
Thrill of the game			

Market Timing

Is it possible to "time the market" successfully?

	TOTAL (100) %	BLUE (44) %	GOLD (42) %
No	73	77	71
Yes	17	16	21
Sometimes	5	*	5
DK/NA	5	5	3

Factors Contributing to Investment Success

How important is each of the following to investment success?

	TOTAL (100) %	BLUE (44) %	GOLD (42) %
<u>"Very Important"</u>			
Self-discipline	90	89	93
Avoid stupid mistakes	77	80	76
Security selection	74	75	79
Asset allocation	60	66	55
Market timing	8	7	12
<u>Other</u>	<u>8</u>	<u>7</u>	<u>10</u>
Consistency			
Coolness			
Flexibility			
Long-term perspective			
Patience			

Track Record

How many years' track record is needed to judge a money manager's performance?

	TOTAL (100) %	BLUE (44) %	GOLD (42) %
1 to 4 years	16	16	19
5 years	42	48	38
6 to 9 years	5	5	5
10 years	28	25	26
11 or more years	2	5	0
DK/NA	7	*	12
Mean years	6	7	6
Median years	5	5	5

Successful Money Manager Characteristics

How important are each of the following characteristics for a successful money manager?

	TOTAL (100) %	BLUE (44) %	GOLD (42) %
"Very Important"			
Inquisitive nature	66	71	68
Investment management experience	61	55	62
Intelligence	56	55	62
Financial analysis	53	43	[62]
Understand money flows	24	21	24
Religious faith	6	9	*
Other	13	14	14

Assumption of risk

Client objectives/goals

Common sense/street smarts

Courage of convictions/dedication to style

Decisiveness

Discipline

Hard work

Modesty

Patience

Personal integrity

Perspective/sense of history

Return Expectations

For investors who characterize their risk profile as moderate, what do *you* think is a satisfactory gross annualized return over a ten-year period assuming a 4% inflation rate?

YOUR OPINION	TOTAL (100) %	BLUE (44) %	GOLD (42) %
6–8% per year	22	21	21
9–10% per year	37	36	33
11–12% per year	26	27	29
13% or more per year	9	7	12
DK/NA	6	8	5
Mean per year	10	10	10
Median per year	10	10	10

What do *most investors* think is a satisfactory gross annualized return over a ten-year period assuming a 4% inflation rate?

INVESTORS' OPINION	TOTAL (100) %	BLUE (44) %	GOLD (42) %
6–8% per year	3	7	0
9–10% per year	23	16	[31]
11–12% per year	17	11	21
13% or more per year	46	[57]	33
DK/NA	11	9	15
Mean per year	12	12	12
Median per year	13	14	12

Risk Tolerance

Do most investors know their true risk tolerance?

	TOTAL (100) %	BLUE (44) %	GOLD (42) %
No	85	84	88

Do you understand your investors' true risk tolerance?

	TOTAL (100) %	BLUE (44) %	GOLD (42) %
Yes	66	61	71

Do you accept more risk with your clients' portfolios, your personal portfolio, or the same level of risk with both?

	TOTAL (100) %	BLUE (44) %	GOLD (42) %
Personal portfolio	54	55	48
Same level of risk	44	43	44
Clients' portfolios	1	0	*
DK/NA	1	*	7

Views of Money Management

Indicate how much you agree with each of the following statements about money management.

STRONGLY AGREE THAT	TOTAL (100) %	BLUE (44) %	GOLD (42) %
Main goal is to beat benchmark	56	55	60
Rely on sell discipline, not gut instinct, when selling	55	48	[62]
Managing clients' expectations integral to my management style	51	57	48
Trust in manager more important than his or her track record	29	27	29
Difficult for manager to be good performer in more than one style	28	32	21
Equity portfolio should include mix of growth and value stocks	24	25	17
Equity portfolio should mix small- and large-cap stocks	24	25	17
Equity portfolio should mix U.S. and international stocks	23	25	21
Use intuition when buying some stocks	22	[25]	14
Portfolio should be balanced between stocks and bonds	19	18	12
Allow position to decline only specific percentage before selling	15	21	12
Have "sixth sense" regarding stock market	10	9	7
Index funds best for novices	10	14	10
Infer clients' risk tolerance rather than ask them	5	5	7

Wealth Building

What advice would you give to individual investors trying to build wealth?

	Total (65) %	Blue (31) %	Gold (25) %
Mentioned by over 5%			
Focus on long-term goals/patience/buy and hold/don't trade too often/get rich slowly	50	51	44
Have plan/style/stick to it/clear objectives	28	19	32
Asset allocation plan/balanced approach/ diversified	26	23	36
Understand own risk tolerance/consider downside/potential loss	25	16	[32]
Invest as much as possible/ invest regularly/systematically	23	19	28
Discipline/consistency	19	19	24
Good professional help/rapport regarding style	17	19	20
Be objective/make decisions rationally/ not on emotion	17	19	12
Buy quality/well-managed companies	14	10	20
Realistic goals/expectations/ don't be greedy/losses part of cycle	14	13	16
Monitor results/reevaluate objectively/ make adjustments	12	13	12
Invest in stocks/equities/particularly well valued	11	13	*
Get started now/start young	11	13	8
Research companies/be knowledgeable/ do homework/avoid investments don't understand/fads	8	7	*
Balance potential profit vs. risk/accept some risk/"no free lunch"	8	10	8
Don't try to outsmart the market/ forget market timing	6	10	*
Consider tax implications	6	3	9
Use "magic of compounding"/reinvest	5	0	*
Be wary of costs/fees/consider low-cost alternatives	5	0	8

Own Investing

When you are investing for your personal portfolio, how does your investment approach differ from your approach to your clients' portfolios? What factors become more important?

	TOTAL (65) %	BLUE (31) %	GOLD (25) %
Portfolio NOT different from clients	40	39	48
Only slightly different from clients	6	13	0
Is different from clients	54	48	52
How own portfolio differs from clients'			
More risk for self	19	23	12
Less diversified/more concentrated positions/fewer and larger positions	17	16	12
More experimental (new-asset classes, microcaps, smaller stocks, emerging markets, short-term opportunities, futures, options)	14	18	*
Longer time frame	9	13	8
Different allocations	6	0	12
No concern about appearances/ "trading errors"/beating benchmarks in short term/answering to others	5	*	8
More active trading/shorter time frame	5	0	3
More equities	3	*	*

Faith and Investing

Many managers we have spoken with are quite religious. Do you believe that faith or involvement with religion plays a significant role in managing money?

FAITH PLAYS A ROLE	TOTAL (100) %	BLUE (44) %	GOLD (42) %
Yes	35	36	29

If "yes," why do you think so?

HOW FAITH PLAYS A ROLE (TOTAL 35)	TOTAL (100) %	BLUE (44) %	GOLD (42) %
Perspective on life/maintains/balance/ keep "up"/deal with hard times	46	38	50
Philosophical framework/inner qualities for good decision making	31	38	17
Moral truths/ethics/right vs. wrong/ honest vs. dishonest important in all aspects of life	23	31	17
"Courage of convictions"/ supports psychological independence	11	19	*
Optimistic mind-set good for investing	9	*	*
Religious qualities translate into strong life skills	9	13	*
Respect for individuals	*	*	0
Helps deal with uncertainty/unknown	*	*	0

MoneyQ Attributes by Pairs

For each set of choices, select the phrase that more accurately describes you at least 51% of the time.

		TOTAL (100) %	BLUE (44) %	GOLD (42) %
1.	Value insights and analogies	51	[66]	36
	Value accuracy and precision	45	30	[62]
2.	Like to be with people of common sense	56	27	[83]
	Like to be with people of vision	41	[73]	12
3.	Find predictable and stable is best	59	32	[93]
	Find new and different best	40	[68]	7
4.	Want to know the practical uses	50	21	[74]
	Want to find innovative uses	46	[80]	21
5.	Tend to be competitive	81	82	81
	Tend to be nurturing	18	18	19
6.	Prefer to be fair	89	91	91
	Prefer to be compassionate	9	9	7
7.	More often skeptical	85	[93]	81
	More often accepting	14	7	19
8.	Persuaded by objective reasoning	88	86	[95]
	Persuaded by passionate conviction	11	[14]	5
9.	Get things done—now	77	70	[88]
	Meet deadlines at the last minute	22	[30]	12
10.	Accommodating when interrupted	63	64	62
	Annoyed when interrupted	35	36	36
11.	Handle problems as they arise	52	[57]	38
	Make detailed plans before you start	46	41	[62]
12.	Make decisions quickly	51	[59]	45
	Stay open to new options	47	41	52
13.	Prefer discussing ideas and theories	52	[75]	31
	Prefer talking about concrete situations	45	23	[67]
14.	Like change	59	[84]	36
	Like set and established procedures	38	16	[60]
15.	Live in and enjoy the present	56	41	[69]
	Prefer to imagine the future	40	[59]	24
16.	Prize strong sense of reality	70	48	[93]
	Prize vivid imagination	27	[52]	*
17.	Value ability to logically analyze	81	84	86
	Value ability to empathize with others	16	14	12

MONEYQ ATTRIBUTES BY PAIRS (continued)	TOTAL (100) %	BLUE (44) %	GOLD (42) %
18. Try to ignore emotional aspects	84	[93]	81
Look for emotional aspects	15	7	[19]
19. Weigh pro and cons	82	84	86
Decide by personal values	16	16	12
20. Always punctual and sometimes early	86	86	93
Tend to be leisurely	13	14	7
21. Want to have things settled in advance	66	59	[88]
Like to be spontaneous	32	[41]	10
22. Like order and structure	67	55	[91]
Like to go with the flow	31	[45]	7
23. Facts only illustrate the general idea	61	[77]	43
Think facts speak for themselves	37	22	[55]
24. Create new and better methods	66	[84]	44
Make existing methods work better	31	14	[56]
25. Handle projects one step at a time	65	42	[86]
Jump in anywhere and leap over steps	30	[55]	7
26. Concerned about underlying principles	63	64	71
Concerned about impact on people	33	34	24
27. See flaws and critique readily	66	68	67
Overlook flaws and support readily	31	32	29
28. Manage by relating sympathetically	51	[59]	41
Manage and deal firmly with others	47	41	[57]
29. Tend to be brief and concise	53	59	55
Tend to be talkative and friendly	44	39	43
30. Most often feel settled	49	34	[71]
Most often feel restless	49	[66]	26
31. Find schedules confining	51	[71]	29
Like to be scheduled	48	30	[71]
32. Like to be systematic	65	46	[95]
Stay unplanned, when possible	34	[55]	5
33. Am orderly	56	48	[76]
Am easygoing	41	[52]	19
34. Look for patterns and relationships	77	[86]	71
Avoid generalities	22	14	29
35. Am an abstract thinker	42	[75]	14
Am a concrete thinker	53	23	[79]

MoneyQ Attributes Individually

For each set of choices, select the phrase that more accurately describes you at least 51% of the time.

	TOTAL (100) %	BLUE (44) %	GOLD (42) %
Prefer to be fair	89	91	91
Persuaded by objective reasoning	88	86	[95]
Always punctual and sometimes early	86	86	93
More often skeptical	85	[93]	81
Try to ignore emotional aspects	84	[93]	81
Weigh pros and cons	82	84	86
Value ability to logically analyze	81	84	86
Tend to be competitive	81	82	81
Look for patterns and relationships	77	[86]	71
Get things done—now	77	70	[88]
Prize your strong sense of reality	70	48	[93]
Like order and structure	67	55	[91]
Create new and better methods	66	[84]	44
See flaws and critique readily	66	68	67
Want to have things settled in advance	66	59	[88]
Like to be systematic	65	46	[95]
Handle projects one step at a time	65	42	[86]
Concerned about underlying principles	63	64	71
Accommodating when interrupted	63	64	62
Facts only illustrate the general idea	61	[77]	43
Like change	59	[84]	36
Find predictable and stable is best	59	32	[93]
Am orderly	56	48	[76]
Live in and enjoy the present	56	41	[69]
Like to be with people of common sense	56	27	[83]
Tend to be brief and concise	53	59	55
Am a concrete thinker	53	23	[79]
Prefer discussing ideas and theories	52	[75]	31
Handle problems as they arise	52	[57]	38
Find schedules confining	51	[71]	29
Value insights and analogies	51	[66]	36
Make decisions quickly	51	[59]	45
Manage by relating sympathetically	51	[59]	41
Want to know the practical uses	50	21	[74]

MoneyQ Attributes Individually (continued)	Total (100) %	Blue (44) %	Gold (42) %
Most often feel restless	49	[66]	26
Most often feel settled	49	34	[71]
Like to be scheduled	48	30	[71]
Manage and deal firmly with others	47	41	[57]
Stay open to new options	47	41	52
Want to find innovative uses	46	[80]	21
Make detailed plans before you start	46	41	[62]
Value accuracy and precision	45	30	[62]
Prefer talking about concrete situations	45	23	[67]
Tend to be talkative and friendly	44	39	43
Am an abstract thinker	42	[75]	14
Like to be with people of vision	41	[73]	12
Am easygoing	41	[52]	19
Find new and different best	40	[68]	7
Prefer to imagine the future	40	[59]	24
Like set and established procedures	38	16	[60]
Think facts speak for themselves	37	22	[55]
Annoyed when interrupted	35	36	36
Stay unplanned, when possible	34	[55]	5
Concerned about impact on people	33	34	34
Like to be spontaneous	32	[41]	10
Like to go with the flow	31	[45]	7
Overlook flaws and support readily	31	32	29
Make existing methods work better	31	14	[56]
Jump in anywhere and leap over steps	30	[55]	7
Prize your vivid imagination	27	[52]	*
Meet deadlines at the last minute	22	[30]	12
Avoid generalities	22	14	[29]
Tend to be nurturing	18	18	19
Decide by personal values	16	16	12
Value ability to empathize with others	16	14	12
Look for emotional aspects	15	7	[19]
More often accepting	14	7	[19]
Tend to be leisurely	13	14	7
Persuaded by passionate conviction	11	[14]	5
Prefer to be compassionate	9	9	7

Self-Descriptors

How well do each of the following statements describe you?

DESCRIBES ME COMPLETELY/VERY WELL	TOTAL (100) %	BLUE (44) %	GOLD (42) %
Optimist	77	80	71
Could be as successful in other job	74	[82]	67
Comfortable delegating	61	59	57
Make quick decisions	60	64	52
Failure is important learning experience	60	59	57
Team player	59	59	60
"Bull" rather than a "bear"	58	[67]	50
Spiritual person	55	61	48
Always interested in stocks and investing	55	52	64
Risk taker	48	[64]	31
Sports contributes to success	36	36	43
Religious faith plays role	26	27	19
Luck contributed to success	14	14	14
Military service contributes to success	12	9	12

How Time Spent

	TOTAL (65) %	BLUE (31) %	GOLD (25) %

How many hours do you work in an average week?

Work Week			
40 hours	11	13	8
41–50 hours	26	23	[36]
51–60 hours	37	36	36
61+ hours	26	29	20
Mean hours	54	55	53

How many hours in an average week, if any, do you spend actively participating in physical activities such as sports and exercise?

Sports and Exercise			
None	8	13	*
1–4 Hours	34	[42]	24
5–9 Hours	43	36	52
10+ Hours	15	10	20
Mean Hours	6	5	7

In an average week, what percentage of time is spent on team sports, individual sports, or other exercise?

Mean percentage of time spent on . . .			
Team sports	9	6	12
Individual sports	47	48	48
Other exercise	44	46	39

How many hours in an average week do you spend reading outside office hours?

Reading outside the office			
1–5 hours	15	16	12
6–9 hours	20	13	[28]
10–14 hours	33	36	32
15+ hours	32	36	28
Mean hours	11	12	11

HOW TIME SPENT (continued)	TOTAL (65) %	BLUE (31) %	GOLD (25) %

In an average week, what percentage of the time you spend reading outside office hours is for business or for pleasure and personal interests?

Mean percentage of time spent on . . .

Business reading	62	58	61
Pleasure and personal-interest reading	39	42	39

How much time do you spend on other activities in an average week?

Do you regularly play . . .

None	54	52	60
Musical instrument	9	10	8
Chess	8	*	[16]
Poker	6	*	*
Bridge	*	0	*
Other (Net)	28	29	28
Golf	6	*	8
Card games	5	7	*
Tennis	5	0	[12]
Sports	3	7	0
Travel	3	*	0
Backgammon	*	0	0
Computer games	*	*	0
Fishing	*	*	0
Motorcycling	*	*	0
Photography	*	0	0
Puzzles	*	*	0
Sailing	*	*	0
Scrabble	*	0	*
Writing	*	*	0

Years in Investment Industry

How long have you been in the investment industry?

	TOTAL (100) %	BLUE (44) %	GOLD (42) %
1–10 years	17	11	[24]
11–15 years	20	21	17
16–20 years	18	18	19
21–30 years	27	34	24
31+ years	17	16	17
Mean years	20	21	19

First Job

What was your first job in the investment industry?

	TOTAL (100) %	BLUE (44) %	GOLD (42) %
Analyst	42	42	44
Stockbroker/sales representative	20	26	16
Money manager	14	10	16
Trader	6	7	8
Operations	6	7	4
Banking	6	3	4
Investment banking	*	0	*
Administrator	*	*	0
Other	8	7	12

Mentoring

	TOTAL (65) %	BLUE (31) %	GOLD (25) %
Has a mentor played a major role in your business success?			
Had Mentor			
No	57	55	56
Yes	43	42	40

Specifically, how has your mentor helped you in your career?

	TOTAL	BLUE	GOLD
How Mentor Helped (27)			
Education/training/skills	44	39	50
Opportunities/doors opened	30	39	20
Philosophy/see big picture/how to think	26	[39]	10
Example/vicarious experience/learn from past	22	*	[40]
Emotional/moral support	19	15	[20]
People/client/sales skills	11	15	0
Halo effect/lend credibility	8	*	*

Education

	Total (100) %	Blue (44) %	Gold (42) %
What university degrees do you hold?			
BA/BS	83	84	83
MBA	59	64	52
Other Master's Degree	8	9	10
Ph.D.	2	*	*
CPA	1	0	0
CFA	7	0	5
What was your undergraduate major?			
Economics	39	32	45
Business	19	16	21
Finance	19	21	14
Accounting	6	*	7
Engineering	5	7	*
Biology/Zoology	5	*	*
Mathematics	4	9	0
Philosophy	4	7	*
English	3	7	0
Political Science	3	*	*
Chemistry	2	*	*
Education	2	*	*
History	2	5	0
Computer Science	1	2	0
Market Research	1	*	0
Marketing	1	2	0
Psychology	1	0	*
Religion	1	0	*
Statistics	1	0	*

EDUCATION (continued)	TOTAL (100) %	BLUE (44) %	GOLD (42) %

What was your graduate school major, if any?

Finance/Investments	40	36	48
Business	17	14	19
Economics	6	14	0
Marketing	6	9	*
Accounting	2	0	*
Law	2	5	0
CFA	1	0	0
Chemistry	1	*	0
East Asian Studies	1	0	*
English	1	*	0

Other Personal Information

	TOTAL (100) %	BLUE (44) %	GOLD (42) %
Attended Ivy League School			
No	75	77	69
Yes	25	23	31
Military Service			
No	72	77	69
Yes	28	23	31
Attend Church/Synagogue			
Yes	58	59	57
No	41	41	41
Gender (from name)			
Male	94	93	93
Female	6	7	7

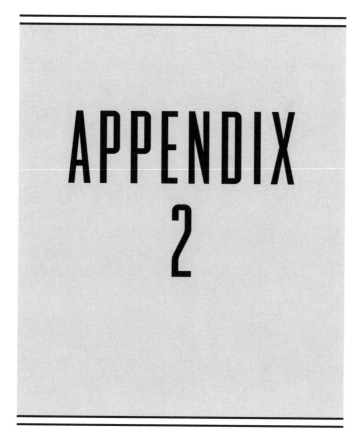

APPENDIX
2

PARTICIPANTS IN INVESTMENT MANAGER SURVEY

The complete listing of investment managers who participated in our survey follows. As you will see, they span the country geographically and represent virtually every style of investment management. What they have in common, as I described earlier in the book, is that each of them has a history of superior investment performance over an extended period of time.

There were 100 participants in all. A few of the managers chose not to be listed. All the others are here.

Rob Arnott
First Quadrant
800 E. Colorado Boulevard
Suite 900
Pasadena, CA 91101

James Barksdale
Equity Investment Corporation
3007 Piedmont Road
Suite 200
Atlanta, GA 30339

Tom O. Barry
George D. Bjurman & Associates
10100 Santa Monica Boulevard
Suite 1200
Los Angeles, CA 90067

William D. Benjes, Jr.
Stratfield Investment Management
40 Broad Street
Suite 825
Boston, MA 02109

Mark Broughton
Badgley, Phelps & Bell, Inc.
1420 Fifth Avenue
Suite 4400
Seattle, WA 98101

Susan M. Byrne
Westwood Management Corporation
300 Crescent Court
Suite 1320
Dallas, TX 75201

Michelle Clayman
New Amsterdam Partners LLC
475 Park Avenue South
20th Floor
New York, NY 10016

Thomas J. Condon
Provident Investment Counsel
300 North Lake Avenue, Penthouse
Pasadena, CA 91101

James P. Cullen
Schafer Cullen Capital Management
645 Fifth Avenue
New York, NY 10022

John Stewart Darrell
Darrell & King
503 Faulconer Drive
Suite 6
Charlottesville, VA 22903

David L. Diamond, CFA
High Rock Capital LLC
28 State Street, 18th Floor
Boston, MA 02109

Joe Engebretson
Engebretson Capital Management, Inc.
840 Newport Center Drive
Suite 490
Newport Beach, CA 92660

Jon W. Erdner
ITS Asset Management, L.P.
1720 Washington Road
P.O. Box 1260
Washington, PA 15301

Jean-Marie Eveillard
SOGEN Asset Management Company
1221 Avenue of the Americas
8th Floor
New York, NY 10020

Ben Fischer
NFJ Investment Group
2121 San Jacinto Street
Suite 1840
Dallas, TX 75201

William H. Fissell
Fissell, Laidlaw & Company, Inc.
42 Main Street
Bedford Hills, NY 10507

John Flippin
Flippin, Bruce & Porter, Inc.
800 Main Street, 2nd Floor
P.O. Box 6138
Lynchburg, VA 24505

Thomas G. Fox
Trend Capital Management
600 South Highway 169
Suite 950 Interchange Tower
Minneapolis, MN 55426

George Froley
Froley, Revy Investment Co., Inc.
10900 Wilshire Boulevard
Suite 900
Los Angeles, CA 90024

Roger Groh
Groh Asset Management
44 Montgomery Street
34th Floor
San Francisco, CA 94104

Peter Gruber
Globalvest Management Company, L.P.
6000 Estate Charlotte Amalie, Suite 4
St. Thomas, VI 00802

Carl W. Hafele
National Asset Management
101 South Fifth Street
Louisville, KY 40202

David Halloran
NCM Capital Management Group, Inc.
103 West Main Street
Durham, NC 27701

Peter J. Hathaway
General Electric Investment Corp.
P.O. Box 7900
3003 Summer Street
Stamford, CT 06904

Fred Hayek
Hayek Investment Counsel, Inc.
117 Fairhope Avenue
Fairhope, AL 36532

Thomas B. Hazuka
Mellon Capital Management Corporation
595 Market Street
Suite 3000
San Francisco, CA 94105

Gerard E. Heffernan
Stratton Management Company
610 W. Germantown Pike
Suite 300
Plymouth Meeting, PA 19462

James R. Henderson, CFA
MetWest Capital Management
610 Newport Center Drive
Suite 150
Newport Beach, CA 92660

Thomas D. Henwood
Emerging Growth Management Co.
One Embarcadero Center
Suite 2410
San Francisco, CA 94111

Bernard R. Horn, Jr.
Polaris Capital Management, Inc.
125 Summer Street
14th Floor
Boston, MA 02110

Richard Huson
The Crabbe Huson Group, Inc.
121 SW Morrison
Suite 1400
Portland, OR 97204

Paul Jackson
Paul J. Jackson & Associates, Ltd.
73 Lexington Street
Suite 104
Newton, MA 02166

Dan Jacobs
Jacobs Asset Management
200 East Broward Boulevard
Suite 1920
Fort Lauderdale, FL 33301

Craig T. Johnson
Leonetti & Associates, Inc.
1130 Lake Cook Road
Suite 300
Buffalo Grove, IL 60089

Kenneth M. Johnson, Vice President
Investment Counselors Incorporated
1010 Market Street
Suite 1540
St. Louis, MO 63101

Scott S. Johnston
Sterling Johnston Capital Management
655 Montgomery St. #600
San Francisco, CA 94111

Gyanendra (Joe) K. Joshi
Systematic Financial Management, L.P.
300 Frank W. Burr Boulevard
Glenpointe East, 7th Floor
Teaneck, NJ 07666

William Jurika
Jurika & Voyles
1999 Harrison Suite
Suite 700
Oakland, CA 94612

Mike Kayes
Eastover Capital Management
212 South Tryon Street
Charlotte, NC 28281

Gerald T. Kennedy
Kennedy Capital Management
10829 Olive Boulevard
St. Louis, MO 63144

James C. King
Voyageur Asset Management
90 South Seventh Street
Suite 4400
Minneapolis, MN 55402

Fred Kuehndorf
Deutsche Morgan Grenfell
31 West 52 Street
15th Floor
New York, NY 10019

James I. Ladge, CFA
Appleton Partners, Inc.
45 Milk Street
Boston, MA 02109

Josef Lakonishok, Ph.D.
LSV Asset Management
181 West Madison
Chicago, IL 60602

Steve Lauck
Ashfield & Company, Inc.
750 Battery Street
Suite 600
San Francisco, CA 94111

Joel Leff
Forstmann-Leff Associates, Inc.
590 Madison Avenue
New York, NY 10022

James P. Leonard
The Leonard Management Group
395 West Avon Road
Avon, CT 06001

John Lindenthal
Oppenheimer Capital
200 Liberty Street, 37th Floor
Oppenheimer Tower
New York, NY 10281

Stan Lipstadt
PSM Investors Incorporated
P.O. Box 692
Carlisle, MA 01741

Justin S. Mazzon
American Blue Chip Investment Management
700 Larkspur Landing Circle
Suite 199
Larkspur, CA 94939

Thomas E. McGowan
Lynch & Mayer, Inc.
520 Madison Avenue
42nd Floor
New York, NY 10022

Ron Muhlenkamp
Muhlenkamp & Company Inc.
12300 Perry Highway
Wexford, PA 15090

A. Deane Nelson
McMorgan and Company
One Bush Street
Suite 800
San Francisco, CA 94104

Frank Peluso
MSR Advisors
Park 80 West
Plaza 2
Saddle Brook, NJ 07663

Lawrence R. Powell
Rohden Funds Management, Inc.
300 W. Adams
Suite 617
Chicago, IL 60606

Todd Rabold
Wachovia Asset Management
2700 Reynolda Road
Suite 1015
Winston-Salem, NC 27106

Arno Rayner
Rayner Associates, Inc.
655 Redwood Highway
Number 370
Mill Valley, CA 94941

John C. Riazzi, CFA
Dean Investment Associates
2480 Kettering Tower
Dayton, OH 45423

Kevin Riley
Roxbury Capital Management
100 Wilshire Boulevard
Suite 600
Santa Monica, CA 90401

Steven H. Rothmann, CFA
PanAgora Asset Management, Inc.
260 Franklin Street
22nd Floor
Boston, MA 02110

Allan M. Rudnick
Kayne Anderson Investment Management, LLC
1800 Avenue of the Stars
Suite 200
Los Angeles, CA 90067

Frederick J. Ruopp
Chelsea Management Company
444 South Flower Street
Suite 2340
Los Angeles, CA 90071

Frank M. Sands
Sands Capital Management
1100 North Glebe Road
Suite 1000
Arlington, VA 22201

S. Van Zandt Schreiber
Bennett Lawrence Management
757 Third Avenue
19th Floor
New York, NY 10017

Donald G. Smith
Donald Smith & Co., Inc.
East 80 Route 4
Suite 360
Paramus, NJ 07652

Ellis C. Smith
Messner & Smith, Theme/Value Investment Management, Ltd.
450 B Street
Suite 780
San Diego, CA 92101

Alan B. Snyder
Snyder Capital Management, L.P.
350 California Street
Suite 1460
San Francisco, CA 94104

Peter F. Spano
Mercator Asset Management, L.P.
2400 East Commercial Blvd.
Suite 810
Fort Lauderdale, FL 33308

Roger Stamper
Spyglass Asset Management, Inc.
P.O. Box 2864
Toledo, OH 43606

Julia Sze
Credit Lyonnais/Nicholas Applegate
3 Embarcadero Center
Suite 2980
San Francisco, CA 94111

Ken Toft
Gateway Advisors
400 TechneCenter Drive
Suite 220
Milford, OH 45150

Bradley E. Turner
Gradison-McDonald Asset Management
580 Walnut Street
Cincinnati, OH 45202

Thomas E. Vass
Business & Family Financial Strategies
5009 Western Boulevard, #C
Raleigh, NC 27606

Nicholas Verbanic
Elias Asset Management
500 Essjay Road
Suite 220
Williamsville, NY 14221

James C. Wadsworth, Chief Investment Officer
Laurel Capital Advisors,
    a wholly owned subsidiary of Mellon Bank
One Mellon Bank Center
Pittsburgh, PA 15258

David Ware
Barrington Capital Management, Inc.
470 Miller Road
Barrington, IL 60010

Josh Weinstein
Aberdeen America Inc.
10 Union Wharf
Boston, MA 02109

Glenn C. Weirick
Westcap Investors
11100 Santa Monica Boulevard
Suite 1850
Los Angeles, CA 90025

Peter D. Wells
Kanne Paris & Hoban
221 N. LaSalle Street
Suite 1740
Chicago, IL 60601

David G. Williams
2511 8th Street
Charlestown, MA 02129

Steven Wilson
Reich & Tang Capital Management
600 Fifth Avenue
8th Floor
New York, NY 10020

T. Scott Wittman
Vantage Investment Advisors
630 Fifth Avenue
Suite 2670
New York, NY 10111

Don Wolcott
Becker Capital Management, Inc.
211 Southwest 5th Avenue
Portland, OR 97204

Kip Wright
Kirr Marbach & Co.
P.O. Box 1729
Columbus, IN 47202

Donald A. Yacktman
Yacktman Asset Management Co.
303 West Madison Street
Suite 1925
Chicago, IL 60606

Art Zaske
Zaske, Sarafa & Associates, Inc.
355 South Old Woodward Avenue
Suite 200
Birmingham, MI 48009

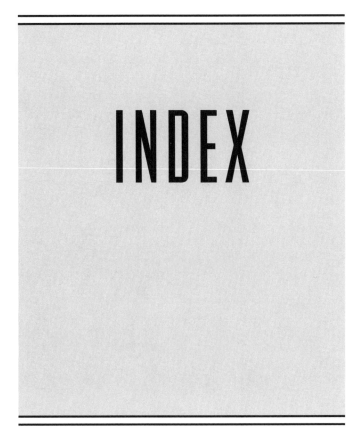

INDEX

Index

A

Aberdeen America Inc., 284
Against the Gods (Bernstein), 62, 70, 84
A. G. Becker, 97
American Association for Individual
    Investors, 93–94
American Blue Chip Investment
    Management, 280
Appleton Partners, Inc., 279
Arnott, Rob, 152, 273
Ashfield & Company, Inc., 280
Asset allocation, 155–68
    and active management, 164–65
    bonds versus stock, 156–59, 161
    importance of, 165–67
    and long–term growth, 157
    versus market timing, 161, 167
    meaning of, 155, 157
    versus picking stocks, 158–64
    and risky investments, 163, 165
    strategies for, 176
    tactical asset allocation, 167
    and volatility, 177
Asset allocation customization,
    174–237

Blue Innovator, 215–21
Blue Strategist, 208–14
Gold Conservator, 187–93
Gold Trustee, 180–86
Green Advocate, 229–36
Green Mentor, 222–28
and MoneyQ profile, 175
one-year range of returns, 178
Red Realist, 201–7
Red Tactician, 194–200
self-managed allocation, 176
20-year range of returns, 178–79

B

Badgley, Phelps & Bell, Inc., 274
Barksdale, James, 273
Baron Asset, 196
Barrington Capital Management, Inc.,
    284
Barry, Tom O., 274
Beating the market, expectations of,
    67

Becker Capital Management, Inc., 285
Beebower, Gil, 157–59
Benartzi, Shlomo, 84
Benchmarks, types of, 55
Benjes, William D., Jr., 274
Bennett Lawrence Management, 282
Berens, Dr. Linda, 19, 20
Bernstein, Peter, 11, 70, 84
 on investor expectations, 62–65
Blue Innovator
 asset allocation for, 215–21
 profile of, 36–37
Blue profile, features of, 22–23
Blue Strategist
 asset allocation for, 208–14
 profile of, 34–35
Bonds
 in asset allocation, 156–59, 161
 prices and interest rates, 156, 157
 return compared to equities, 85
 use in portfolio, 156–57
Boston Chicken, 110
Brandywine Blue, 189, 224
Brandywine Fund, 11, 148, 151, 210, 231
Brazos/MIC Small Cap Growth, 210, 217, 231
Briggs, Katherine, 19
Brinson, Gary, 11, 157–64
 on asset allocation, 160–63
Broughton, Mark, 274
Buffett, Warren, 6, 14, 57, 77, 158–59
Business & Family Financial Strategies, 284
Byrne, Susan, 11, 274
 on avoiding investment mistakes, 134–36

C

Call option, 106–7
Capital Asset Pricing Model, 75
Capital Ideas (Bernstein), 62
Cataclysmic risk, 88–90

Catch-up, avoiding, 139–40
Chavalier, Judith, 44
Chelsea Management Company, 282
Chicago Board of Option Exchange, 121
Clayman, Michelle, 165, 274
Coca-Cola, 76, 81, 135
Cohen & Steers Real Estate, 182, 189, 224, 231
Coleman, Ellen, 115
Commodities, 110–11, 124
 avoiding, 124, 142
 guidelines for investors, 111, 124
 nature of, 110–11
Compounding, 60–61
 example of, 60
 results of, 85
Condon, Thomas J., 146, 274
Contrarians, strategies for, 114–16
Corning Glass, 115
Corrections, 95
Coupon clippers, 156
Cover, in selling short, 105
Crabbe Huson Group, Inc., 278
Credit Lyonnais/Nicholas Applegate, 283
Cullen, James P., 274

D

Dalbar, Inc., 66
Darrell & King, 103, 147, 275
Darrell, John Stewart, 103, 147, 275
Davis NY Venture, 196, 201, 203
Dean Investment Associates, 82, 281
Dell Computer, 81
Deutsche Morgan Grenfell, 279
Diamond, David, 61, 76, 275
Diversification, 75
 with hedge funds, 125
 and risk reduction, 91
 See also Asset allocation
Dividends, in calculation of return, 60
Donald Smith & Co., Inc., 282

Dow Jones Average, drop in, 87–88
Driehaus, Richard, 46, 97

E

Eastover Capital Management, 279
Educational background, investment
    managers, 44–45, 269–70
Education of a Speculator, The
    (Niederhoffer), 112, 126
Efficient Market Theory, 68, 139
Elias Asset Management, 284
Ellison, Glenn, 44
Emerging Growth Management Co., 277
Engebretson Capital Management, Inc.,
    275
Engebretson, Joe, 275
Equities, return compared to bonds, 85
Equity Investment Corporation, 273
Equity premium, meaning of, 85
Erdner, Jon W., 275
Eveillard, Jean-Marie, 275
Expectations, 61, 64–66
    beating the market, 67–68
    and goal-setting, 56–57
    returns expected by investors,
        49–50, 66
    and risk versus reward, 61–66
    and stock market efficiency, 67–68
    unrealistic, effects of, 66

F

Faith and investing, 145–54
    meaning of, 146–47
    money managers on, 146–52, 259
    and optimism, 152
Fama, Eugene, 75, 78
Fidelity Spartan High Income, 196,
    203, 217
First Quadrant, 152, 273
Fisher, Ben, 275
Fissell, Laidlaw & Co., Inc., 154, 275

Fissell, William H., 275
Flippin, Bruce & Porter, Inc., 276
Flippin, John, 276
Forbes, Peter, 160
Forstmann-Leff Associates, Inc., 280
Fox, Thomas G., 145, 146, 276
Franklin Small Cap Growth, 182, 189, 224
Freezing price, 106
French, Ken, 75, 78
Friess, Foster, 11
    on faith and investing, 148–51
Froley, George, 59, 276
Froley, Revy Investment Company, 59,
    276

G

Gabelli Value, 210, 231
Gain, stock picks versus asset alloca-
    tion, 158–64
Galen Associates, 98
Galen Group, 11
Gates, Bill, 114
Gateway Advisors, 283
General Electric Investment Corp., 277
General Motors, 75
George D. Bjurman & Associates, 274
Gillette, 76
Globalvest Management Company,
    L.P., 276
Goal-setting, 55–72
    beating the market concept, 67
    and benchmarks, 55
    and expectations, 56–57, 61, 64–66
    long-term goals, 56
    and money personality, 70–71
    and time horizons, 57–61
Gold Conservator
    asset allocation for, 187–93
    profile of, 28–29
Goldman Sachs Global Income, 182
Gold profile, features of, 21–22
Gold Trustee
    asset allocation for, 180–86
    profile of, 26–27

Gradison-McDonald Asset
      Management, 86, 283
Grant, William, 11
   on contrarian strategies, 114–16
   on timing, 98–101
Great Depression, 78, 88
Green Advocate
   asset allocation for, 229–36
   profile of, 40–41
Green Mentor
   asset allocation for, 222–28
   profile of, 38–39
Green profile, features of, 22–23
Groh Asset Management, 276
Groh, Roger, 276
Growth stocks
   characteristics of, 76
   examples of, 76
   versus value stocks, 76–82
Gruber, Peter, 276

H

Hafele, Carl W., 147, 276
Haga, Michael William, 90
Halloran, David, 276
Harbor International Growth, 196, 203,
      210, 217, 231
Hathaway, Peter J., 277
Hayek, Fred, 277
Hayek Investment Counsel, Inc., 277
Hazuka, Thomas B., 277
Hedge funds, 111–13, 124–25
   examples of, 112–13
   fees, 125
   fund of hedge funds, 125
   guidelines for investors, 125
   minimum investment, 124–25
   nature of, 111–12
   risk of, 111–12
Heffernan, Gerard E., 277
Henderson, James R., 76, 277
Henwood, Thomas D., 277
High Rock Capital, LLC, 61, 76, 275

Hood, Randolph, 157–59
Horn, Bernard R., Jr., 147, 277
Hotchkis & Wiley Total Return, 196,
      203, 210, 217, 224, 231
Hot issues, IPOs, 124
Hubris, and investment losses, 132–33
Huson, Richard, 278

I

IAI mutual fund group, 66
Ibbotson/Sinquefield series, 85
IBM, 105–8
Index funds, 67
Initial public offerings (IPOs), 109–10,
      124
   example of, 109–10
   guidelines for investors, 110, 124
   hot issues, 124
   nature of, 109–10
   versus waiting to buy, 110
"In the money" options, 120
Interest rates
   and bond prices, 156, 157
   Fed raising/lowering rates, 62–63
Investment Counselors Incorporated,
      278
Investment Gurus (Tanous), 117, 145,
      148
Investment managers
   basic advice to investors, 51–52
   choosing money manager, 48–51
   educational background, 44–45
   goals of, 48
   methodology of, 47–48
   personality profile of, 43–44
   professional profile of, 46–48
   reading behavior, 45–46
   return expected of, 49–50
   work week per-hours, 46
Investment managers survey
   competitive orientation, 248
   determination of investment style,
      247

educational profile, 269–70
faith and investing, 259
first job, 267
investing success, affecting factors, 251
investment orientation, 246
investment styles of, 244
investment styles utilized, 244–46
manager characteristics for success, 253
market timing, 250
mentors, views on, 268
money management views, 256
MoneyQ attributes, 260–63
MoneyQ profile, 243
motivations for activities, 249
participants in survey, 273–85
personal investing approach, 258
return expectations, 254
risk tolerance, 255
self-descriptors, 264
time spent by, 265–66
track records, 252
wealth building approach, 257
years in investment industry, 267
Investment mistakes, 7
anxiety, 133
hubris, 132–33
overtrading, 133, 136–38
playing catch–up, 139–40
stock tips, 138–39
unlimited losses, 140–43
Investment profile. See MoneyQ profile
Investment shortcuts, 56
Investment wisdom, meaning of, 8–9
IPOs. See Initial public offerings (IPOs)
ITS Asset Management, L.P., 275

J

Jackson, Paul, 131, 147, 278
Jacobs, Dan, 278
Johnson, Craig T., 82, 147, 278
Johnson, Kenneth M., 278

Johnston, Scott, 118, 152, 278
Joshi, Gyanendra (Joe) K., 131, 147, 278
Jung, Carl Gustav, 19
Jurika & Voyles, 71, 279
Jurika, William, 71, 279

K

Kahneman, Daniel, 70, 84
Kanne Parris & Hoban, 59, 284
Kayes, Mike, 279
Kayne Anderson Investment Management, LLC, 282
Keirsey, Dr. David, 19, 20
Kennedy Capital Management, 147, 279
Kennedy, Gerald T., 147, 279
King, James C., 279
Kirr Marbach & Co., 285
Kuehndorf, Fred, 157, 279

L

Laboratory Corporation of America, 115–16
Ladge, James I., 279
Lakonishok, Josef, 11, 279
on risk, 78–81
Large-cap stocks, 75, 79
Lauck, Steve, 280
Laurel Capital Advisors, 284
Leadership Style of Women (Zichy), xvii
LEAPS, 121
Leekley, Gregory H., xviii, 175
Leff, Joel, 280
Leonard, James P., 280
Leonard Management Group, 280
Leonetti and Associates, 82, 147, 278
Lindenthal, John, 280
Lipstadt, Stan, 280

Lloyd's of London, 118–19
Longleaf Partners Small Cap, 203
Long-term goals
    advantages of, 59, 69
    and asset allocation, 157
    benign neglect strategy, 86
    and growth stocks, 76
    holding versus active trading, 69, 86
Losses
    most common losses, 142
    unlimited, 140–43
    See also Investment mistakes
LSV Asset Management, 78, 279
Lynch & Mayer, Inc., 146, 280
Lynch, Peter, 6, 14, 46, 95, 117, 158–59

M

MacKay Shields Financial Corporation,
    11, 98, 114
Market multiple, 135
Market risk, 74–75
Market timing. See Timing market
Master Keys, 12, 15, 42
    asset allocation, 155–68
    faith and investing, 145–54
    goal-setting, 55–72
    identification of, 11
    investment mistakes, 131–44
    purpose of, 9–10
    risk and investing, 73–91
    speculation, 103–30
    timing market, avoiding, 93–101
Mazzon, Justin S., 280
McGowan, Thomas E., 146, 280
McMorgan and Company, 281
Mellon Bank Corp., 146
Mellon Capital Management
    Corporation, 277
Mental accounting, 70
Mercator Asset Management, L.P., 283
Messner & Smith, Theme/Value
    Investment Management, Ltd.,
    283

MetWest Capital Management, 76, 277
Microsoft, 75, 76
Mistakes. See Investment mistakes
Momentum investing, 97
MoneyQ profile, 12–13, 18–42
    Blue Innovator, 36–37
    Blue Strategist, 34–35
    foundations of, 19–20
    Gold Conservator, 28–29
    Gold Trustee, 26–27
    Green Advocate, 40–41
    Green Mentor, 38–39
    MoneyQ1, 24–25
    Money Q2, 172–74
    Red Realist, 32–33
    Red Tactician, 30–31
Montag & Caldwell Growth, 196, 203,
    210, 217, 231
Montgomery Asset Management, 62,
    66, 87
Morningstar, 79, 178
MSR Advisors, 281
Muhlenkamp & Company Inc., 281
Muhlenkamp, Ron, 147, 281
Mutual Beacon, 189, 224
Mutual Series funds, 117
Myers-Briggs Type Indicator (MBTI),
    19–20
Myers, Isabel, 19
Myopic loss aversion, 85

N

Naked puts, 112
NASDAQ, 108
National Asset Management, 147, 276
Nations Managed Small Cap Index,
    182
Natural disasters, 119
NCM Capital Management Group, Inc.,
    276
Nelson, A. Deane, 281
Netscape, 109–10
New Amsterdam Partners LLC, 274

NFJ Investment Group, 275
Nicholas-Applegate Mini-Cap Growth, 203
Niederhoffer, Victor, 11, 112–13
 on speculating, 126–29
Nikkei 225 index, 162
NY Davis Venture, 217

O

Oakmark Small Cap, 217
Odean, Terrance, 69
OEX options, 121–22
Oil embargo, 89
On the Brink: How to Survive the Coming Great Depression (Haga), 90
Oppenheimer Capital, 280
Optimism, and success, 152
Options, 106–8, 120–22
 buying options, 108
 call option, 106–7
 example of, 106–8
 expiration dates, 120–21
 guidelines for investors, 120–22
 LEAPS, 121
 meaning of, 106
 "in the money," 120
 OEX options, 121–22
 "out of the money," 120
 put option, 107
 writing options, 107–8
"Out of the money" options, 120
Overtrading, as investment mistake, 133, 136–38

P

PanAgora Asset Management, Inc., 282
Panic selling, 87–88
Pascal, Blaise, 84
Paul J. Jackson & Associates, 131, 147, 278

Peluso, Frank, 281
Pension plans, study of different returns, 158–59
Personality type
 Blue profile, 22–23
 financial temperament assessment (MoneyQ profile), 12–13, 18–42
 and goals, 70–71
 Gold profile, 21–22
 Green profile, 22–23
 investor psychology, 68–71
 Red profile, 22
 and risk tolerance, 51
Personal liability, avoiding in investing, 142
Pfizer, 99–100
Pharmaceutical companies, 76, 99–100, 115, 138
PimCo Foreign Bond, 196, 203
PimCo Low Duration, 182, 189, 196, 203, 210, 217, 224, 231
PimCo Total Return, 182, 189
Polaris Capital Management, 147, 277
Polaroid, 135
Portfolios
 for Blue Innovator, 215–21
 for Blue Strategist, 208–14
 for Gold Conservator, 187–93
 for Gold Trustee, 180–86
 for Green Advocate, 229–36
 for Green Mentor, 222–28
 for Red Realist, 201–7
 for Red Tactician, 194–200
Powell, Lawrence R., 66, 73, 281
Premium value, options, 106–7, 120
Price earnings ratio, 135
Price, Michael, 6, 14, 46, 117
Private placements, 108–9, 122–23
 guidelines for investors, 109, 122–23
 meaning of, 108–9
 shareholders' agreement, 123
 sources for, 122–23
Provident Investment Counsel, 146, 274
PSM Investors Incorporated, 280

Psychological risk, 82–83
Psychology of Financial Planning
    (Zichy), xvii
Put option, 107
    naked puts, 112

Q

Quantum Fund, 111
Quest Diagnostics, 115–16

R

Rabold, Todd, 131, 281
Rayner, Arno, 281
Rayner Associates, Inc., 281
Red profile, features of, 22
Red Realist
    asset allocation for, 201–7
    profile of, 32–33
Red Tactician
    asset allocation for, 194–200
    profile of, 30–31
Reich & Tang Capital Management, 73
Return
    expectations of investors, 49–50, 66
    expectations of money managers,
        254
    stocks versus bonds, 85
Riazzi, John C., 82, 281
Riley, Kevin, 57, 282
Risk, 73–91
    cataclysmic risk, 88–90
    and growth versus value stocks,
        76–77, 80–82
    guidelines for dealing with, 91
    interest-rate risk, 125
    market risk, 74–75
    psychological risk, 82–83
    real risk, 74, 87
    risk/reward theories, 83–85

risky investments and asset alloca-
    tion, 163, 165
size risk, 75
small versus large cap stocks, 75
style risk, 75
time factors, 85–86
Risk tolerance, 64–66
    and average investor, 65–66
    of investment managers, 255
    and personality profile, 51
Robertson, Julian, 65, 111
Rohden Funds Management, 66, 73,
    281
Rothman, Steven H., 282
Roxbury Capital Management, 57, 282
Rudnick, Allan M., 282
Ruopp, Frederick J., 282
Russell 2000 index, 55

S

Sands Capital Management, 282
Sands, Frank M., 282
Schafer Cullen Capital Management,
    274
Schmitt, Jennifer, 175
Scudder Small Cap Value, 182, 189,
    203, 210, 224, 231
Security Capital US Real Estate/Self-
    Managed, 210, 217
Selected American Shares, 100–101
Selling short, 105–6, 118–20
    example of, 105–6
    guidelines for investors, 118–20
    as investment mistake, 142
    meaning of, 105, 142
Shareholders' agreement, 123
Sharpe, Bill, 75
Shiller, Robert J., 69
Short sales. *See* Selling short
Short-term goals, 58–59
Siegel, Jeremy, 63
Size risk, 75
Sloate, Laura, 46

Small-cap stocks, 89
  as speculative stocks, 104
  versus large-cap stocks, 75, 79
Smith, Donald G., 282
Smith, Ellis C., 283
SmithKline Beecham, 98
Snyder, Alan B., 61, 283
Snyder Capital Management, L.P., 61, 283
SOGEN Asset Management Company, 275
SOGEN Overseas, 189
Soros, George, 65, 111
Spano, Peter F., 283
Speculation, 103–30
  commodities, 110–11, 124
  contrariness, 114–16
  guidelines for, 113, 116–25
  hedge funds, 111–13, 124–25
  initial public offerings (IPOs),
    109–10, 124
  options, 106–8, 120–22
  private placements, 108–9, 122–23
  selling short, 105–6, 118–20
  speculative stocks, 104–5, 116–18
Speculative stocks, 104–5, 116–18
  guidelines for investors, 116–18
  nature of, 104–5
Spyglass Asset Management, 76, 283
Stamper, Roger, 76, 283
Standard & Poor's 500 index, 55, 80
  index funds, 67
  1926 to 1997 returns, 59
Standish International Fixed Income,
    217, 231
Steinhardt, Michael, 65, 111
Sterling Johnston Capital Management,
    118, 152, 278
Stock
  equity premium, meaning of, 85
  return versus bonds, 85
  small-cap versus large-cap, 75, 79
  value versus growth stock, 76–77,
    80–82
Stock market crashes
  as buying opportunity, 90
  declines in 1973–74, 88, 89
  declines, investor reactions to,
    88–89

future view, 90
Great Depression, 78, 88
number since 1900, 88
October 1987, 88, 89, 183, 211, 218,
    226, 232
psychological effects of, 89
Stocks for the Long Run (Siegel), 63
Stock tips, avoiding, 138–39
Stratfield Investment Management, 274
Stratton Management Company, 277
Style risk, 75
Systematic Financial Management, L.P.,
    131, 147, 278
Sze, Julia, 283

T

Tactical asset allocation, 167
TeamVest, LLC, xvii, 175
Templeton Developing Markets, 182,
    189, 196, 201, 203, 210, 217,
    224, 231
Templeton Foreign, 224
Thaler, Richard H., 69, 84
Three Factor Model, 75
Time frame and investing, 57–61
  benign neglect strategy, 86
  compounding, 60–61
  and different objectives, 58
  and equity premium, 85
  examples of, 58–59
  long–term goals, 59, 87–88
  panic selling, incidence of, 87–88
  and risk, 85–86
  selling, disadvantages of, 69
  short-term goals, 58–59
Timing market
  actions during rising market, 94–95
  versus asset allocation, 161, 167
  and corrections, 95
  Momentum investing, 97
  money managers on, 250
  negative aspects of, 93–101
Tisch, Larry, 114–15

Toft, Ken, 283
Total return, meaning of, 155
Treasury bills, 85
Trend Capital Management, 146, 276
T. Rowe Price Blue Chip Growth, 196, 203, 217
T. Rowe Price Equity–Income, 210, 224, 231
T. Rowe Price International Stock, 182, 189
T. Rowe Price Small Cap Stock, 217
Turner, Bradley E., 86, 283
Turner Small Cap (TIP), 196
Tversky, Amos, 70, 84

V

Value stocks, 75
  benefits of, 78–80
  characteristics of, 76
  versus growth stocks, 76–82
Vanguard Index 500, 182
Vanguard US Growth, 189, 224
Vantage Investment Advisors, 146, 285
Van Zandt Schreiber, S., 282
Vass, Thomas E., 284
Verbanic, Nicholas, 284
Viagra, 76, 99
Volatility, and asset allocation, 177
Voyager Asset Management, 279

W

Wachovia Asset Management, 131, 281
Wadsworth, James C., 146, 284
Warburg Pincus International Equity Common, 210, 217, 231
Ware, David, 284
Wealth Equation
  components of, 12, 15, 42
  Master Keys, 12, 15
  MoneyQ questionnaire, 12–13

Weinstein, Josh, 284
Weirick, Glenn C., 155, 157, 284
Wells, Peter D., 59, 284
Westcap Investors, 155, 157, 284
Westwood Equity Fund, 134
Westwood Management Corporation, 134, 274
Williams, David G., 285
Wilson, Steven, 73, 285
Wittman, T. Scott, 59, 146, 285
Wolcott, Don, 285
Wright, Kip, 285
Writing options, 107–8

Y

Yacktman Asset Management Co., 100, 133, 285
Yacktman, Donald, 100, 131, 285

Z

Zaske, Arthur, 166–67, 285
Zaske, Sarafa and Associates, 166, 285
Zichy & Associates, xvii
Zichy, Shoya, xvii, 13, 18, 20, 24

About the Author

PETER J. TANOUS is President of Lynx Investment Advisory, Inc., of Washington, D.C., a registered investment advisor. Lynx provides consulting services relating to the selection and monitoring of money managers. Its clients include institutions and individuals worldwide. Before founding Lynx, Tanous was Executive Vice President and a director of Bank Audi (U.S.A.) in New York City.

Prior to joining Bank Audi, he was Chairman of Petra Capital Corporation, a New York Stock Exchange member firm, which he co-founded. During his 15 years at Smith Barney, Inc., Tanous served as the International Director. He was also manager of its Paris office and a director and member of the Executive Committee of Smith Barney, International. He currently serves on the board of directors of Modis Professional Services, Inc. (formerly Accustaff, Inc.), Cedars Bank in Los Angeles, Kistler Aerospace in Seattle, and Interstate Resources Inc., a paper manufacturing company based in Virginia.

Mr. Tanous has written articles on the securities industry that have appeared in French and English publications. In addition, he has co-authored three novels that have been translated into several foreign languages.

Mr. Tanous received a Bachelor of Arts degree in economics from Georgetown University in 1960. He has served as a member of the board of advisors of Georgetown's College of Arts and Sciences. A long-time resident of New York City prior to moving to Washington, D.C., he served as a trustee of the Browning School, a private school in Manhattan.

In 1991, Mr. Tanous was the recipient of the American Task Force for Lebanon Philip C. Habib Award for Distinguished Public Service, whose prior recipients have included Senator George Mitchell, Governor John Sununu, and Senator Bob Dole. He was awarded the Ellis Island Medal of Honor in 1994.

Peter Tanous is married to the former Ann MacConnell. They have three grown children.